PRAISE FOR
DESIGNING ACCESSIBLE LEA

Every eLearning designer needs this book on their desk! So much of the accessibility guidance out there is written for programmers and assumes you are creating websites. Finally, we have a resource just for us. This book will save you countless hours of frustratingly confusing research. This masterful reference guide on eLearning accessibility demystifies everything from why accessibility matters all the way down to complying with each individual WCAG standard. Complete with clear language explanations and helpful screen captures, you'll finally have the answers you've been searching for.
Diane Elkins, Co-owner, Artisan E-Learning and E-Learning Uncovered

This invaluable guide for L&D practitioners gives the how and why of making learning content accessible. It brings together an extensive range of resources and practical advice in one place and will likely become a standard work in our field.
Donald H Taylor, Chair, Learning Technologies Conference

Susi Miller combines her own and others' lived experience into an empathy-fueled work that creates clarity and removes barriers for anyone seeking to understand how to produce accessible learning content and why. Her book has a compelling and comprehensive approach to digital accessibility and disability inclusion, which really brings the subject to life. This is recommended reading for any professional producing digital content.
Michael Vermeersch, Digital Inclusion Lead, Microsoft

I know from working with Susi Miller through the eLearning Network that she is not only passionate about accessibility in eLearning design but also extremely knowledgeable about what is required by those of us creating eLearning. It comes as no surprise that she's made this book accessible in the way she's structured it and the language she uses! This will surely become a

must-read for all eLearning professionals; after all, making better learning experiences for all learners is what we are (or should be) all about!
Joan Keevill, Director, Designs on Learning, and Chair of the eLearning Network

I wish I had this book when I started working with accessible eLearning. Susi Miller does a fantastic job of showing why eLearning professionals need to ensure that their training needs to be accessible, while also providing, through the eLearning accessible framework that she proposes, a practical way of making it happen. I'm looking forward to putting what I learned here into practice and recommending the book whenever I'm discussing eLearning and accessibility.
Kevin Gumienny, Senior Consultant, Guidehouse

Digital accessibility can be a tough and technical subject to tackle, but Susi Miller has broken down complex guidelines and carefully brought them to life through using her personal learning journey, practical examples and how-to illustrations. It is an essential read for any eLearning practitioner.
Grant Broome, Digital Inclusion Strategist and Director, DIG Inclusion Ltd

Designing Accessible Learning Content is a unique and much-needed resource for L&D practitioners struggling with the complexities of eLearning accessibility. The wealth of background knowledge it provides, combined with practical frameworks, clear explanations and examples make this a vital handbook for anyone who believes that designing inclusive learning content is the right thing to do.
Dr Nasser Siabi OBE, CEO, Microlink PC

Before instructional designers understand how to develop accessible eLearning, they often fall back on providing a written course transcript. However, armed with modern eLearning authoring tools and the information found in this book, author Susi Miller suggests that 'as eLearning professionals become more familiar with designing accessible content, they find ways of making *all learning content inclusive* without needing to provide accessible alternatives' (emphasis mine). If you aspire to develop universally accessible eLearning, look no further than this comprehensive, plain-language guide.
Chris Willis, Director of Product, Lectora, eLearning Brothers

At a time where everything is changing, acquiring new skills is of paramount importance. Now more than ever learning is being delivered online and remotely. If we want everyone to have an equal chance of acquiring new skills, learning content needs to be accessible. In this book Susi Miller demystifies and explains what learning and development professionals need to know in order to make their content work for the widest possible learner base. The work recognizes the difference between standard web content and learning materials and offers practical and pragmatic advice on accessible content creation.

Neil Milliken, Global Head of Accessibility (Atos Group), Atos

Designing Accessible Learning Content

A practical guide to applying best-practice accessibility standards to L&D resources

Susi Miller

KoganPage

First published in Great Britain and the United States in 2021 by Kogan Page Limited

2nd Floor, 45 Gee Street
London
EC1V 3RS
United Kingdom
www.koganpage.com

122 W 27th St, 10th Floor
New York, NY 10001
USA

4737/23 Ansari Road
Daryaganj
New Delhi 110002
India

Kogan Page books are printed on paper from sustainable forests.

ISBNs
Hardback   978 1 78966 807 0
Paperback   978 1 78966 805 6
Ebook   978 1 78966 806 3

British Library Cataloguing-in-Publication Data

A CIP record for this book is available from the British Library.

Library of Congress Cataloging-in-Publication Data

Names: Miller, Susi, author.
Title: Designing accessible learning content: a practical guide to applying best-practice accessibility standards to L&D resources / Susi Miller.
Description: 1st Edition. | New York: Kogan Page Inc, 2021. | Includes bibliographical references and index.
Identifiers: LCCN 2021010276 (print) | LCCN 2021010277 (ebook) | ISBN 9781789668070 (hardback) | ISBN 9781789668056 (paperback) | ISBN 9781789668063 (ebook)
Subjects: LCSH: Computer-assisted instruction–Design. | Internet in education. | Digital media.
Classification: LCC LB1028.5 M549 2021 (print) | LCC LB1028.5 (ebook) | DDC 371.33/44678–dc23
LC record available at https://lccn.loc.gov/2021010276
LC ebook record available at https://lccn.loc.gov/2021010277

Typeset by Hong Kong FIVE Workshop, Hong Kong
Print production managed by Jellyfish
Printed and bound by CPI Group (UK) Ltd, Croydon CR0 4YY

For Farisai Moyo and Ananya Chittolla

CONTENTS

List of figures xii
Foreword by Alistair McNaught xiv
Preface xvii

Introduction 1

PART ONE
Accessibility fundamentals 5

01 How to use this book 7
Introduction 7
Part One: Accessibility fundamentals 8
Part Two: Accessibility frameworks 9
Part Three: WCAG 2.1 level A and AA accessibility standards 10
Part Four: WCAG 2.1 level AAA and WCAG 2.2 draft accessibility
standards 11
Disclaimer 11
Summary 12

02 Getting started 13
Introduction 13
Key terms 14
The Web Content Accessibility Guidelines (WCAG) 16
Authoring tool considerations 20
Accessibility testing 30
Team and organizational accessibility strategy 32
Summary 33

03 Exploring disability 37
Introduction 37
Disability definitions 38

Types of disability 38
Disability facts and figures 42
Temporary and situational impairments 44
Disability personas 45
Learner case studies 46
Summary 53

04 Designing for assistive technology and impairments 56

Introduction 56
What is assistive technology? 57
Assistive technology users 58
Visual impairments 59
Hearing impairments 63
Motor impairments 65
Cognitive impairments 68
Summary 69

05 The case for digital accessibility 71

Introduction 71
The ethical case 72
The legal case 73
The business case 77
The learning case 79
Industry perspectives 81
Summary 86

PART TWO

Accessibility frameworks 91

06 The WCAG (Web Content Accessibility Guidelines) framework 93

Introduction 93
Principle 1 – Perceivable 94
Principle 2 – Operable 102
Principle 3 – Understandable 107
Principle 4 – Robust 110

07 The eLa (eLearning accessibility) framework 112

Introduction 112
Step 1 – Resource design and tool settings 114
Step 2 – Text, information and instructions, and images 119
Step 3 – Interactive items and assessments 127
Step 4 – Audio and video content, moving content and timing 137
Step 5 – Keyboard and global content 143
Step 6 – Mobile and code 146

PART THREE
WCAG 2.1 level A and AA accessibility standards 151

08 Perceivable 153

1.1.1 Non-Text Content 153
1.2.1 Audio-Only and Video-Only (Prerecorded) 159
1.2.2 Captions (Prerecorded) 163
1.2.3 Audio Description or Media Alternative (Prerecorded) 167
1.2.4 Captions (Live) 171
1.2.5 Audio Description (Prerecorded) 173
1.3.1 Info and Relationships 175
1.3.2 Meaningful Sequence 180
1.3.3 Sensory Characteristics 183
1.3.4 Orientation 186
1.3.5 Identify Input Purpose 187
1.4.1 Use of Color 189
1.4.2 Audio Control 192
1.4.3 Contrast (Minimum) 194
1.4.4 Resize Text 198
1.4.5 Images of Text 200
1.4.10 Reflow 204
1.4.11 Non-Text Contrast 206
1.4.12 Text Spacing 209
1.4.13 Content on Hover or Focus 212

09 Operable 222

2.1.1 Keyboard 222
2.1.2 No Keyboard Trap 228

2.1.4 Character Key Shortcuts 230

2.2.1 Timing Adjustable 233

2.2.2 Pause, Stop, Hide 237

2.3.1 Three Flashes or Below Threshold 239

2.4.1 Bypass Blocks 241

2.4.2 Page Titled 243

2.4.3 Focus Order 246

2.4.4 Link Purpose (in Context) 248

2.4.5 Multiple Ways 253

2.4.6 Headings and Labels 256

2.4.7 Focus Visible 258

2.5.1 Pointer Gestures 261

2.5.2 Pointer Cancellation 263

2.5.3 Label in Name 265

2.5.4 Motion Actuation 268

10 Understandable 273

3.1.1 Language of Page 273

3.1.2 Language of Parts 275

3.2.1 On Focus 278

3.2.2 On Input 279

3.2.3 Consistent Navigation 281

3.2.4 Consistent Identification 282

3.3.1 Error Identification 284

3.3.2 Labels or Instructions 288

3.3.3 Error Suggestion 290

3.3.4 Error Prevention (Legal, Financial, Data) 293

11 Robust 299

4.1.1 Parsing 299

4.1.2 Name, Role, Value 301

4.1.3 Status Messages 302

PART FOUR
WCAG 2.1 level AAA and WCAG 2.2 draft accessibility standards 307

12 WCAG 2.1 level AAA accessibility standards 309

Introduction 309
Principle 1 – Perceivable 310
Principle 2 – Operable 312
Principle 3 – Understandable 315

13 WCAG 2.2 draft accessibility standards 318

Introduction 318
Principle 2 – Operable 319
Principle 3 – Understandable 320

Conclusion 322

Acknowledgements 325
Index 327

LIST OF FIGURES

Figure 0.1   The Be My Eyes mobile app 2

Figure 2.1   Access HTML source code (Lectora Online) 22

Figure 2.2   Alternative conforming interactivity (CourseArc) 26

Figure 2.3   Impairment focused accessibility guidance (Xerte Online Toolkits) 28

Figure 2.4   Accessibility guidance embedded in the tool (Evolve) 29

Figure 2.5   Accessible theme selector (dominKnow | ONE) 30

Figure 3.1   A simulated visual impairment and how it affects an eLearning resource 40

Figure 7.1   The eLa (eLearning accessibility) framework 113

Figure 8.1   Alternative text for images that convey meaning (dominKnow | ONE) 157

Figure 8.2   Alternative text for complex images (CourseArc) 157

Figure 8.3   Alternative text for decorative images (Lectora Online) 158

Figure 8.4   Alternative text for interactive items (Articulate Storyline) 158

Figure 8.5   Audio description track (Evolve) 162

Figure 8.6   Upload a captions file for an embedded video (Lectora Online) 165

Figure 8.7   Manually add captions to an embedded video (Articulate Storyline) 166

Figure 8.8   Auto-generated transcript link for video (CourseArc) 170

Figure 8.9   HTML source code for an unordered list (Xerte Online Toolkits) 178

Figure 8.10   Assign table header properties (CourseArc) 178

Figure 8.11   Set the correct focus order (Articulate Storyline) 181

Figure 8.12   Place content blocks in the correct order (CourseArc) 182

Figure 8.13   Quiz feedback supplemented with icons and text (iSpring) 191

Figure 8.14   Contrast ratio on inbuilt button states (Articulate Storyline) 197

Figure 8.15   Text added as an image (Evolve) 203

Figure 8.16   Contrast ratio requirements for buttons with text 208

Figure 8.17   Text spacing causes no loss of content or functionality (CourseArc) 211

Figure 8.18   Dismissible pop-up content 214

Figure 8.19   Hoverable pop-up content 215

Figure 9.1   Hotspot interaction alternative (Articulate Storyline) 225

Figure 9.2   Drag-and-drop multiple choice alternative (CourseArc) 226

Figure 9.3   Drag-and-drop ordering alternative (iSpring) 226–27

Figure 9.4   Drag-and-drop simulation with animation paths (Articulate Storyline) 227

Figure 9.5   Keyboard shortcut for a button (Adobe Captivate) 232

Figure 9.6   Quiz timing options (iSpring) 236

Figure 9.7   Skip to lesson bypass link (Articulate Rise) 242

Figure 9.8   Page titles displayed in a menu (Articulate Rise) 245

Figure 9.9   Logical focus order for interactive items (Articulate Storyline) 247

Figure 9.10   Non-descriptive links shown in the Elements List of a screen reader (Articulate Rise) 251

Figure 9.11   Descriptive links shown in the Elements List of a screen reader (Articulate Rise) 252

Figure 9.12   Multiple ways to navigate (Articulate Rise) 255

Figure 9.13   Visible focus indicator for radio buttons (CourseArc) 259

Figure 9.14   Customizable focus indicator (Lectora Online) 260

Figure 9.15   Visible name and accessible name mismatch (Articulate Storyline) 267

Figure 10.1   Language of page tool settings (Xerte Online Toolkits) 274

Figure 10.2   Identify the language of an individual phrase (Adobe Captivate) 277

Figure 10.3   Quiz answer error feedback message (Articulate Rise) 287

Figure 10.4   Formatting information in a quiz question (Articulate Rise) 289

Figure 10.5   Error suggestion message (Articulate Storyline) 292

Figure 10.6   Check and reset option for quiz question (CourseArc) 296

Figure C.1   Key takeaways eLearning resource slide 323

FOREWORD

Digital accessibility is not renowned for being inclusive or easy to grasp.

The Web Content Accessibility Guidelines assume a knowledge of coding which is beyond that of many eLearning professionals. They also assume an awareness of the needs of disabled users and their assistive technologies. Accessibility can seem like a mountain to climb – and for what purpose? How much extra time will you have to invest? Who will pay for it? How many actual users will benefit?

These are natural questions to ask and are worth addressing. But they are not the right questions to start with. Digital accessibility is less about standards and more about mindset, opportunity and professional 'value added'.

With non-digital resources – like a printed handbook – the difference in user experience and accessibility between an amateur version and a professional version is minimal. The professional one might have glossy paper and neater typesetting but from the user's experience they both contain words and pictures. Neither is more 'accessible' than the other because neither can be personalised to suit user needs. On a hard copy document, font size, type, spacing and colour are set. Neither the professional nor the amateur version will read its content to you. What you see is exactly what you get.

Digital resources are different. An amateur can create an eLearning resource which may be capable of some personalization. For example, it may reflow when magnified just because the authoring tool they have used has a responsive template. But a professional with accessibility expertise would bring enormous added value. Their version of the resource may be fully capable of text-to-speech, adaptable in terms of fonts, colours and contrasts and equally navigable by mouse and keyboard. It may be entirely perceivable to a blind person using their assistive technology and entirely operable by a paraplegic who accesses the content using a blink operated switch. Digital accessibility is an exercise in opportunity and imagination. It will only make your practice better, your repertoire wider and your problem solving more agile.

But where do you begin?

You have already made a good start by recognizing your need and buying this book. Even as eLearning professionals, it is easy to forget that learning is driven by the recognition that there are things you don't know about and perhaps ought to.

When I started my own eLearning journey, I came across a model of education technology innovation where the limiting factor changed through time, starting with:

- hardware – the availability of networked PCs or personal devices; then

- software – the availability of suitable software tools; then

- liveware – the skills, competence and imagination of the users.

But liveware does not represent the end of the process. Something is still missing if thousands of developers use software tools to deliver eLearning to millions of hardware devices only to find that more than 10% of the end users cannot adapt the content to meet their needs. The final bullet in the model should be culture – a professionalism determined to create content with as few barriers as possible.

An excellent place to start such a cultural shift is here. Susi's wisdom has been distilled from experience; from trying to improve her own practice, shift her own skill set, learn from end users and learn from other professionals. That gives the book authenticity. It doesn't pretend that digital accessibility is always an easy process, but it offers a pragmatic approach which makes it achievable for everyone. This is the book I wish I had read 15 years ago. It would have saved me an enormous amount of time having to learn things a harder way.

Writing books on technology is a thankless task because technology changes so quickly. Susi has been careful to focus on principles rather than products but the inclusion of products to illustrate those principles is very helpful. We each have favourite tools we use. Understanding the constraints and opportunities within those tools is vital in our journey to creating better content. In some cases, we might even decide to change tools. As global legislation tightens up on accessibility requirements for digital content, the last thing you need is to have your accessibility practice constrained by an authoring tool that makes life difficult for you rather than easy.

Accessibility belongs to everybody. It should be at the core of every eLearning project. Creating accessible content is a marketable skill. If a client hasn't asked about accessibility, ask them yourself. 'How many end users do you want to have a bad learning experience?' is a great conversation opener and brings home the fact that if you're not planning for 'good experiences for all learners' you can guarantee bad experiences for some.

So, learn from this book. There's a clear logic to the layout and a detailed structure that helps you dip in and out as you need to. The book will take you on a journey through digital accessibility.

From a professional point of view, it might be the most important journey you embark on.

Alistair McNaught
Director, Alistair McNaught Consultancy Ltd

PREFACE

Growing up in the eighties meant that my beliefs surrounding disability were firmly rooted in the medical model which was common at the time. This model focuses on a person's disability first and is based on the idea that disability is caused by impairments that need to be treated, managed or cured. Fortunately, one of my first jobs after qualifying as a teacher allowed me to work first-hand with a disabled student. This experience challenged all of my assumptions and preconceptions about disability and marked the beginning of my interest in accessibility.

I met Farisai Moyo in the first class I taught as an English teacher at Gutu High School in Zimbabwe. I'd been teaching for a few years but was horribly nervous, mainly because it was the first opportunity I'd had to teach English literature since studying it at university, but also because it was the first time I'd taught a group of advanced level students not much younger than I was at the time. Soon after beginning my class, I noticed that every time I wrote something on the board, one of the students called Mercy would murmur what I'd written to Farisai. I wasn't sure why this was but was so concerned with maintaining my credibility as a teacher that I didn't want to ask. Luckily at the end of the class, the two girls explained that Mercy was Farisai's 'principal reader'.

Farisai had a condition called corneal opacity caused by measles as a child, which meant that she was blind. Mercy had been chosen by the headteacher to support Farisai during lessons, and to organize a small group of the other students in the class who also helped her by reading the literature texts we were studying. When I found this out, my first reaction was panic. Like so many other teachers and trainers who discover they have a student with access needs, I had no idea how to adapt my teaching methods to be inclusive. Things didn't go smoothly to begin with, mainly because I wasn't willing to ask for help, fearing that I'd undermine any confidence that anyone had in my teaching ability. It soon became obvious, however, that my reluctance to ask for advice was affecting Farisai's ability to learn. As a result, I admitted to Farisai and Mercy that I was struggling and together we worked out how I could adapt my teaching style and ways of working to accommodate them. The strategies we implemented were very simple. All they needed were a bit of extra thought and planning before each class and around homework assignments. Yet, although these were relatively easy to achieve, they made a noticeable difference to how effectively Farisai could participate and learn.

There was one aspect of Farisai's learning support, however, which was clearly holding her back. This was her dependence on Mercy and the other students to read aloud the literature texts we were studying. Farisai was without a doubt one of the most gifted students in the class, but it was clear that in order to achieve what she was capable of she needed to be able to study in a way and at a pace that suited her. Access to assistive technology was not an option in our school at that time, but Farisai could read braille. Although we had originally thought it would be impossible to source braille versions of the texts we were studying, after a lengthy search we did manage to find copies of most of them. Since our school was on a remote compound in a rural district of Zimbabwe, we arranged to have these books sent by post. One of my most abiding memories of Farisai is seeing her absolute joy as she unwrapped the huge braille version of *Hamlet* which had been sent from the central library in Harare.

Although Farisai's braille books were not an immediate fix to all of the barriers she faced, they made a huge impact on her ability to learn. What was most noticeable was the confidence that she gained from being able to study independently. It was clear that with the help of the braille texts, she felt that she had the opportunity to achieve what she was capable of and to fulfil her academic potential. This turned out to be the case. Farisai passed her English Literature A Level with a good grade and went on to study at a local teacher training college. Although this was an exceptional achievement, she once confided to me that her dream was to study literature at the University of Zimbabwe. I have often wondered since then whether Farisai would have been able to achieve this ambition if she'd been able to take advantage of the extraordinary developments in technology which have happened over the last 30 years. I am certain that she would.

Working with Farisai was one of the greatest privileges in my career. The experience forced me to reevaluate all of my assumptions about teaching and learning. It taught me to be more aware of the needs of my students and made me realize how important it was to be able to adapt to those needs, ultimately making me a better teacher. Even more importantly, however, it made me rethink my attitude to disability. Working with Farisai showed me that her impairment, in the form of her blindness, was not in itself something which disabled her. She was just as bright and capable as the other students in her class, and with strategies and accommodations which allowed her to become more confident and independent she was able to fulfil her potential. Farisai's achievements were a perfect demonstration of the social model of disability. This model is based on the idea that disability is caused by barriers which are created when products and services are not designed to accommodate impairments. If these barriers are removed, a person may still have an impairment, but they don't experience disability. The social model of disability often focuses on physical barriers imposed by inaccessible environments or digital barriers imposed by inaccessible technology such as websites. Working with Farisai showed me that it was just as relevant to barriers in learning.

The social model of disability promotes equality and inclusivity because it is centred around the idea that we are all equal, we just have differing needs. This is a concept which is central to this book. If we design inaccessible learning content, we create barriers which disable people's abilities and potential. If we design accessible learning content, we allow everyone to participate equally. We also promote the idea enshrined in the first article of the 1948 Universal Declaration of Human Rights that 'All human beings are born free and equal in dignity and rights.'[1] I wrote this book for Farisai, because I believe that everybody has the right to be treated equally in their learning experience. If you agree, I also wrote it for you.

Endnote

[1] United Nations (1948) The Universal Declaration of Human Rights, 10 December, https://www.ohchr.org/EN/UDHR/Documents/UDHR_Translations/eng.pdf (archived at https://perma.cc/G29P-KM9V)

Introduction

I begin many of the talks and training sessions I deliver on designing accessible learning content by focusing on two numbers taken from the Be My Eyes mobile app. The first is 266,353 and the second is 4,329,505. If you have a neurodiversity like mine, which means you struggle to process large numbers written in figures, I'll also give you those numbers in text. The first number is two hundred and sixty-six thousand, three hundred and fifty-three. The second number is four million, three hundred and twenty-nine thousand, five hundred and five. By the time you come to read these numbers they will be completely out of date. They will, however, be no less relevant.

The Be My Eyes app connects visually impaired users with sighted volunteers from all over the world through a live video call. It allows the volunteers to be the eyes of the user and complete any task that they ask for help with. This could include identifying the colour of clothes, reading out a WIFI code or a recipe, giving directions or even helping to find a lost cat. One of the numbers I've given you is the number of people with visual impairments who use the app, the other is the number of volunteers. Take a moment to decide which is which.

As you may have guessed, the volunteers for Be My Eyes vastly outnumber the people who use the service. My own experience of the app confirms this. I've been a volunteer since the beginning of 2020, yet during that time have received only a handful of requests for help. Each of the calls I received was answered by another member of the community before I could reach my phone. This is the typical experience of many Be My Eyes volunteers and is caused by the sheer number of people in the community who are willing to give up their time to help out. But why do I focus on Be My Eyes when I talk about designing accessible content? It is a valuable story for two reasons.

FIGURE 0.1   The Be My Eyes mobile app

The front page of the Be My Eyes mobile app.
SOURCE Reproduced with permission of Accessibly, Inc.

The first lesson to be learnt from Be My Eyes is just how transformational the impact of technology can be for disabled people. For Hans Jørgen Wiberg, the visually impaired founder of Be My Eyes, one of the primary drivers for creating the app was to allow disabled people more autonomy.[1] By connecting people with visual impairments to a global community who were happy to volunteer and to offer help, he effectively bypassed the need for friends, family, neighbours and colleagues who normally had to be relied on. Designing accessible learning content has exactly the same positive impact because it empowers learners and allows them to be autonomous.

The second lesson we can learn from Be My Eyes is that its success relies not only on technology but also on human commitment. Before launching Be My Eyes, the app's creators considered using incentives such as badges and leader boards to encourage people to become volunteers. As CCO Alexander Hauerslev Jensen explains, 'When we launched, we didn't know if people would be willing to volunteer time to help complete strangers.'[2] What happened when they released the app, however, convinced them that people didn't need incentives to join. Within the first 24 hours, they had more than 10,000 volunteers. As we know, that number has now reached over 4 million. By the time you read this book it will be tens of thousands, if not hundreds of thousands, more.

But is it possible to draw a parallel between the Be My Eyes volunteers and eLearning professionals? I think it is. I believe that the time and effort needed to create inclusive learning resources means that eLearning professionals are most likely to succeed if they are motivated, at least in part, by the type of altruism shown by the Be My Eyes volunteers. As more and more people look to find purpose and meaning in the work they do, especially as a result of the COVID 19 pandemic, the good news for eLearning professionals is that we are in the privileged position of being able to positively impact people's lives, simply by changing the way we work. No one has articulated this better than the user experience designer Steve Krug who wrote:

> The one argument for accessibility that doesn't get made nearly often enough is how extraordinarily better it makes some people's lives. How many opportunities do we have to dramatically improve people's lives just by doing our job a little better?[3]

As eLearning professionals we can make disabled people's lives better by designing content in ways which allows them to learn effectively and independently. And although many people may believe that this has very little impact, nothing could be further from the truth. When we consider how vital access to digital learning is in both education and professional development, the contribution we make to people's lives by creating accessible eLearning resources is indeed 'dramatic'. It also has the potential to affect many more people than we commonly believe. In most Western countries the size of the disabled population ranges from 12% to 26%,[4] while globally it is estimated to be about 15%.[5] That equates to over 1 billion people whom we have the potential to help, just by 'doing our job a little better'.

In the future, I hope there is an app as brilliant as Be My Eyes which offers a simple technological solution to the challenges eLearning professionals face when designing inclusive learning resources. Yet, the lessons we have learnt from using accessibility overlays and automatic testing tools are a good demonstration of the pitfalls of relying on technology to fix our accessibility issues. As a result, I believe that a book offers the best chance of practically solving the challenges involved with designing accessible learning content, for the moment at least. Although we will never be able to measure how many people it helps in the same way as we can with Be My Eyes, I'd like to think that at some time in the future it will mean that thousands of eLearning professionals are helping millions of people to enjoy better learning experiences.

Endnotes

1   Be My Eyes. Our story. Small acts of kindness with global impact, https://www.bemyeyes.com/about (archived at https://perma.cc/N7GD-GJQH)

2   Salam, E (2019) I tried Be My Eyes, the popular app that pairs blind people with helpers, *Guardian*, 12 July, https://www.theguardian.com/lifeandstyle/2019/jul/12/be-my-eyes-app-blind-people-helpers (archived at https://perma.cc/BB6W-ESSE)

3   Krug, S (2000) *Don't Make Me Think Revisited: A common sense approach to web usability*, New Riders, Pearson, London

4   Hassel, J (2019) *Inclusive Design for Organisations: Including your missing 20% by embedding web and mobile accessibility*, Rethink Press, Gorleston-on-Sea

5   World Health Organization (2020) Disability, https://www.who.int/health-topics/disability#tab=tab_1 (archived at https://perma.cc/7U9W-K8XC)

Accessibility fundamentals

01

How to use this book

Introduction

In her book *Accessibility for Everyone* Laura Kalbag writes:

> Accessibility is often presented as something that should be left to 'experts'. We do need experts for their specialized knowledge and guidance, but there aren't enough accessibility experts in the world to leave the task of building an accessible web in their hands alone.[1]

It was this quote which convinced me to write *Designing Accessible Learning Content*. It made me realize that as eLearning professionals we all have a responsibility to learn how to make the content we design and create inclusive. I also agreed with Kalbag that although accessibility can seem like a technical and complex subject which is best supported with the help of experts, it is not something that we can leave 'in their hands alone'. Because if we do, there is no hope that it will ever become mainstream.

Luckily, increasing awareness of the importance of inclusive design coupled with changes in legislation mean that more and more eLearning professionals are beginning to agree with me. Yet this leaves us facing a dilemma which, as an instructional designer passionate about eLearning accessibility, I have had direct experience of. The issue we face is that there are very few experts and barely any resources available to support us. The emphasis of accessibility is often still focused on commercial and informational websites and not on online content designed to provide an engaging learner experience. The purpose of *Designing Accessible Learning Content* is to address this issue. It is centred on a pragmatic and practical approach designed to help eLearning professionals become competent and confident applying accessibility to learning content. Yet, while designing eLearning resources that are more accessible is easy to achieve, creating content which is legally compliant with the Web Content Accessibility Guidelines (WCAG) is not without its challenges.

Simplicity and usability were at the forefront of my vision when I began writing. I wanted to create a handbook which made designing fully accessible learning content so easy that there could be no excuse for not doing so. In effect, I wanted to write an 'eLearning Accessibility Made Simple' manual. I soon came to realize, however, that it would be both disingenuous and demotivating to describe it as a simple process. Nevertheless, I have tried to make it as straightforward as possible. This first chapter gives you an overview of the best way to use the book in order to suit the way you learn and the way you work. I hope that it helps to make your eLearning accessibility journey a smooth and positive experience.

Part One: Accessibility fundamentals

Chapter 2, Getting started, provides information which is essential to be aware of before you begin. It contains crucial background information on topics such as the WCAG, authoring tools, testing and organizational strategy. It also focuses on some of the challenges faced by eLearning professionals and gives guidance on how to overcome them. The other chapters in Part One also contain supplementary information. It can be easy to get bogged down in the complicated intricacies of the WCAG, but digital accessibility can also be a fascinating and inspiring subject. Chapter 3, Exploring disability, helps you to understand disability from a digital perspective. As well as factual information such as statistics and examples of different types of disabilities and impairments, this chapter includes case studies from disabled learners. Their experiences highlight how inaccessible content can create barriers and allow you to consider the human aspect of accessibility which is often lost when we focus only on technical requirements.

Chapter 4, Designing for assistive technology and impairments, is a key chapter for making sense of the WCAG standards. I found that it wasn't until I had a better understanding of how assistive technology worked that I could fully appreciate what was required by many of the standards. This chapter also provides a useful overview of some of the key requirements for making learning content accessible for learners with a range of different needs. The final chapter in Part One is The case for digital accessibility. This provides the ethical, legal, business and learning arguments for accessibility. It also includes a number of industry perspectives which highlight why accessibility is becoming a 'must have' feature of eLearning products and services in today's increasingly competitive market. This chapter gives you the information to allow you to advocate for accessibility. It can also provide a welcome source of motivation if at any point you feel overwhelmed or become discouraged when you are learning more about designing accessible content which, rest assured, happens to everyone.

Part Two: Accessibility frameworks

Since I believe that the complex language and structure of the WCAG are primary factors in making accessibility difficult for eLearning professionals to apply, I have designed two frameworks which form Part Two of the book. These frameworks both give summarized, plain English explanations of the WCAG standards and how they apply to learning content. They both cover all 50 WCAG 2.1 level A and AA standards, which are the legal benchmark for most international accessibility legislation. The frameworks, however, are structured differently to allow you to dip in and out as you wish and to give you different ways to access the content and to apply the guidelines.

The WCAG (Web Content Accessibility Guidelines) framework

The WCAG framework divides the standards into the World Wide Web Consortium's (W3C) POUR principles. These stand for Perceivable, Operable, Understandable and Robust. Each of the principles is further subdivided into guidelines. While the WCAG framework can be useful when developing content, the way it is structured means you may find it is better suited to testing for conformance or for formulating an accessibility statement.

Each of the standards in the framework has an icon set which indicates what it applies to in an eLearning context. For example, WCAG **1.1.1 Non-text Content** has the following icon set:

These icons indicate that you need to consider this standard when you set up your eLearning resource. They also show that the standard is relevant for images, interactive items, and audio and video content.

The eLa (eLearning accessibility) framework

The eLa framework also covers all the 50 WCAG 2.1 level A and AA standards. Rather than grouping the guidelines into the four POUR principles, however, the framework is divided into six steps. These are each relevant to a particular eLearning theme or subject area and are structured in a contextual order which is logical for designing and developing learning content with a range of authoring tools. I initially developed this framework to help make my own learning content accessible. It is now at the core of the successful training programmes I provide at www.elahub.net.

Checklists

To accompany the frameworks there are additional checklist versions which can be accessed at www.koganpage.com/DALC (archived at https://perma.cc/6UCY-FE7F). They are provided in an online format so that they can be easily reproduced, but also so that they can be customized and adapted to suit your way of working and your authoring tool.

Part Three: WCAG 2.1 level A and AA accessibility standards

Part Three contains detailed explanations of each of the WCAG 2.1 level A and AA standards. As with the WCAG framework, the standards are ordered according to the W3C POUR principles, with one chapter dedicated to each principle. To make them easier to understand and cross reference they also include the icon sets used in the WCAG framework and are broken down into the following topics:

- Key information
- How to conform
- Exceptions
- Why?
- Examples
- How to test
- Useful resources

Part Four: WCAG 2.1 level AAA and WCAG 2.2 draft accessibility standards

WCAG 2.1 level AAA accessibility standards

The first chapter in this section provides a brief overview of each of the advanced AAA standards. Bearing in mind that conforming to this level requires 28 additional criteria, it is understandable that many content authors are often primarily concerned with meeting the requirements of levels A and AA. The pragmatic approach adopted in the book is to include a brief explanation of the best-practice AAA guidelines in this separate chapter for reference. If they are related to the requirements of any of the level A and AA standards, they are also included in the detailed explanations of these standards in Part Three.

WCAG 2.2 draft accessibility standards

The second chapter in this section provides the nine WCAG 2.2 standards which were released in August 2020. As with all new W3C standards they are first released in draft form and are then finalized after feedback from accessibility experts has been taken into consideration. They are included for reference and because they give an indication of future requirements and best practice. These are not plain English interpretations of the guidelines, but simply the WCAG wording.

Disclaimer

No resource which gives guidance on meeting the requirements of the WCAG standards is complete without a disclaimer. *Designing Accessible Learning Content* is no exception. It is important to be aware that the information and advice it contains are not intended to guarantee that learning content will be fully compliant with legal regulations. It is well known that the WCAG standards are open to differing interpretations. I have based my explanations on commonly referenced and recommended digital accessibility sources. They have also been verified and approved by experts both in the fields of accessibility and online learning. As with all guidance created to help people make sense of the WCAG standards, however, my explanations are ultimately only interpretations and should not be considered legal advice.

Summary

- To get the most out of this book, it's important to understand the information it contains and how it is structured.

- Part One contains useful accessibility background information which can either be read before you begin or can be referred back to at any time if you need further support. It also includes the Getting started chapter which contains crucial information to be aware of before you start.

- Part Two contains the WCAG and the eLa frameworks. These frameworks both give summarized, plain English explanations of each of the WCAG standards and how they apply to learning content. They are structured in different ways to support the way that you work and suit the task you are trying to achieve.

- Part Three contains detailed explanations of each of the 50 WCAG 2.1 level A and AA standards.

- Part Four contains a brief overview of all 28 level AAA standards. It also contains the nine 2.2 standards which were available only in draft format at the time of publishing.

- The guidance in this book should not be considered legal advice which guarantees conformance to the WCAG standards.

Endnote

[1] Kalbag, L (2017) *Accessibility for Everyone*, A Book Apart, New York

02

Getting started

Introduction

The word accessibility is often shortened to A11Y, with the number 11 replacing the 11 letters in between the A and the Y. When I began trying to find out how to design accessible learning content, I wasn't aware of this. It took me at least a month before I realized that A11Y was connected with accessibility, and another couple more before I thought to run a search on what it meant. When I eventually did find out, I was genuinely elated. It felt like I had finally cracked a code, or at least found a missing piece of the puzzle which could help me to solve the mysteries of eLearning accessibility. While I was doing research into the origins of A11Y, I discovered that it was based on 'an information and communications orientated convention used mostly in the software community.'[1] And this was a lightbulb moment. I finally understood that I wasn't woefully ignorant about accessibility, nor embarrassingly technologically unaware, I was just doing the wrong job.

I'm not part of the software community. I am an instructional designer who uses rapid authoring tools to develop learning content. While I'm familiar with using many authoring tools, and proficient in a few, I have only ever used tools which do not need any understanding of the underlying source code. Before carrying out the research for this book, my knowledge of HTML was limited to what I'd learnt in the first few chapters of a 'teach yourself' manual in the late nineties. I had a vague idea that CSS had something to do with styling content and that WAI-ARIA was somehow related to coding for accessibility. If you have had any experience of working with the WCAG, you will understand that this left me ill-equipped to deal either with the challenges of making sense of them or with applying them to an eLearning context. Yet, applying the WCAG criteria to learning content is exactly what eLearning professionals need to do to meet the legal accessibility requirements in an ever-increasing number of countries.

I know I am not the only content author who has faced this challenge. I also know that I am not the only one who has felt so utterly out of their depth that it is easier simply to ignore accessibility and hope it goes away. This book doesn't assume that you are a software developer or a coding expert, or that you have any prior knowledge about accessibility. It follows the same principles essential to designing likeable software as identified by Alan Cooper: 'Respectful, generous and helpful.'[2] This chapter follows that approach by providing useful background information, like the meaning of A11Y, which I wish I'd known before I started trying to design accessible learning content.

Key terms

In my experience, much of the language around eLearning and accessibility can mean different things to different people. As a result, the first section of this chapter provides definitions of some key terms used throughout this book in order to avoid any confusion or misunderstanding.

eLearning professional/content author

The content of this book is suitable for anyone involved in any part of the creation, design or development of eLearning. You may be an HR or a finance officer, a lecturer or a tutor, or a student intern responsible for creating online learning content. Your role could be an instructional designer, an art director, an eLearning developer or a learning technologist. You may be involved in testing or quality assurance or have an 'end-to-end' role, which means you are responsible for all the different aspects of designing and creating learning content. For ease, and as a result of the lack of standardization around job roles and responsibilities in the industry, I use 'eLearning professional' and 'content author' as umbrella terms throughout the book.

Learning content/eLearning

The terms 'learning content' and 'eLearning' can cover a wide variety of resources, including online documentation, video material, online textbooks and web pages with learning content. In this book, however, they refer specifically to any online learning content created using an authoring tool.

Authoring tool

'Authoring tool', or sometimes 'rapid authoring tool', is used to describe any software, either web based or locally hosted, which gives eLearning professionals the ability to create online learning experiences. Although creating digital learning content is possible with a wide range of tools and software, in this book it refers to standalone tools developed to create eLearning content.

Accessibility

I often find that when I use the term accessibility in an eLearning context people misunderstand me. This is because they think I am using it in the sense of either 'easily obtained or used' or 'easily understood or appreciated'. Although accessibility can have these meanings, in this book it is used to mean specifically 'able to be used by disabled people'.

Digital accessibility

The W3C gives a useful definition of digital or web accessibility which I follow in this book. 'Web accessibility means that people with disabilities can equally perceive, understand, navigate, and interact with websites and tools. It also means that they can contribute equally without barriers.'[3]

WCAG standard

The official W3C term for each of the WCAG standards is 'success criterion'. I find this term awkward and overly technical and use the word 'standard' instead.

The language of disability

There are many different opinions about the language of disability and people often have strong preferences around how they prefer to be identified. Throughout this book I use the identity first terms 'disabled people' or 'disabled learners'. This is because they are in line with the social model of disability, which is based on the idea that people are disabled by barriers in society, not by their impairment or difference. I also use person first language and refer to people with visual, cognitive, hearing and motor impairments. This is in order to encourage inclusive thinking and the idea that having impairments is something that can affect all of us, whether this is due to a disability, ageing, a temporary situation or the particular environment that we are in.

Having defined the key terms, the rest of this chapter focuses on background information which is useful to be aware of before moving on to the practicalities of designing inclusive learning content.

The Web Content Accessibility Guidelines (WCAG)

Why the WCAG?

For many years one of the main difficulties faced by content authors who wanted to design accessible learning content was a lack of clarity from the eLearning industry on how this should be achieved. Much of the accessibility support from authoring tool providers focused on 'hints' and 'tips' rather than definitive advice about which standards to follow and guidance on how to implement them. In 2015, this led a leading content provider to call for the industry to work together to produce a 'collective agreement and a specific set of standards for best practice when it comes to accessibility'.[4] There is now an increasing awareness, however, that the WCAG are the definitive standards to follow for accessibility compliance in eLearning products and services.

This is primarily because they are the internationally recognized guidelines produced by the Web Accessibility Initiative (WAI), which are part of W3C, the organization responsible for developing standards for the web. W3C describes the WCAG as the 'single shared standard for web content accessibility that meets the needs of individuals, organizations, and governments internationally'.[5] They are technical standards developed collaboratively with stakeholders from industry, disability organizations and government. Without them, it is impossible for eLearning professionals to be sure they are designing content which is accessible to agreed standards. Content authors might know, for example, that they should have good colour contrast in their resources, but without further technical details from the WCAG they wouldn't know that, depending on the size of the font, the minimum contrast ratio between text and the background it appears on should be at least 4.5:1.

Another reason the WCAG are increasingly considered to be the definitive guidelines for achieving accessibility in learning content is as a result of legal developments. An overview of international accessibility laws provided by W3C demonstrates that it is currently the WCAG, or a derivative of them, which are the legal standards used in most countries.[6] Recent updates to the law in the EU, the UK and the US provide compelling evidence to support this case. More information about these developments can be found in Chapter 5. Even for those eLearning professionals working in countries which have not yet formally adopted the WCAG, due to the global reach of so many companies and organizations, they are increasingly considered the definitive digital accessibility guidelines to meet.

WCAG key facts

- The WCAG are 'stable referenceable standards that do not change.'[7] They are, however, updated continuously. The first version, WCAG 1.0, was published in 1999, the second, WCAG 2.0, in 2008, the third, WCAG 2.1, in 2018. The most up-to-date version, WCAG 2.2, has a release date of 2021.

- Accessibility experts always advise working to the most recent version of the guidelines as this incorporates any significant technological advances, such as with version 2.1 and mobile technology.

- There are three levels of conformance in the WCAG. Level A is the most basic, level AA is intermediate and level AAA is the most advanced.

- For WCAG 2.1 there are 78 standards altogether: 30 at level A, 20 at level AA and 28 at level AAA.

- WCAG 2.2 introduces a further nine standards, eight at level AA and one at level AAA, although at the time of writing these were still in draft and subject to change.

- International legislation varies with regard to which version and which level is the legal benchmark, although levels A and AA are the most common requirement.

- Level AAA conformance is considered best practice. W3C concedes, however, that it may not be possible to achieve all the standards at this level.

- The WCAG are divided into four principles and subdivided into 13 guidelines. The principles are Perceivable, Operable, Understandable and Robust. These are often referred to as the POUR principles.

- o Perceivable means that the design of learning resources is presented in ways that are available to all the senses, eg alternative text is provided for images for non-visual learners.

- o Operable means that resources can be operated by all learners, including those who use assistive technology.

- o Understandable means that learners can understand not only the content but also how to navigate and work with interactions, etc.

- o Robust means that content can be interpreted by a wide range of technologies, including different browsers and assistive technologies.

- The WCAG are undergoing an extensive overhaul at the time of writing, with recommendations for the new guidelines scheduled to be published in 2023.

  - o The project and the task force involved in this work are often referred to by the name 'Silver'. This is taken from the symbol for the chemical element for silver, 'Ag', standing for 'Accessibility Guidelines'.

  - o The new guidelines will be known as W3C Accessibility Guidelines 3.0 to reflect that their scope is wider than just web content, but they will still have the acronym WCAG.[8]

  - o WCAG 3.0 defines three levels of conformance: bronze, silver and gold.[9] The current structure only allows pass or fail.

  - o While the new guidelines are scheduled to be published in 2023, many accessibility experts believe this is likely to be delayed. Many also believe that the new guidelines will need to be adopted into legal regulations before they are widely implemented which could take several years.

  - o Although WCAG 3.0 will update and revise the standards and present them in a different way, the fundamental principles of accessibility will remain largely the same as for the standards covered in this book.

WCAG challenges

Despite the benefits of the WCAG, it is undoubtedly true that they have limitations which cause issues for eLearning professionals. The most significant of these is that they were created for web developers building standard websites who are able to modify the underlying code used to create content.

They are not aimed at eLearning professionals who create highly engaging and interactive learning resources using rapid authoring tools and who commonly do not access underlying code. This creates a constant tension and can make it difficult to understand how some of the WCAG standards are relevant to learning content at all.

Another challenge is that the language of both the standards themselves and the supporting guidance is unhelpfully technical and complex. If you have never read a WCAG standard, the following is a good example of the type of language used:

> 3.1.2 Language of Parts – Level AA
>
> *The human language of each passage or phrase in the content can be programmatically determined except for proper names, technical terms, words of indeterminate language, and words or phrases that have become part of the vernacular of the immediately surrounding text.*

One of the justifications used to defend the language of the WCAG is that it needs to be deliberately generalized in order to be 'technology neutral', ie applicable to a wide range of technology. This may well be the case, but having spent several months translating the WCAG standards into plain English, I believe there are many instances where they could be explained in a much clearer way. This is particularly frustrating when W3C's own recommendation is to provide an easily readable alternative if the language used is more advanced than would be suitable for someone with a lower secondary education reading level, ie with about nine years of education. It is encouraging to know at least that one of the key requirements for the new W3C accessibility guidelines is that they will be explained in 'plain or clear language'.[10]

I believe the language of the WCAG also causes an issue when it comes to the way they are structured. Since many people struggle to remember what the four POUR principles mean, structuring the standards based on these principles offers most people very little help when trying to navigate the WCAG and find information. I challenge anyone who doesn't routinely work with the standards, for example, to work out whether they should look in the Perceivable, Operable, Understandable or Robust category if they are trying to find information about ordering page items logically for assistive technology. If you want to try this for yourself, you can check if you were right by finding the **Meaningful Sequence** standard in Part Three. Admittedly, the subgroup 'guideline' headings under POUR are generally easier to understand but some, such as 'time-based media', 'adaptable' and 'input modalities', still cause confusion for many people.

The final challenge of the WCAG is the number of standards which content authors need to understand. As we discovered in the 'WCAG key facts' section, there are 78 standards altogether, 50 of them at levels A and AA. WCAG 2.2 provisionally introduces a further eight at level AA. This means that if legislation catches up with the latest 2.2 guidelines there will be a total of 58 standards to meet in order to achieve legal compliance. While it is true that not all standards apply to all learning content, eLearning professionals still need to have an understanding of the requirements of each of them to find out if they are applicable. It is not surprising, then, that many feel overwhelmed by the sheer number of standards they have to understand and implement in order to comply with legislation.

I have included these challenges not because I want to discourage or demotivate content authors, but rather to reassure people that if they have struggled with eLearning accessibility and the WCAG standards in the past, there are good reasons for this. Many of the clients I work with are apologetic if they have found it difficult to design accessible learning content. They often confess to being frustrated that eLearning accessibility makes them feel incompetent or inadequate in a role in which they are otherwise highly skilled and professional. I don't believe this should be the case. My initial driver for creating the eLearning accessibility framework was to address my own feelings of incompetence and inadequacy. I soon realized, however, that it could also help my clients and delegates to overcome similar barriers.

Authoring tool considerations

As an eLearning accessibility consultant, one of the things that I am asked for most often is advice about which authoring tools are the best for accessibility. This is a difficult question to answer, not least because authoring tools are continually updated, and many are now focusing on improving their accessibility functionality on an ongoing basis. Another reason this is not a simple question is because 'being accessible' covers many different aspects and also needs to be balanced with other requirements which are important for eLearning professionals. For example, some tools may have good accessibility features but may not have the flexibility in design and functionality which clients demand. Some tools may have good accessibility features but may not give content authors the support and guidance they need to implement those features. And some tools may have good accessibility features but these may be difficult to find and cumbersome to apply, making them a chore rather than part of the standard workflow for content authors. Due to these challenges, my approach in this book is to use a selection of the many tools available to demonstrate examples and best practice wherever possible. Each tool has advantages and disadvantages and including them in this book is not intended to be an endorsement of any of the tools featured.

Approaches to content creation

Since it can be rare for content authors to specialize in only one authoring tool, it is important to be aware of the different approaches to creating content in the wide variety of tools available. Although each tool has unique features it is possible to identify several broad approaches to content creation. The first option is to build content from scratch using code. This was the approach traditionally used in the early days of eLearning authoring, but it is much rarer nowadays and doesn't strictly speaking qualify as using an authoring tool. Another option is for content authors to use tools which allow them to view and amend the source code when creating content. Open source tools typically have this functionality. The final option used by the vast majority of eLearning content authors is to use tools with a graphical interface. These types of tools are sometimes known as WYSIWYG (What You See Is What You Get) tools. They allow content authors to see what the end result will look like when they are designing content. Some WYSIWYG authoring tools have functionality which easily allows content authors to view and amend the source code (see Figure 2.1). With other tools content authors can access and change the code but this may require additional guidance and support.

Access to underlying code is significant because achieving some of the WCAG standards requires that they are coded correctly so that they are compatible with assistive technology. If content authors have access to this code it can make it easier to check whether this is the case, and to amend the code if necessary.

A final issue to be aware of with regard to content creation is that broadly speaking there are two approaches to creating content using WYSIWYG authoring tools. More traditional authoring tools tend to have what I describe as a 'blank page' approach. This allows content authors to add all the components to a page and to have control over how they look and how they function. A more common approach, particularly among the latest tools, is

FIGURE 2.1   Access HTML source code (Lectora Online)

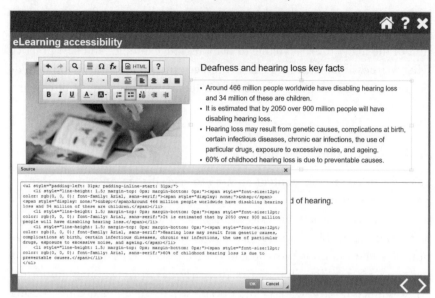

The Lectora Online authoring tool has an Edit HTML source code option in the text box formatting tool bar. This allows content authors to view and change the underlying code of the output.
SOURCE Reproduced with permission of eLearning Brothers

to have an interface which is less configurable and allows content authors to add set components or blocks of content. This is important in relation to meeting the WCAG standards because the second approach often means that content authors have less control over the content they are creating and rely more on the inbuilt accessibility functionality of the authoring tool.

This book is designed to be useful for content authors regardless of which authoring tool or approach they are using. This does mean, however, that it is not possible to give tool-specific instructions for how to achieve each of the WCAG standards. Instead I give generic guidance, or sometimes a comparison of different approaches between tools. The best-practice examples I provide are also designed to give a better understanding of how the WCAG standards can be achieved using a variety of tools and approaches. It is ultimately the responsibility of authoring tool providers to give guidance on how to meet accessibility standards with their tool. This book will at the very least allow content authors to know what they should be trying to achieve and what they should be asking their authoring tool providers for if they are not able to do so.

Relevance of WCAG standards

Although it may seem like an obvious point to make, it's important to be aware that not all of the WCAG standards are relevant to all learning content. This depends on the purpose and functionality of the content. In addition, the standards themselves contain exceptions which may mean that some content is exempt. Although it is tempting to try to identify WCAG standards which are not likely to be relevant to any eLearning resources, this approach is risky. This is mainly due to the sheer number of tools available, which means it is impossible to make assumptions about the functionality available in all of them. Another reason it is not a recommended approach is due to technological advances which mean that tool functionality is constantly being updated. A good example to demonstrate this is standard **2.5.4 Motion Actuation**, which applies to content that can be triggered by motion in mobile devices. While this standard is unlikely to apply to many eLearning resources currently, it may well do so in the future.

A final reason the approach is risky is because of the grey area surrounding the definition of authoring tools. In the case of learning content this is particularly relevant for learning management systems (LMS) or virtual learning environments (VLE), which may have content creation functionality or allow this to be achieved with plugins. While most authoring tools do not have the functionality to provide live content, such as presentations or lectures, this may exist in the LMS or VLE. This means that standard **1.2.4 Captions (Live)** may be relevant to some content authors and organizations. Another example concerns data entry fields which in most authoring tools are generally used to allow learners to answer quiz or assessment questions. Many of the WCAG standards, however, relate to fields which collect personal data, since this is often their purpose on standard websites. While it would be tempting to discount these standards as not being relevant to learning content, they may apply to LMS and VLE functionality and so will still be useful for some content authors. As a result, this book includes an overview of all the WCAG standards and allows content authors to decide which of them are relevant to the content they are designing and creating.

Tool provider responsibilities

Since the W3C Authoring Tool Accessibility Guidelines (ATAG)[11] were published in 2015, there have been specific accessibility standards for authoring tool providers. Although there are no legal imperatives to enforce these standards, they nevertheless provide comprehensive guidance for authoring tool providers on the accessibility support they should offer. The ATAG contain a large number of detailed recommendations, but they have two key aims. The first is to make authoring tools themselves accessible. The second is to help authors create accessible content by ensuring that the tool output conforms to the WCAG standards and also by providing support and guidance on how to achieve this. Many accessibility experts believe that the ATAG are even more significant than the WCAG in the struggle to make digital accessibility the norm rather than the exception. This is because without accessibility functionality in software and tool-specific guidance, it can be extremely difficult or even impossible for content authors to create accessible content.

In light of the ATAG recommendations, a useful way of evaluating the accessibility credentials of authoring tool providers is to assess not only the information they provide about the accessibility of their tool but also the guidance they offer on how to implement this functionality. Since we have established that the WCAG are the legal requirement for accessibility in many countries, authoring tool providers should ideally provide information on how their tool complies with these standards. This is most commonly done in the form of an accessibility conformance statement or in the US a Voluntary Product Accessibility Template (VPAT™). Articulate Storyline[12] and CourseArc[13] both offer best-practice VPAT™ examples. Not only do both providers offer detailed information about how their tools allow content authors to conform to WCAG 2.1 standards, but they also adhere to the requirements of the ATAG by providing further information and links to additional support which show content authors how to use their tools to implement them. In addition to supporting content authors, best-practice VPAT™ documents have the added advantage of being a resource which can be linked to in an accessibility statement.

Note: The information provided in some VPAT™ documents focuses on US Section 508 requirements. While Section 508 was aligned with the WCAG in 2017,[14] at the time of publishing this was only to WCAG 2.0, leaving 12 WCAG 2.1 standards at levels A and AA not covered by Section 508.

Authoring tool limitations

In a 2019 Learning Guild report on authoring tools, Jane Bozarth noted that problems with accessibility were a common frustration cited by eLearning professionals.[15] Several complained that accessibility features too often seemed like an afterthought, or that they were surprised that major vendors had done so little to make their products meet accessibility guidelines. The industry perspectives provided in Chapter 5 of this book provide encouraging evidence that authoring tool providers are becoming more engaged with accessibility. We are, however, still a very long way away from all tools providing the functionality and support which content authors need to make learning content fully accessible as standard. While as eLearning accessibility expert Kevin Gumienny states, 'some accessibility is always better than no accessibility',[16] this still leaves many eLearning professionals facing the challenge of what to do if their authoring tool does not allow them to meet all the WCAG standards required to conform to legislation. There are two common approaches to addressing this problem.

CONFORMING ALTERNATE VERSIONS

One strategy is to create an alternative accessible version of the content. W3C call these 'conforming alternate versions'.[17] The key W3C requirements for these versions are as follows:

1 The content is fully accessible.

2 The content is at the same level and is in the same language as the non-accessible version.

3 Learners are provided with the same information and the same functionality as for the non-accessible version.

4 The content remains up to date.

5 Learners can access the conforming version from the non-conforming version, through a mechanism which is accessible.

In most eLearning resources, alternate conforming versions are provided as a PDF or a text document which is either uploaded as a resource or which learners access via a link. Although this approach is acceptable as long as the same information and functionality is provided, it is far from ideal, for learners or for content authors. From the learners' perspective it cannot be considered fully inclusive because it continues to provide a solution which is not equivalent for all learners. This reinforces the perception of otherness and exclusion. For content authors the disadvantage of conforming alternate versions is the extra time and effort that it takes to create two versions of the content and the additional resource needed to maintain two versions when updates are made.

FIGURE 2.2   Alternative conforming interactivity (CourseArc)

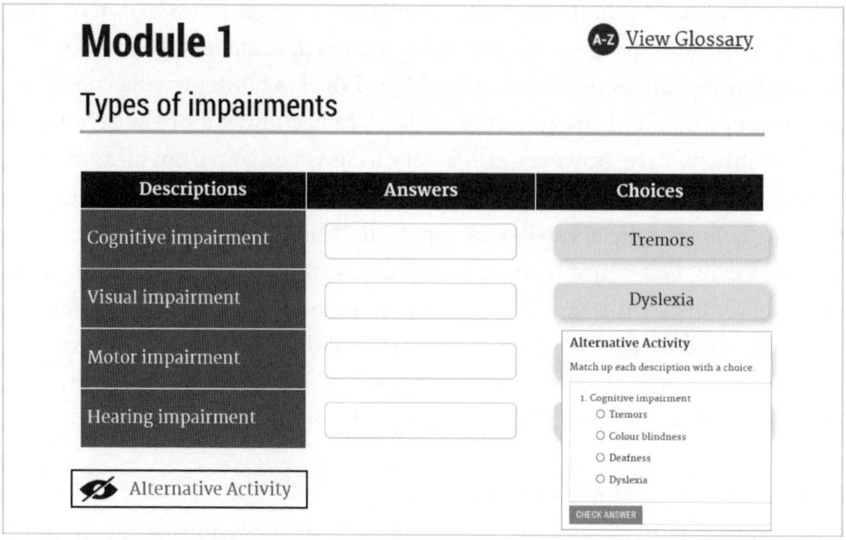

The CourseArc authoring tool automatically creates accessible alternatives for non-accessible interactivity. This example shows a drag-and-drop activity which is not keyboard accessible. When content authors add the drag-and-drop interaction, CourseArc automatically generates an Alternative Activity link. Learners can select this link to access the keyboard-accessible, multiple-choice version of the interaction shown in the insert.
SOURCE Reproduced with permission of CourseArc

A recommended approach is to create only one version of the eLearning resource wherever possible. If, however, the content includes interactivity which cannot be made accessible, such as a drag-and-drop interaction which is essential for learning, then an alternative for that particular interactivity can be provided. Some authoring tools, such as CourseArc, have this functionality built in (see Figure 2.2). While this is a useful approach, I have often found that as eLearning professionals become more familiar with designing accessible content, they find ways of making all learning content inclusive without needing to provide accessible alternatives.

ACCESSIBILITY STATEMENTS

Another commonly used strategy to deal with authoring tool limitations is to provide an accessibility statement. This has been good practice for websites for many years and is an approach I recommend for all eLearning resources, but particularly for those which cannot be made fully accessible due to tool limitations. Although it is a useful strategy, however, it is important to be aware that accessibility statements are not simply a tick-box exercise to ensure legal compliance. Their purpose is to improve the user experience of disabled learners by detailing what is not achievable in the eLearning resource, thereby saving time and frustration. Some accessibility legislation requires organizations to provide an accessibility statement. This is the case with the UK Public Sector Bodies Accessibility Regulations 2018,[18] which are explored in more detail in Chapter 5. The requirements of this law are a useful example of the information which should be provided in an effective accessibility statement:

1 An explanation of those parts of the content that are not accessible and the reasons why.

2 Where appropriate, a description of any accessible alternatives provided.

3 A description of, and a link to, a contact form which enables a person to notify the organization of any failure to comply with accessibility requirements.[19]

In addition to providing effective support to disabled learners, accessibility statements have the added advantage of engendering trust. They do this by allowing content authors to be transparent about any accessibility failings while still demonstrating a willingness to try to rectify them and offer support to learners. According to Dafydd Henke-Reed, Principal Accessibility and Usability Consultant with AbilityNet, 'Being honest about inaccessibility is a form of accessibility itself.'[20]

While the purpose of this book is to enable content authors to design content which is fully accessible to the WCAG standards, I believe it is important to be aware that many accessibility experts agree that '100% conformance with any level of the WCAG is very difficult to accomplish'.[21] They recommend instead seeing accessibility as a journey rather than a destination and aiming for progress rather than perfection. It can be argued that providing an accessibility statement and accessible alternatives for essential non-accessible elements of eLearning resources is the best way of achieving this. It offers a pragmatic solution rather than giving up on accessibility altogether, which can often be the result if content authors find that their tools have accessibility limitations. However, I also encourage eLearning professionals to actively advocate for accessibility with their authoring tool providers and to challenge them on any limitations of their tools. I believe that this is one of the best ways to influence better engagement with accessibility in our industry.

Best-practice accessibility features for authoring tools

While it is important to know about authoring tool limitations and how to tackle them, it is also useful to be aware of the good accessibility practice which exists. As we have discovered, in addition to allowing eLearning professionals to create accessible content, another key ATAG requirement for authoring tool providers is to give good accessibility guidance. While some tools offer support through their VPAT™ statement centred around WCAG requirements, other tool providers offer information with a different focus. The Xerte Online Toolkit, for example, offers guidance on how to use its tool features to optimize accessibility for learners with a range of impairments (see Figure 2.3).

Although providing accessibility support in the form of external documentation is a good start, it becomes even more effective if the guidance is embedded into the workflow of the tool. The Evolve authoring tool provides a good example of this when content authors add video content to resources (see Figure 2.4).

FIGURE 2.3   Impairment focused accessibility guidance (Xerte Online Toolkits)

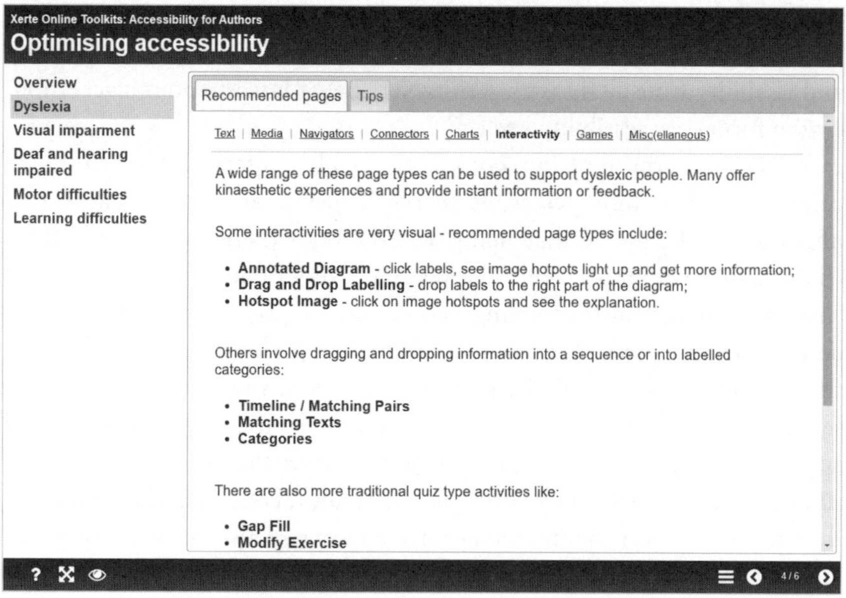

The Xerte Online Toolkit offers detailed guidance on accessibility issues and which of its tool activities best suit learners with different types of impairments.[22] The example given advises which interactivities are best suited for learners with dyslexia.
SOURCE Reproduced with permission of The Xerte Project 2020

FIGURE 2.4   Accessibility guidance embedded in the tool (Evolve)

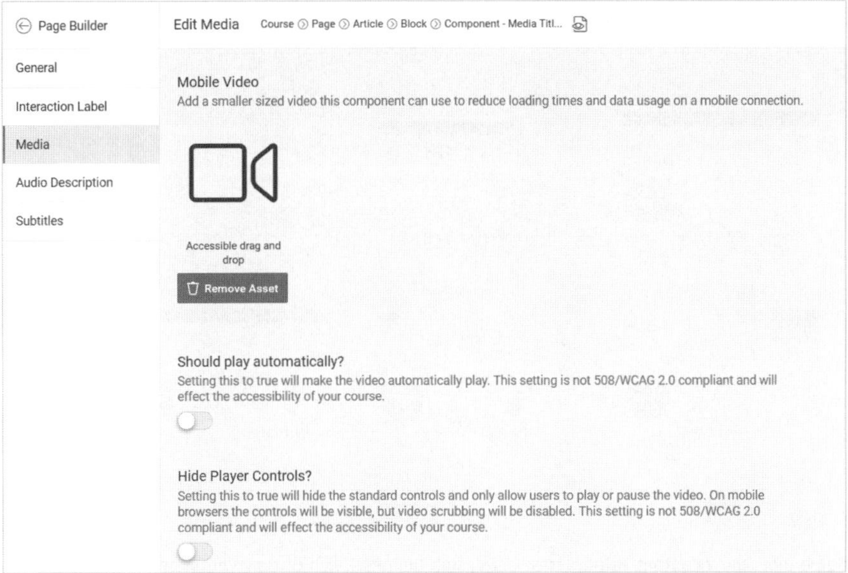

The Evolve authoring tool demonstrates how accessibility guidance is embedded into the workflow of the tool. When content authors add a video component to the resource, they are given the option for the video to play automatically. This, however, comes with the warning that the content will not then conform to WCAG standards.
SOURCE Reproduced with permission of Intellum UK Limited

Another example of accessibility best practice in authoring tools are features which are easy to find and implement. The dominKnow | ONE authoring tool, which prides itself on making accessibility part of the standard workflow for content authors so that it is not perceived as extra work or a chore, provides many examples. These include a review workflow, which allows reviewers to see and comment specifically on accessibility aspects, and a theme selector, which clearly indicates which of the tool's themes are WCAG compliant (see Figure 2.5).

Another important feature of best practice in authoring tools is that accessibility is a mainstream feature of the tool output and not one which needs to be activated in a separate mode. The open source Adapt Framework demonstrated this shift in focus in its V4 release, which removed the need to have an accessibility mode that assistive technology users had to enable.[23] Adapt also demonstrates best practice in its commitment to keeping up with advances in accessibility and making ongoing improvements to its features. Since Adapt is open source, advances and improvements are often suggested by a community of developers committed to improving accessibility. Other tools also have the benefit of being supported by a thriving accessibility

FIGURE 2.5   Accessible theme selector (dominKnow | ONE)

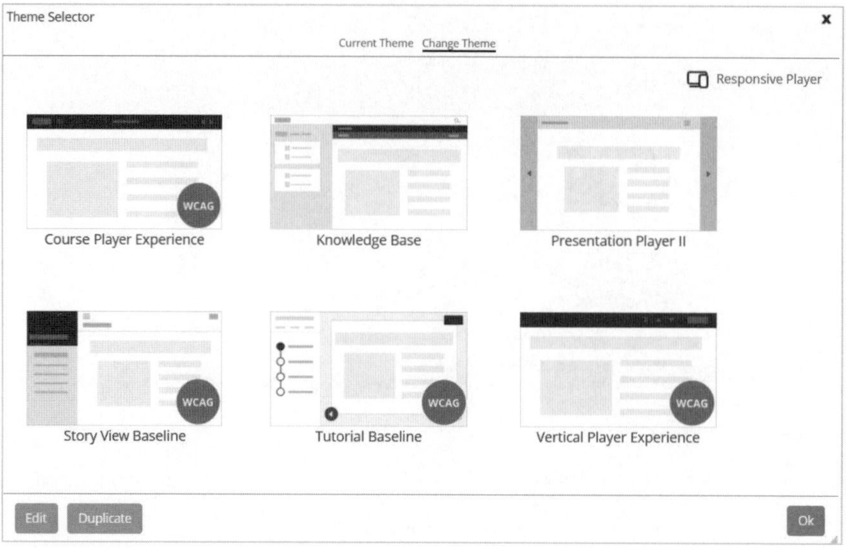

Some tools allow content authors to select design themes which comply with accessibility standards. This example from the dominKnow | ONE authoring tool shows a best-practice example of themes which are clearly flagged as WCAG compliant.
SOURCE Reproduced with permission of dominKnow, Inc.

community, with the Lectora Accessibility User Group being a notable example.

Although this is only a brief overview of some authoring tool best-practice accessibility functionality and support, I hope it is a useful indication of some of the features which are useful to look out for when evaluating tools. I also hope it serves as a good demonstration of some of the things that all authoring tool providers can do to better support content authors to create accessible learning content.

Accessibility testing

Since the purpose of this book is to make accessibility achievable for all eLearning professionals, the explanations for the WCAG standards in Part Three contain advice on how to test for conformance. While the majority of the standards can be tested by content authors, it is important to be aware that some may require additional support. In order to clarify this, I have grouped the standards into the following categories according to what is required from a testing perspective.

Test without tools

These are standards which content authors should be able to test for themselves without any tools, just with some basic understanding of accessibility requirements. Examples include checking that the resource is keyboard accessible, checking that any time limits imposed can be controlled by learners, and checking that audio and video content has captions and audio description.

Test with basic tools

Content authors can check these standards with basic tools. Examples include checking that the content is understandable for people who are colour blind by changing the display to greyscale, checking that it is possible to resize text to 200% using browser zoom and using a colour contrast checker to make sure the resource conforms to WCAG colour contrast ratios, and so on.

Note: There are several automated testing tools which identify accessibility errors across all the standards, generally to WCAG 2.1 A and AA levels. These include WAVE[24] from WebAIM, Axe[25] from Deque and Google Lighthouse.[26] While automated testing tools are useful for highlighting some errors, they are problematic. This is mainly due to the fact that they rely on machine rather than human testing and so are able to identify only a limited number of accessibility issues. Another issue with automatic testing tools is that they often require an in-depth understanding of coding in order to be able to interpret and action their results.

Test with assistive technology

Some standards can only be properly checked with assistive technology, most commonly screen readers. This can be done by content authors, but requires more expertise and commitment than testing with basic tools. Although it is recommended that content authors undergo training to become proficient in thorough screen reader testing, carrying out basic checks can still be valuable. Examples include checking alternative text for images and other non-text items, checking that page items are in a meaningful sequence, and checking that the language of the resource and of individual phrases have been correctly set.

Test with accessibility expert support

The standards in this final category require a more in-depth knowledge of both assistive technology and coding. As a result it is generally recommended that they are best supported with the help of accessibility experts. Examples of standards in this category include checking that the underlying source code is error free, checking that the resource is coded correctly to allow learners to modify the spacing between text, and checking that structures convey the correct information to assistive technology. The main advantage of working with accessibility experts is that in addition to the accessibility and coding expertise they provide, it offers the assurance that the content will be thoroughly tested with different technologies, including a range of browsers, assistive technology and mobile devices. Another important advantage is that testing is often carried out by people with lived experiences of disabilities who routinely use assistive technology. This allows a much more thorough analysis of the user experience provided by the content.

Another option for checking specific coding requirements is to confirm with authoring tool providers that the underlying code for the tool conforms with these standards. This information is sometimes supplied in the VPAT™ documentation. It is important to be aware, however, that information provided by authoring tool providers can be subjective so is not always a 100% guarantee that resources conform.

I believe that grouping the standards into these four categories helps content authors to formulate a more realistic strategy on the best way to tackle accessibility testing. Any approach chosen will depend on factors such as budget, time and resources available and the degree to which the content must conform to legislation. It will also very often be a team or organizational decision, rather than an individual one. For further detailed information and a useful guide on the technicalities and processes around accessibility testing I recommend Laura Kalbag's book *Accessibility for Everyone*, which has a chapter dedicated to accessibility evaluation and testing.[27]

Team and organizational accessibility strategy

The approach taken throughout this book is to focus on how much can be achieved by individuals working alone. As the information on testing suggests, however, content authors very often work as part of a team. Adopting a strategic approach within a team provides the best chance of successfully establishing and maintaining eLearning accessibility initiatives in the long term. Although an in-depth analysis of team strategy is beyond the scope of this book, there are many practical steps which can be taken to help embed a commitment to designing and creating accessible content. An important first step is to ensure that everyone in the process is on board. This could involve providing team-wide training and support to all roles, including managers, team leaders, project managers, designers, content creators, developers, testers and people involved in quality assurance roles. Other strategies to consider are assigning clear accessibility roles and accountabilities, developing accessibility champions, creating accessible templates and style sheets for learning content, producing standard templates for accessibility statements, etc.

In order to succeed in the long term, team strategies also need to receive wider support. In his book *Inclusive Design for Organisations*, Professor Jonathan Hassell explains that in order to be sustainable, accessibility needs to be embedded into every process, 'so that like a stick of seaside rock, you can take a cross section of any aspect of your organization and find the same values at play'.[28] Organizational strategy plays such an essential part in ensuring the long-term success of any accessibility initiative that I recommend taking time to explore it in more detail. The following resources have different perspectives but offer useful approaches which are applicable to an eLearning context. The Section 508 Program Maturity Levels[29] and the HE and FE Accessibility Maturity Model[30] both enable organizations to benchmark their digital maturity. Standard ISO 30071-1[31] is also useful for organizations that want to embed accessibility considerations into their 'business as usual' processes.

Summary

- The WCAG are universally recognized technical standards which are used internationally for legal accessibility compliance.

- It is useful to acknowledge the challenges involved for eLearning professionals working with the WCAG because it is reassuring to know that there are legitimate reasons for struggling with eLearning accessibility.

- There is a wide range of authoring tools and approaches involved in creating content, which means that the advice in this book is generic but supported with examples which cover different approaches and tools.

- W3C authoring tool guidelines state that tool providers should ensure that it is possible for content authors to create accessible content and provide guidance on how to achieve this.

- Providing accessibility statements and accessible alternatives for any non-accessible content are good ways of supporting disabled learners and addressing authoring tool limitations.

- Despite authoring tool limitations, more and more are evolving to allow accessible output and there are many examples of good practice.

- There are various approaches to accessibility testing which need to be considered in order to devise an appropriate testing strategy.

- In order for accessibility implementation to succeed in the long term it needs to be embedded in the working practices and culture of a team and organization.

Endnotes

[1] Techopedia (Updated 2019) Definition – what does Accessibility (a11y) mean? 27 February, https://www.techopedia.com/definition/10165/accessibility-a11y (archived at https://perma.cc/K89F-WGGJ)

[2] Stevens, E (2018) 15 Inspirational UX design quotes that every designer should read [blog], 20 April, https://careerfoundry.com/en/blog/ux-design/15-inspirational-ux-design-quotes-that-every-designer-should-read/ (archived at https://perma.cc/5EDS-K942)

[3] Lawton Henry, S, Abou-Zahra, S and White, K (Updated 2016) Accessibility, usability, and inclusion, March 2016, https://www.w3.org/WAI/fundamentals/accessibility-usability-inclusion/ (archived at https://perma.cc/R259-9GAN)

[4] Sponge (2015) 6 ways to improve accessibility in elearning, 2 April, https://wearesponge.com/insights/2015/04/6-ways-to-improve-accessibility-in-elearning/ (archived at https://perma.cc/2ZRP-D7CQ)

[5] Lawton Henry, S (Updated 2020) Web Content Accessibility Guidelines (WCAG) overview, 12 August, https://www.w3.org/WAI/standards-guidelines/wcag/ (archived at https://perma.cc/5RRT-ZYBR)

[6] Mueller, M, Jolly, R, Eggert, E (Updated 2018) Web accessibility laws & policies, 21 March, https://www.w3.org/WAI/policies/ (archived at https://perma.cc/C2AF-YGWQ)

[7] Lawton Henry, S (Updated 2020) WCAG 2 FAQ, 12 August, https://www.w3.org/WAI/standards-guidelines/wcag/faq/#done (archived at https://perma.cc/77WS-QMA6)

8   Silver Task Force Main Page (Updated 2020) https://www.w3.org/WAI/GL/
     task-forces/silver/wiki/Main_Page (archived at https://perma.cc/8HR4-VZET)

9   Spellman, JF (2021) WCAG 3 FPWD published, 21 January,
     https://www.w3.org/blog/2021/01/wcag-3-fpwd/ (archived at https://perma.cc/
     F2DB-9794)

10   Content Creation Process for Migrating WCAG SC (Q4 2019)
     https://docs.google.com/document/d/1gfYAiV2Z-FA_
     kEHYlLV32J8ClNEGPxRgSIohu3gUHEA/edit (archived at https://perma.cc/
     DL4D-H8EU)

11   Lawton Henry, S (Updated 2020) Authoring Tool Accessibility Guidelines
     (ATAG) overview, 01 July, https://www.w3.org/WAI/standards-guidelines/atag/
     (archived at https://perma.cc/ZJ8S-KZSK)

12   Articulate (Updated 2020) Articulate Storyline 360 accessibility conformance
     report, 14 October, https://articulate.com/support/article/Storyline-360-
     Accessibility-Conformance-Report-VPAT (archived at https://perma.cc/
     LRF4-YDHS)

13   CourseArc, Accessibility, CourseArc is WCAG 2.1 AA compliant,
     https://www.coursearc.com/vpat/ (archived at https://perma.cc/GCG8-KDJH)

14   Kuykendall, H (2017) Section 508 and WCAG: What's changed for federal
     government website accessibility requirements? 22 February,
     https://www.microassist.com/digital-accessibility/section-508-and-wcag/
     (archived at https://perma.cc/3FCH-SLMR)

15   Bozarth, J (2019) The Learning Guild Authoring Tools 2019, 12 June,
     https://www.learningguild.com/insights/239/authoring-tools-2019/ (archived at
     https://perma.cc/8CP9-YJ46)

16   Gumienny, K (2018) The training manager's guide to accessible elearning,
     6 December, https://www.microassist.com/learning-dispatch/training-managers-
     guide-to-accessible-elearning/ (archived at https://perma.cc/GXW6-XTUC)

17   W3C, Understanding conforming alternate versions, https://www.w3.org/TR/
     UNDERSTANDING-WCAG20/conformance.html#uc-conforming-alt-versions-
     head (archived at https://perma.cc/J9NE-5867)

18   Legislation.gov.uk, The Public Sector Bodies (Websites and Mobile Applications)
     (No. 2) Accessibility Regulations 2018, https://www.legislation.gov.uk/
     uksi/2018/952/made (archived at https://perma.cc/92BL-HDCR)

19   Legislation.gov.uk (2018) Accessibility statement, 23 September,
     https://www.legislation.gov.uk/uksi/2018/952/regulation/8/made (archived at
     https://perma.cc/R2S5-B4EC)

20   Henke-Reed, D (2020) Accessibility anti-patterns webinar with Dafydd Henke-
     Reed [online video], https://youtu.be/SY0u11sWND0 (archived at
     https://perma.cc/PNH7-QP6P)

21   Perkins Access (2020) What is conformance? And why 100% conformance is
     not the only goal on your digital accessibility journey, 18 August,

https://www.perkins.org/access/blog/what-is-conformance-and-why-100-conformance-is-not-the-only-goal-on-your-digital (archived at https://perma.cc/4B5B-MCSN)

[22] Xerte Online Toolkits, Meeting the needs of all users: An author's guide to Xerte accessibility, https://xot.xerte.org.uk/play.php?template_id=153#page1 (archived at https://perma.cc/3RRU-8H2L)

[23] Leathes, M (2019) Adapt Framework v4 released! 24 January, https://community.adaptlearning.org/mod/forum/discuss.php?d=3567 (archived at https://perma.cc/HZY5-BER4)

[24] WAVE Web Accessibility Evaluation Tool, https://wave.webaim.org/ (archived at https://perma.cc/58VD-WKUR)

[25] Deque – axe™ – the standard in accessibility testing, https://www.deque.com/axe/ (archived at https://perma.cc/E7FU-XKMM)

[26] Lighthouse, https://developers.google.com/web/tools/lighthouse (archived at https://perma.cc/ZA3K-D4S2)

[27] Kalbag, L (2017) *Accessibility for Everyone*, A Book Apart, New York

[28] Hassell, J (2019) *Inclusive Design for Organisations, Including your missing 20% by embedding web and mobile accessibility*, Rethink Press, Gorleston-on-Sea

[29] Section 508.gov, Play 2: Assess your Section 508 program maturity, https://www.section508.gov/tools/playbooks/technology-accessibility-playbook-intro/play02 (archived at https://perma.cc/Z5VY-VSU6)

[30] HE and FE Accessibility Maturity Model, https://abilitynet.org.uk/he-and-fe-accessibility-maturity-model#request-maturity-model (archived at https://perma.cc/Q6TH-MWS8)

[31] Hassell Inclusion ISO 30071-1 digital accessibility standard – all you need to know, https://www.hassellinclusion.com/iso-30071-1/ (archived at https://perma.cc/7T5S-9MS6)

03

Exploring disability

Introduction

A few years ago, I went to the Learning Technologies exhibition in London to assess the level of engagement with accessibility in the industry. At a stand belonging to a leading content supplier, I asked a representative if his company's work with the public sector had led to better engagement with digital accessibility. He explained that this wasn't the case because the majority of the public sector clients they worked with were in the transport industry and 'you don't get many blind train drivers'. While it is important to be very clear that this remark is not representative of the entire industry, it is nevertheless worth exploring. In the past, I have used it as an example to highlight my belief that a lack of understanding about disability is one of the chief reasons there is so little engagement with accessibility in some areas of the eLearning profession. Although I believe this is true, I also think it demonstrates the danger that a lack of awareness can lead to ableism. 'Ableism is the discrimination of and social prejudice against people with disabilities based on the belief that typical abilities are superior. Like racism and sexism, ableism classifies entire groups of people as "less than".'[1] Ableism often leads to harmful stereotypes, misconceptions and generalizations about disabled people.

Whether the indifference to accessibility shown by some members of our industry is caused by a lack of awareness or an underlying current of ableism, there is no doubt that a better understanding of disability has an important part to play in promoting accessibility and tackling commonly held misconceptions. It is also crucial background knowledge for content authors who want to design accessible learning content. As a result, this chapter gives you key information about disability and allows you to explore some important related concepts.

Disability definitions

Legal definitions of disability have traditionally been based on the medical model which focuses on physical and health perspectives. In the UK, the legal definition is set out in the UK Equality Act. It states that you are disabled if you have 'a physical or mental impairment which has a substantial and long-term adverse effect on your ability to carry out normal day-to-day activities'.[2] In the US, the Americans with Disabilities Act (ADA) defines an individual with a disability 'as a person who has a physical or mental impairment that substantially limits one or more major life activities'.[3]

There is, however, increasing recognition that definitions based on the medical model fail to take into account the external barriers central to the social model of disability. Article one of the United Nations Convention on the Rights of Persons with Disabilities (CRPD) states: 'Persons with disabilities include those who have long-term physical, mental, intellectual or sensory impairments which, *in interaction with various barriers*, may hinder their full and effective participation in society on an equal basis with others.'[4] It is important to be aware that as eLearning professionals, if we create inaccessible learning content, we are directly responsible for creating barriers which prevent disabled learners from participating in society 'on an equal basis with others'.

Types of disability

There are many different viewpoints about types of disability and how they should be categorized. This can lead to a confusing range of terminology and classifications. In order to simplify things when trying to make sense of digital accessibility, we look at disability in relation to how people interact with technology. This means that disabilities are grouped into four broad categories: visual, hearing, motor and cognitive. It's important to remember, however, that people do not fit neatly into these four categories. Research suggests that almost 75% of disabled people have more than one type of impairment.[5] It is also essential to understand that each of these categories includes a wide range of conditions and that everyone's experience of disability is unique.

Visual impairments

The misconception that accessibility is only important for blind people is a common one. Many people are surprised to learn, therefore, that the proportion of blind people in the disabled population is approximately 2%.[6] If we have a better understanding of the whole range of visual impairments included in this category, it is easier to understand how this rises to 10%.[7] According to the World Health Organization, the leading causes of visual impairment globally are:

- uncorrected refractive errors;
- cataracts;
- age-related macular degeneration;
- glaucoma;
- diabetic retinopathy;
- corneal opacity;
- trachoma.[8]

As eLearning professionals we need to be aware of the impact these conditions have on our learners when they are viewing digital content. Conditions such as farsightedness (hyperopia), nearsightedness (myopia) and astigmatism which cause difficulty focusing and blurriness are very common if not corrected with glasses, contact lenses or surgery. Other conditions cause a whole range of issues which make it more difficult for people to see content because their field of vision is blocked in different ways. Macular degeneration, for example, causes blocking of the central visual field. Glaucoma causes blocking of the peripheral field. Diabetic retinopathy causes large spots which block vision. Using a visual impairment simulator[9] is a good way to get a better understanding of some of the visual impairments your learners may experience (see Figure 3.1).

Colour blindness is another visual impairment which can affect your learners' digital experience. There are different types of colour blindness which affects people's ability to see a range of colours. The most common are deuteranopia, which affects green, protanopia, which affects red, and

FIGURE 3.1   A simulated visual impairment and how it affects an eLearning resource

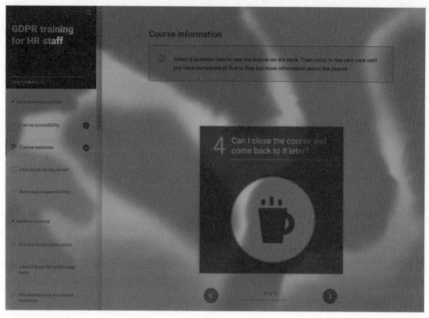

A visual impairment simulator shows how diabetic retinopathy can cause large spots to obstruct the field of vision.

tritanopia, which affects blue. In addition there is a rare form of colour blindness called achromatopsia which means that people can see in monochrome only. There are many colour blind simulators[10] available which allow you to check how your resources will be viewed by people with different types of colour blindness.

Hearing impairments

Hearing impairments range from complete deafness to mild hearing loss. Impairments can be caused by a range of factors, including genetic causes, complications at birth, infectious diseases, exposure to excessive noise, and ageing. There are different types of hearing loss which have different effects on learners. Auditory processing disorders occur when the brain has difficulty processing the information in sound, such as in understanding speech. Conductive hearing loss is caused by problems with the outer ear, which disrupts passing sound to the inner ear and makes it more difficult to hear.

Sensorineural hearing loss occurs when the cochlea and/or auditory nerve are damaged and make sound distorted.[11]

Conditions associated with hearing impairments include:

- spatial processing disorder;
- auditory neuropathy;
- Ménière's disease;
- noise-induced hearing loss;
- otosclerosis;
- tinnitus.

Motor impairments

Unlike visual and hearing impairments, which are sensory, motor impairments are physical. While this category includes a whole range of limitations, for digital accessibility we are primarily concerned with dexterity issues. These affect learners' ability to interact with technology such as a mouse, keyboard, touch pad or computer screen.

Conditions associated with motor impairments which affect dexterity include:

- arthritis;
- paralysis;
- multiple sclerosis (MS);
- cerebral palsy;
- essential tremor;
- Parkinson's;
- motor neurone disease;
- congenital or acquired limb deficiency.

Cognitive impairments

The cognitive category contains not only the widest range of impairments we need to be aware of but also the largest amount of differing terminology used to define and categorize those impairments. The wide variance among the capabilities of people with cognitive impairments can also complicate matters. As WebAIM states, 'Some web content is too complex by its nature to ever be fully accessible to users with profound cognitive disabilities.'[12] For the purposes of digital accessibility, our definition of cognitive impairments includes any condition which creates difficulties with memory and problem solving, difficulties processing text, numbers or symbols, slower processing speeds, and attention or concentration difficulties. These can be caused by learning disabilities, neurodiverse conditions or mental health issues. We also need to be aware of seizure and vestibular disorders in order not only to make our learning accessible but also to make it safe.

Learning difficulties such as Down syndrome or Fragile X are defined as 'a reduced intellectual ability and difficulty with everyday activities which affects someone for their whole life'.[13] Neurodiversity refers to the different ways a person's brain processes information. It is used to describe alternative thinking styles and includes conditions such as dyslexia, dyspraxia, dyscalculia, autism spectrum disorder (ASD), and attention deficit hyperactivity disorder (ADHD). Mental health problems include anxiety, depression, post-traumatic stress disorder (PTSD) and bipolar disorder. All have the potential to affect cognitive ability. Seizure disorders such as photosensitive epilepsy make people sensitive to flickering or flashing content. Finally, vestibular disorders, which include conditions such as labyrinthitis and Ménière's disease, can cause dizziness and nausea as a result of moving content.

Disability facts and figures

Providing statistics on the number of people who are affected by different conditions and impairments is a common way to encourage people to become more engaged with accessibility. There are, however, a few important limitations to this approach to be aware of. The first is that due to international and local differences in how disability is defined and measured there are often wide variations in the statistics given in different sources. Another limitation is that not all conditions considered a disability have an impact on digital accessibility. Mobility impairments, for example, are only relevant if they affect manual dexterity and the ability to interact with digital hardware. Finally, in my experience, giving statistics on how many people are affected by different impairments is not a particularly effective driver for change. Despite these drawbacks, there are a few key figures which are useful in making the case for digital accessibility. By far the most compelling is that 'one billion people, or 15% of the world's population, experience some form of disability'.[14] In most Western countries the size of the disabled population ranges from 12% to 26%.[15] If we design inaccessible content in the UK, we risk excluding a potential one in five of our learners. In the US this rises to a potential one in four.

Hidden disability

The number of disabled people in society often comes as a surprise to people. This is particularly true if they do not have experience of disability themselves or have not seen much evidence of disability in their social environments or workplaces. It becomes easier to understand if we consider how many of the impairments we have already explored in this chapter are not visible. It has been estimated that up to 80% of disabilities are hidden.[16] This makes it much easier to understand how designing accessible learning content has a positive impact on many more learners than the small niche audience that disabled people are often perceived to be.

Undisclosed and undiagnosed disability

Another important point to be aware of with regard to the number of disabled people in our society is the fact that the statistics given are very likely to be a significant underestimate. This is due to two known issues. The first is that people are often reluctant to disclose a disability. This could be for many reasons, but it is particularly common in the workplace where people fear that disclosure could lead to discrimination. Recent research in the US suggests that only 39% of employees with disabilities have disclosed their disability to their manager. 'Even fewer have disclosed to their teams (24%) and HR (21%) and almost none (4%) have revealed their disability to clients.'[17]

The second reason which contributes to underreporting is that many people are not aware that they have a disability. This is most commonly the case for adults with neurodiverse conditions such as dyslexia and ADHD who may not have been diagnosed when they were young. I have first-hand experience of this. At school I was told that I was dyslexic but was given hardly any support. I didn't think much of it until many years later when I was carrying out research into assistive technologies. Discovering just how much I benefitted from technology designed to help people with cognitive impairments made me recognize that there may well have been some truth in my teacher's casual observation. While I haven't had a formal assessment, becoming aware that it was very likely that I was neurodiverse had a profound impact on my role as a content author. It helped me to finally understand why I found some learning experiences so difficult to engage with and also motivated me to find out more about how to accommodate learners with cognitive impairments in the learning content I designed and created.

Disability and the ageing population

A final point to be aware of with regard to the number of disabled people in our society is that it is likely to increase dramatically in the future. This is as a result of the ageing population. According to the United Nations (UN), 'Population ageing is poised to become one of the most significant social transformations of the twenty-first century, with implications for nearly all sectors of society.'[18] This trend is set to have a significant impact on our learners and their access needs. It is particularly relevant to workplace learning. In the UK, for example, 31% of the workforce are over 50 and this is steadily increasing.[19]

If we look beyond statistics, there is another reason why the ageing population makes digital inclusion so significant. It makes the case that designing accessible learning content is the best guarantee we have of making it usable for our future selves. The idea that we are all only temporarily able bodied is common among accessibility advocates. I believe, however, that it was best articulated by Professor Mike Wald when he said, 'Everybody can think of themselves as only temporarily not having a disability, because at some point in their life, as they get older, they will.'[20]

Temporary and situational impairments

While a focus on disability or permanent impairments is essential for a better understanding of accessibility, it is also useful to be aware of temporary and situational impairments. By considering these concepts we broaden the benefit of accessibility to encompass everyone. In medical terms a temporary impairment is anything which lasts less than 12 months. In the digital context it simply means any impairment which temporarily prevents us from interacting with technology, or makes it more difficult. An example of a visual impairment could be recovering from eye surgery or suffering from a migraine. A hearing impairment could be caused by a heavy cold or an ear infection. An example of a motor impairment could be a broken wrist or a condition such as carpal tunnel syndrome. Finally, a cognitive impairment could be caused by everyday stress or anxiety which has a detrimental impact on concentration and cognitive abilities.

Situational impairments are caused by external or environmental factors. An example of a visual impairment could be slow broadband which prevents images downloading, or using an old monitor with poor colour contrast. A situational hearing impairment could be caused by not having headphones in a noisy public environment such as on public transport or in a quiet space such as a library. A motor impairment could be caused by something as simple as a wireless mouse which has run out of charge, while a cognitive impairment could be the result of working in a noisy and distracting home environment.

While some disabled people are understandably frustrated that temporary and situational impairments are necessary in the argument to justify accessibility, I include them because I have found that they can be effective, particularly when I have had to tackle the scepticism of stakeholders and clients. I believe this is because it makes accessibility personal, without the uncomfortable acknowledgement that a permanent disability is something that could happen to any of us at any point in our lives. If we reframe accessibility to be about everyone's access needs, including our own, rather than thinking of it only as something that helps disabled people, it sends a powerful message. I believe that it helps tackle the misconception that digital accessibility is an 'us' versus 'them' issue and allows it instead to become just an 'us' issue. This idea is echoed by the charity AbilityNet in its definition of accessibility:

> Accessibility isn't just about disability. It's about universality. It's about making something that can be used by as many people as possible. Different environments, different devices, elderly, different cultural backgrounds, non-English speakers, and impaired abilities.[21]

Disability personas

An important principle of disability activism, known as the 'nothing-about-us-without-us principle', is based on the idea that 'persons with disabilities know what is best for them and their community'.[22] It helps to avoid any assumptions or misconceptions about disability which can influence products and services if disabled people are not involved in designing and creating them. However, this leaves many eLearning professionals facing a challenge unless they have a lived experience of disability or work with disabled people who have experience of a range of impairments and disabilities. While the best long-term solution to this situation is for organizations to employ more disabled people, in the short term, one way of mitigating against assumptions and misconceptions is to use disability personas. These highlight common barriers which disabled users face and can be very helpful, particularly when content authors are starting out with accessibility. 'Understanding disabilities and impairments' from the Government Digital Service[23] and 'Stories of Web Users' from W3C[24] are both recommended resources.

Another useful strategy is to gather first-hand learning experiences of disabled people. The following case studies give an overview of some of the strategies disabled learners use to overcome inaccessible learning content and are a good introduction to some of the barriers to avoid.

Learner case studies

Visual impairment – Kirsty Major, trainer and consultant

I am Kirsty Major. Through my two businesses, I teach English to adults and provide online accessibility training. I am blind and cannot use a mouse when I am interacting with digital content. Instead I use a screen reader called JAWS on my laptop. This allows me to navigate to all areas of web pages and eLearning content using keyboard commands and also reads out the contents of the page. To make my screen reader work, I need the page to be coded correctly and all elements to be accurately labelled.

I have had both good and bad experiences with online learning content. A good experience means that I have an equivalent learning experience to everyone else on the course. My current distance learning provider puts all the information online, on accessible web pages or as PDFs. When information is provided visually, the graphics and diagrams also have text descriptions, which my screen reader reads out. This means that I have the same access to information and that I'm able to learn independently. Ideally, I wouldn't promote a two-system approach, but I appreciate it when the learning provider creates alternatives to inaccessible online activities. These often involve selecting options from dropdown lists rather than dragging elements around the screen. This works well for me and allows me to have an equivalent way of taking part.

Bad experiences can happen before the course even begins. If in order to take part in a course I have to write several emails, make phone calls and chase around till I get an answer about accessible materials, this is definitely a case of the organization in question not making it easy for me. It isn't an equivalent experience to everyone else because I can't just sign up and go. Other issues can happen once the course has begun. On a self-study course that I started recently, I got part-way through module one before hitting the roadblock of a question called 'Label this diagram'. The content was easy. The diagram made it impossible for me to complete the task. Another big problem that I have faced in the past is inconsistency across a learning provider's offerings. It doesn't help if all the learning materials are completely accessible but the testing activities, which must be completed in order to move on or complete the training, are not. Most frustrating of all is the 'Can't you get a sighted person to help you?' response which I've encountered many times. Then my only option is to ask a sighted person to do the inaccessible practical tasks following my directions and I focus on ensuring that I understand the theory. It gets the job done, but it's not a satisfactory solution. Not all people have assistants available to them to read information, describe diagrams or click mouse buttons when page elements are unlabelled or inaccessible. Ultimately, it's not the job of my friends and family to fix a product or learning resource that isn't designed accessibly.

The onus should not be on the disabled user to compensate for inaccessible materials. We want to concentrate on learning, the same as everyone else. Having to work twice as hard just to access the material takes all the enjoyment out of the learning process. Ultimately, it's much better to design accessibly than to retrospectively try to fix an inaccessible course. Also, measures that make materials more accessible for me often end up helping others, too. For example, not relying on colour to convey important information helps me, but it also helps colour-blind users. I think that accessible learning content is better for everyone because it makes content authors think about the needs of all their learners.

Hearing impairment – Jake Harrison, student

I am Jake Harrison. I am studying an HND in computing at a higher education college. I am deaf and have two cochlear implants which help me to recognize sound. I rely heavily on lip reading and also use British Sign Language (BSL) and Sign Supported English (SSE) to understand people and to communicate. I also rely on captions on videos and for live video conferencing. I sometimes find it difficult to understand written English, especially if the language is technical and complex and the sentences are long. It helps me if there is a BSL interpretation as this breaks down the English and makes it easier and less stressful for me to understand.

Now that I am in higher education, I have a Disabled Students Allowance (DSA) which gives me the extra support I need to study. It meant that I could get a new laptop when I started my course which is very important especially now that so much of my learning is online because of the COVID 19 pandemic. I also have a communication support worker (CSW) who interprets my tutor's spoken English into BSL. She also supports me by making learning materials easier to understand and by helping me with my written assignments. One of the things I find very useful on my course is using eBooks. This is because I can highlight things in colour, which makes it much easier for me to process and understand written English. Another thing which has been very helpful is the support of my peers, both hearing and hearing impaired. They have given me advice and strategies to help me with my studies, like keeping a record of all the resources I have found. This helps me because it saves me time doing all the extra work I have to do as a hearing-impaired learner, which makes me feel less frustrated.

Learning is a positive experience for me when people and technology work together to help me overcome barriers. A good demonstration of this is online learning and video conferencing. When I get feedback on my assignments, for example, I work with my personal tutor and my CSW. My tutor shares his screen so that I can see my assignment and he uses colour to highlight information for me, such as red to show me information that I don't need and yellow to show me when I need to change the sentence structure or tenses. I use the video of my tutor to lip read but have my CSW on video at the same time so that I can see her BSL interpretation. Learning doesn't work well and is frustrating and demotivating when technology and people create barriers which make it more difficult for me. When we first started using video-conferencing calls to get feedback on my assignments, for example, as soon as my tutor shared his screen so that I could see my work, it meant that the video of him and my CSW were so small that I could not lip read or see the BSL interpretation. I got over this in the end by using two video-conferencing services, with my tutor on MS Teams and my CSW on MS Skype. This meant that I could see the BSL interpretation on a full screen next to my assignment.

Another example of when people and technology create barriers which make my learning more difficult is captioning. This can be with live video conferencing or with videos which have had captions added to them. In video conferencing there is usually no option to choose the language that the automatic captioning is interpreting. It is often American English, which makes it a lot less accurate at interpreting people who are speaking British English. The accuracy of live automatic captioning is a real problem because often there are so many mistakes that I can't understand what is being said at all. The captions are often too fast for me to read. This is why it is really helpful if people provide transcripts for live video calls and videos because the transcript is usually more accurate than the captions, and when I read them I have more time to understand and process the information.

I find videos a really helpful way to learn because they make it easier for me to get a good understanding of a topic. If they don't have captions, though, this can make it very difficult or sometimes impossible for me to use them. This makes me feel totally isolated and left out because I am missing out on information which other people have access to. Another thing which I find very frustrating is if videos have captions but people have relied on automatic captioning and not taken the time to make them useful for hearing impaired people. Automatic captions always have spelling and punctuation mistakes, which make it more difficult for me to read and interpret what is being said. Another problem with them is that they don't include important background information like sound effects. If there is more than one person talking, another issue with automatic captions is that they don't make it clear who is saying what. This can make it impossible for me to understand what is happening. I often have to give up on watching videos which don't have good captions because it is just pointless and a waste of my time.

One thing I would like people to take away from my experience is how much extra time and effort it takes for me to learn and to achieve the grades I want. Technology and the way that people use it can make it easier for me to learn, or it can create more barriers which mean that I have to spend even more time and effort just to have the same access to learning as every-one else. If people understand how to use technology to meet the needs of all their students, they can make the learning experience so much better. I also think that there is still much more that can be achieved in developing technology so that it benefits disabled people but also helps everyone. For example, I would love to see text-to-speech functionality in video conferenc-ing, which could help hearing impaired people who might be struggling to speak, or automatic captions in different colours to show who is speaking. Another really important key to the success of video conferencing is devel-oping internet access to make sure that everyone has good coverage.

Motor impairment – Esi Hardy, disability inclusion expert

I am Esi Hardy. I am an entrepreneur, a business owner and a student. I am a physically disabled person. I have cerebral palsy and have limited mobility in all four of my limbs and very limited dexterity in my hands. The way I describe it is that 'I can do a little bit of most things but nothing of everything'. When I was at school everything needed to be done for me. Throughout my education that made it harder for me to learn because I learn by doing. Now technology means I can study independently. This has opened up learning for me and I am currently studying for an online degree in business management. I use a keyboard and trackpad to navigate around my computer and Siri to read aloud content. I also use Siri to dictate notes to my phone. If I'm writing something that's going to be long, I'll either dictate through Siri or speak it into my phone and then upload it onto a transcription service. I can then send this to my personal assistant who types it up for me. I also download books onto my Kindle to read course material.

Although technology has made learning more inclusive and I have had some very good experiences of learning online, there are still many cases where eLearning continues to create barriers and exclude disabled people. My learning experiences while studying for my degree have provided examples of both. Before I began my course, I had a disability assessment which allowed me to outline my access requirements and everything I needed to learn successfully. This was taken into account in my first two years. I was given the tools I needed to succeed without question. I felt that the university were genuinely inclusive and mindful of disability and access requirements. This boosted my confidence and helped me to achieve high merits in all my assignments and distinctions for my modules. Unfortunately, this changed in my third year when one of the modules I studied had an assessment method which was inaccessible for me, yet the faculty refused to make reasonable adjustments to accommodate my disability. Despite making a formal complaint and the university accepting that my disability profile had been incorrectly recorded, this was not taken into account and I barely scraped a pass mark for this module.

From an eLearning perspective, the issue I had was simple. It was a problem caused by the fact that only one form of assessment was allowed, and that the criteria for that assessment didn't take into account the diversity and differing learning needs of the students. Yet, the implications of the issue and the university's refusal to take responsibility or to make accommodations had far-reaching consequences. I felt I had no option other than to take legal action. Eventually, however, the stress and anxiety involved with this process took such a toll on my mental health that I wasn't able to carry on. I still feel bad about this. I am someone who always tells people to stand up for what they believe in and not to back down when they face oppression. I'm saddened that because of the mindset that I was in at the time I didn't feel able to do this. But I'm also saddened that the only way to make some universities take action over discriminatory practice is to sue so that it becomes public knowledge. I am determined not to let this experience stop me getting my degree, but it has definitely undermined my confidence and it still affects my mental health. I shouldn't have had to go through this, and neither should other disabled people.

We are people who are disabled by the barriers which we encounter all the time in our daily lives. Equal rights to services and learning should not be an option or luck of the draw, it should be taken for granted by us as students and consumers. Too many disabled students still put up with less than average support because society has made us feel as though we do not deserve this. Educational establishments have a duty to role model equality and best practice for others to follow so that disabled people and their families expect and are empowered by true inclusion. We must have equal rights to access learning and educational services so that we can move on in life, instead of being forced into situations which perpetuate the stereotype that disabled people aren't able to achieve. The main message that I'd like people to take away from my story is to be aware that disability and impairments affect so many people at different points in their journey in so many different ways. This means that the only way to be inclusive of the majority of people is to gather their lived experiences and learn from what they are telling you. I urge you to take this understanding and use it to create better and more inclusive learning experiences.

Cognitive impairment – Luke Westwood, eLearning developer and mental health advocate

I am Luke Westwood. I am an eLearning developer. At school I had learning difficulties and today I still struggle with some kinds of learning. I have dyspraxia, which makes it more difficult for me to learn certain subjects such as maths and topics which are logic based, including programming or coding. I find it particularly difficult to process long lists of instructions. Other things which affect my ability to learn online are my mental health and also a condition I have which causes chronic pain. Many of the issues I have around learning are linked to negative experiences I had at school. Due to my learning difficulties I was made to feel stupid, which led to the belief that I'd never be able to have a career or be successful. Although some of the things I struggle with are probably the same as for a lot of other people, because of my past associations with learning they often bring up negative memories and sometimes trigger a feeling of panic. This undermines my confidence and can even affect my mental health. My chronic pain also affects my ability to learn. Although it is a long-term condition which I've learnt to manage, if I am having a bad day with the pain it affects my ability to concentrate. This then leads to stress, which in turn makes the pain worse as managing my anxiety is a vital factor in being able to control the pain. Stress also intensifies my dyspraxia, so it sometimes feels like a vicious circle.

The language that is used in eLearning is a huge issue for me. The way the course is written is really important because sometimes my learning difficulties mean that my vocabulary might be limited. If the learning uses a lot of complicated language or technical terms and is written in long, complex sentences, I can find this very difficult to understand. One of the most challenging things for me is if assessment questions and instructions aren't written in clear language. Sometimes it feels like the content author has written them to be deliberately confusing, almost because they want to trip learners up. While for some people this might be frustrating, for me it causes real problems because it undermines my confidence and triggers all the negative associations I have with learning. This is especially true if the training is mandatory and something which I need to pass to keep my job. This is where the real stress kicks in, because if I can't get through these courses, I need to explain why. There's still such a lot of stigma around learning difficulties and neurodiversity that this is something that I am reluctant to do. Instead I can spend hours and hours on compliance training just so I can pass it without having to ask for support.

Another barrier I face is when I am given a set amount of time to complete training or activities such as quizzes. I know from experience that I need more time to understand and process questions and tasks than many other people. Having a time limit imposed just makes me feel stressed and anxious. I can also struggle with various issues around course assessments. If I fail a test, for example, I find it very frustrating when I am given no clues about which questions I have answered incorrectly, especially if I have to repeat the test until I pass it. If the order of repeated questions is randomized, I also find this distracting and it can really affect my ability to concentrate. It is much easier for me to interact with content which is consistent and predictable.

My main strategy for coping with the barriers I encounter in learning content is to use the internet to try to make sense of the vocabulary and concepts I find difficult to understand. I'm reluctant to ask other people for help because it brings up all the negative feelings associated with struggling with learning and again because of the stigma around learning difficulties. I've been developing online learning content for about five years now, but one of the things which motivated me to first get involved in the industry was wanting to make learning experiences better for people. I find it frustrating that as an industry we strive to make our resources as interactive and engaging as we can but we assume that everyone learns in the same way. This means that instead of engaging people, often our resources create barriers and exclude people, which can have profoundly negative consequences. My own experiences help me to empathize with other people and some of the issues they may be facing when they learn. I know first-hand that learning can be a demotivating and demoralizing experience. I don't think many eLearning professionals are aware just how much the learning they create can affect the confidence and even the mental wellbeing of their learners. My key takeaway is that by designing learning which is accessible and inclusive for everyone, we have the potential to make a huge difference to the confidence and ability to succeed of so many people.

Summary

- Lack of awareness about disability can make it more difficult to understand accessibility and how to implement it. It can also lead to harmful assumptions and misconceptions.

- Definitions of disability were traditionally based on the medical model centred on the idea of deficiency but are now increasingly moving to the social model which considers social and environmental barriers.

- In the digital accessibility context, disability is divided into four categories: visual, hearing, motor and cognitive.

- People are sometimes sceptical about the value of accessibility and how many learners it benefits because they are unaware of the prevalence of disability in society. This is often attributed to the fact that an estimated 80% of disabilities are hidden.

- Disability is often underreported. This can be due to a reluctance to disclose or because people are unaware that they have a disability.

- The ageing population will have a significant impact on the number of people who have disabilities and impairments in the future.

- Considering temporary and situational impairments makes it easier to understand that the positive impact of accessibility is universal.

- Disability personas and learner case studies help content authors to better understand the barriers which face disabled learners and how to avoid them.

Endnotes

[1] Eisenmenger, A (2019) Ableism 101: What it is, what it looks like, and what we can do to fix it [blog], 12 December, https://www.accessliving.org/newsroom/blog/ableism-101/ (archived at https://perma.cc/HQ9L-GM8G)

[2] UK Equality Act 2010 (2010) https://www.legislation.gov.uk/ukpga/2010/15/section/6/2010-07-06 (archived at https://perma.cc/Y5RV-SG8S)

[3] US Department of Justice (2020) A guide to disability rights laws – Americans with Disabilities Act (ADA), https://www.ada.gov/cguide.htm#anchor62335 (archived at https://perma.cc/WQ8B-E3DN)

[4] European Commission, The International and European Framework of Disability Law, http://www.era-comm.eu/UNCRPD/e_learning/B/definition.html (archived at https://perma.cc/SW7S-EUAS)

[5] Sport England (2016) Mapping disability – the facts, https://sportengland-production-files.s3.eu-west-2.amazonaws.com/s3fs-public/mapping-disability-the-facts.pdf (archived at https://perma.cc/U9RN-YFL9)

[6] Hassell, J (2019) *Inclusive Design for Organisations, Including your missing 20% by embedding web and mobile accessibility*, Rethink Press, Gorleston-on-Sea

[7] Sport England (2016) Mapping disability – the facts, https://sportengland-production-files.s3.eu-west-2.amazonaws.com/s3fs-public/mapping-disability-the-facts.pdf (archived at https://perma.cc/U9RN-YFL9)

[8] World Health Organization (2019) Blindness and vision impairment, 8 October, https://www.who.int/news-room/fact-sheets/detail/blindness-and-visual-impairment (archived at https://perma.cc/BB5D-8K8J)

[9] Leventhal, A, NoCoffee vision simulator, https://chrome.google.com/webstore/detail/nocoffee/jjeeggmbnhckmgdhmgdckeigabjfbddl (archived at https://perma.cc/637V-8MNB)

[10] Colour Blind Awareness, Colour blindness: Experience it, https://www.colourblindawareness.org/colour-blindness/colour-blindness-experience-it/ (archived at https://perma.cc/8S64-H2RF)

11 HEARnet online, Types of hearing loss, https://hearnet.org.au/hearing-loss/
    types-of-hearing-loss (archived at https://perma.cc/8SX7-UGZH)

12 WebAIM (Updated 2020) Cognitive, 21 August, https://webaim.org/articles/
    cognitive/ (archived at https://perma.cc/5M9M-224W)

13 Mencap, What is a learning disability? https://www.mencap.org.uk/learning-
    disability-explained/what-learning-disability (archived at https://perma.cc/
    S3KL-Z72G)

14 The World Bank (Updated 2020) Disability Inclusion, May 15, https://www.
    worldbank.org/en/topic/disability (archived at https://perma.cc/F8XT-FCV6)

15 Hassell, J (2019) *Inclusive Design for Organisations, Including your missing
    20% by embedding web and mobile accessibility*, Rethink Press, Gorleston-on-
    Sea

16 What is a hidden disability? https://hiddendisabilitiesstore.com/what-is-a-
    hidden-disability (archived at https://perma.cc/D7BC-QUK7)

17 Jain-Link, P and Taylor Kennedy, J (2019) Why people hide their disabilities at
    work, 3 June, hbr.org/2019/06/why-people-hide-their-disabilities-at-work
    (archived at https://perma.cc/WS6C-37KS)

18 United Nations, Ageing, https://www.un.org/en/sections/issues-depth/ageing/
    (archived at https://perma.cc/KEH7-P4AS)

19 Center for Ageing Better (2018) Greater support needed for older workers as
    number of over 50s in UK workforce reaches record 10 million, 24 January,
    https://www.ageing-better.org.uk/news/number-over-50s-uk-workforce-10-million
    (archived at https://perma.cc/DY74-8RMS)

20 Wald, M, Taken from introduction to Digital accessibility: Enabling
    participation in the information society, https://www.futurelearn.com/courses/
    digital-accessibility (archived at https://perma.cc/M8MC-D3T5)

21 Ability Net (2018) Web accessibility, what does it all mean? (online video),
    https://youtu.be/cY8zxPiSyug (archived at https://perma.cc/6HX3-QNVF)

22 Lockwood, E (2020) 'Nothing about us without us': Disability, the SDGs and
    the UNCRPD, https://www.futurelearn.com/courses/global-disability/0/
    steps/37575 (archived at https://perma.cc/9A9J-EAAF)

23 Government Digital Service (2017) Understanding disabilities and impairments:
    User profiles, 25 October, https://www.gov.uk/government/publications/
    understanding-disabilities-and-impairments-user-profiles (archived at
    https://perma.cc/8SWB-7MSE)

24 Abou-Zahara, S and Sinclair, N (Updated 2017) Stories of web users, 15 May,
    https://www.w3.org/WAI/people-use-web/user-stories/ (archived at
    https://perma.cc/M38K-XQT2)

04

Designing for assistive technology and impairments

Introduction

The first learning resource I designed and developed included a link for learners to send feedback about their learning experience. One of the emails I received was another reason I became so interested in eLearning accessibility. It was from a colleague called Carol Simmonds, who explained that she was a screen reader user and that the headings I had used in my eLearning module made it difficult for her to navigate. At the time, I knew nothing about how to use my authoring tool to make learning content compatible with assistive technology and I had no idea what this meant. Fortunately, Carol agreed to give me a demonstration of her screen reader so that I could see the problem for myself. When I met her in person, I was surprised to find that Carol didn't seem to have a visual impairment. Because I knew that she was a screen reader user I had been expecting to meet someone who was blind. It wasn't until I saw her using her assistive technology that everything made sense. Carol had severe repetitive strain injury, which meant that she couldn't use a mouse. Instead she used a screen reader and her keyboard to navigate through online content. She was used to navigating by jumping from heading to heading, but I hadn't programmed my headings correctly so that she was able to do this.

Not only did this experience give me the clue I needed to fix the problem, it also taught me two valuable lessons. First, it was an important reminder about how easy it is to make assumptions about people's access needs if these are based on misconceptions rather than knowledge. Second, finding out that screen readers could be useful for people with motor as well as visual impairments demonstrated just how little I knew about assistive technology. This prompted me to begin a training course in accessible learning design which involved a research project on the subject. As I was carrying out my research I realized that the more I understood about assistive technology and the reasons behind why I needed to work in a certain way, the more likely I was to invest the time I needed to do this. This echoed something I had discovered during many years of digital systems training. As long as my delegates understood the 'why?' behind a procedure or process, there was a much better chance that they would do what was needed, even if it took them longer.

I believe that a better understanding of assistive technology is critical for the motivation needed to design accessible learning content. If you know, for instance, that some people navigate using voice activation software, it becomes much easier to understand why it is so important that accessible names match visible labels for buttons. This is because if you use a button which has the visible label 'Next', but accidentally give the button the accessible name 'Forward', anyone who tries to activate the button by saying the word 'Next' won't be able to move on in the eLearning resource. I believe that if people understand this and can empathize with how frustrating this would be, they are much more likely to check that the visible labels of buttons match accessible names rather than simply trying to comply with the WCAG standard **2.5.3 Label in Name**.

The purpose of this chapter is to give you an overview of the most common forms of assistive technology likely to be used by your learners and a better understanding of what you need to do to make your learning content compatible. The chapter also gives you some of the key accommodations you need to be aware of to make learning content accessible for learners with impairments who don't use assistive technology. For ease, I have organized the information according to the four categories we identified for disabilities: visual, hearing, motor and cognitive. It is important to remember, however, that this is an oversimplification of the many different and overlapping requirements of disabled people and those who use assistive technology.

What is assistive technology?

There is a strong case for arguing that 'all technology is assistive technology'.[1] This is because it helps to make everyday tasks easier for everyone.

In this chapter, however, I focus on technology which is developed specifically for the purpose of benefitting disabled people. Although the umbrella term assistive technology includes products such as glasses, wheelchairs, prosthetic limbs, etc, it is most commonly used to refer to technology-enhanced tools or systems. It describes devices such as hearing aids, adapted keyboards, eye-tracking cameras or refreshable braille displays. It also covers third-party software such as screen readers, text-to-speech tools and screen magnifiers. In addition, it incorporates assistive functionality built into the operating systems of desktops, laptops and mobile devices. This includes features such as text-to-speech, cursor and pointer customization, colour filters and high contrast. Browser extensions and apps created for specific accessibility needs are also considered assistive technology. There are many ground-breaking and innovative examples of apps which are worth exploring further. Seeing AI,[2] BlindSquare[3] and Soundscape[4] are just a few examples if you are interested in finding out more.

Assistive technology users

The best way to find out more about assistive technology is to see it being used by people who have a lived experience of a disability. This not only gives a better understanding of the challenges which they face as a result of inaccessible content, it also allows you to appreciate the different skills and expertise that users develop. One of the most surprising things I discovered in my screen reader demonstration from Carol was the speed at which she was able to listen to content. According to WebAIM, 'experienced users often like to speed up the reading rate to 300 words per minute or more'.[5] This is much faster than most listeners can understand. It is a powerful example of the capacity that people have to develop existing skills and learn new ones in order to adapt to their environment and circumstances. Having said that, it is important not to make assumptions about these skills. A common misconception often held by content authors is that all assistive technology users are confident with technology and have knowledge of the advanced features of their tools which allow them to apply workarounds for inaccessible content. This is often far from true. People who use assistive technology have just as wide a range of experience, competence and confidence with technology as anyone else.

If you don't have the opportunity to see people using assistive technology first hand, a good compromise is to use the many video resources available.

Running a search for a particular assistive technology on a video-hosting platform will often allow you to find examples of disabled people demonstrating how they use their devices and software. This brings the experience to life and can help you to get a better understanding of how assistive technology works. A good introduction is provided by W3C's Web Accessibility Perspectives.[6] Pacercenter's Assistive Technology in Action series[7] is another recommended resource.

Visual impairments

Assistive technology for visual impairments

Assistive technology for learners with visual impairments includes screen readers, refreshable braille displays and screen magnifiers.

SCREEN READERS
Screen readers convert what is on a computer screen into information that can be output through synthetic speech or braille. Some screen readers also play sound cues when certain actions are performed, such as activating a link or menu item. In addition to outputting information, screen readers enable users to navigate content. They use keyboard commands or shortcuts to allow users to move between items such as headings, images, paragraphs and lists. They also have commands which allow users to move to tables and to navigate the rows and columns inside them so that the data they hold can be successfully interpreted. Common specialized screen reader keyboard commands include 'L' to jump to the next list, 'K' to jump to the next link and 'G' to jump to the next graphic. Screen reader users also use the same standard keyboard commands as people who navigate using the keyboard. These include 'Tab' to jump to interactive items, 'Enter' to activate links and 'Enter' or 'Space Bar' to activate buttons.

INBUILT SCREEN READERS
New computer hardware and the majority of mobile devices come with inbuilt screen readers. Voiceover is the screen reader for macOS and iOS for Apple mobile devices. Talkback is used for Android devices. Narrator is the screen reader supplied with Windows machines.

THIRD-PARTY SCREEN READERS

The two most commonly used third-party screen readers for Windows are NVDA[8] (NonVisual Desktop Access) and JAWS[9] (Job Access With Speech). Together they represent more than 80% of the screen reader market on desktops and laptops.[10] NVDA is an open source, globally accessible screen reader. It is free, although a donation is requested to support its mission of 'empowering lives through non-visual access to technology'.[11] JAWS is a commercially available screen reader which has excellent functionality but can be prohibitively expensive. There is a demo mode currently available for testing non-commercial material, but this requires you to restart your machine every 40 minutes.

TESTING WITH SCREEN READERS

There are a few caveats to be aware of if you intend to test your learning content with screen readers. The first is that all are unique and perform differently with a range of browsers. This means that what may work with a screen reader when testing with one browser may not necessarily work with another. In a useful article on designing for screen reader compatibility[12] WebAIM suggests the following pairings for optimum testing:

- Firefox with NVDA;
- Chrome or Internet Explorer with JAWS;
- Safari with VoiceOver;
- Edge with Narrator.

Another thing to be aware of is that the keyboard commands or shortcuts used to operate screen readers vary. This is often why people tend to stick with one screen reader once they become familiar with the commands. There are many resources which detail these specific commands, including recommended WebAIM overviews for NVDA[13] and JAWS.[14] It is also important to understand that screen readers are highly configurable. They have many options available depending on their users' needs or preferences. This means that it is unlikely that anyone will use the software with its default settings as we tend to do when we begin using screen readers for testing purposes. It is also unlikely that we will be able to replicate anything like an authentic screen reader user experience without training and a significant amount of practice. These issues understandably lead some people to conclude that screen reader testing is best left to accessibility experts. Even with basic skills, however, there is a great deal that we can learn from testing using screen readers which can lead to significant improvements in the accessibility of learning content.

TEXT-TO-SPEECH VS SCREEN READERS

A common misconception is to confuse text-to-speech and screen reader functionality. There are many inbuilt versions of text-to-speech software and third-party tools available. Some examples include Read Aloud,[15] NaturalReader[16] and ClaroRead.[17] A key difference between the two is that while screen readers are able to convert text into either speech or braille output, text-to-speech can only output in speech. Most crucially, text-to-speech software does not allow users to navigate using keyboard shortcuts in the same way as screen readers do. As a result it's not possible to use text-to-speech software to test for screen reader compatibility.

MAKING CONTENT ACCESSIBLE FOR SCREEN READER USERS

Many of the requirements needed to make content accessible for screen reader users are achieved using the underlying code of the tool. This applies to the ability to identify and interpret structures such as tables, lists and page regions. Navigating using keyboard commands is also reliant on coding. This is done using appropriate HTML elements, for example <h1> for level one headings, <li> for lists, <img> for images.

Note: For further detailed information I recommend Laura Kalbag's book *Accessibility for Everyone*, which has a chapter dedicated to accessibility and HTML.[18]

Good screen reader user experience, however, does not rely solely on underlying code. Content authors are responsible for adding alternative text, ordering items correctly so that they are read out in a logical linear order which makes sense to screen reader users and avoiding programming single character key shortcuts which can interfere with screen reader commands. It is also important that they set the correct language for the learning resource so that the screen reader voices content with the correct pronunciation. Either avoiding or allowing learners to control moving content such as animated text is also a key consideration, as often text which moves can be missed by screen readers. Providing descriptive transcripts for video content can also benefit screen reader users as this allows them to use their screen reader settings to control the speed they listen to the content.

REFRESHABLE BRAILLE DISPLAYS

Refreshable braille displays are used by people who are blind or have low vision and also by deafblind people. They are electronic devices which create six or eight dot braille characters using moving pins. These are lowered and raised to form braille in cells which are arranged in a linear order. The number of cells typically range from 12 to 88, with mobile displays and less expensive models tending to have fewer cells. Braille displays have traditionally needed a screen reader in order to work. As a result of recent advances in technology, however, this is no longer always the case. Some displays, for example, can work with Windows Narrator.

MAKING CONTENT ACCESSIBLE FOR BRAILLE DISPLAY USERS

An important consideration for content authors to be aware of is that it may take braille display users longer to process content. This could be due to the time it takes to convert text into braille and the number of cells that are available on the device being used. This makes it important that any time limits imposed are adjustable, or better still that they are avoided. It also makes clear and concise text extremely helpful. Providing descriptive transcripts for audio and video content is also vital for deafblind users who use refreshable braille displays and who may not be able to see or hear the content.

SCREEN MAGNIFIERS

Screen magnifiers enlarge the size of text and images on the screen for better visibility. They can be used to magnify small areas of the screen around the mouse cursor or to enlarge the whole page and zoom in on a particular area. They can be operated by using either the mouse or keyboard commands to enlarge portions of the screen and can also be programmed so that the cursor moves automatically depending on a pre-set speed. Screen magnifiers sometimes have additional functionality, such as allowing users to invert colours, using shading to help people find their place on the page and customizing the cursor to make it more visible. Many of the leading screen magnifiers also come combined with screen reader functionality. Popular third-party screen magnifiers include ZoomText[19] and SuperNova.[20]

Operating systems for desktop and mobile devices have functionality which allows either full-screen or text-only magnification. In addition, the zoom function in browsers allows content to be enlarged. Neither of these options, however, has the same advanced functionality as screen magnifiers.

MAKING CONTENT ACCESSIBLE FOR SCREEN MAGNIFIER USERS

The key takeaway for screen magnifier functionality is that as the size of the area that is enlarged increases, the amount of the original screen image being displayed reduces. This means that it is important for the layout of learning content to be as clear as possible. Navigation items need to be in a consistent place and order so that they are easy to find. Good colour contrast and clear, simple text make for a better learning experience for screen magnifier users since reading large print on a screen can be tiring. Another key requirement is alternative text since many screen magnifiers also have screen reader functionality. It can often be quicker and easier to listen to the description of an image rather than trying to work out what is being conveyed when looking at a small portion of it at a time.

Additional considerations for all visual impairments

In addition to the requirements which are needed to accommodate assistive technology, there are some other key measures content authors can take to make content accessible for people with visual impairments. Choosing good colour contrast between text and interactive items and the background they appear on is crucial as it benefits learners with many different types of visual impairments. Accommodating colour blind learners is achieved by making sure that no information is conveyed using colour alone – for example, supplementing the colour red to show that a question has been answered incorrectly by using a cross icon and the word 'incorrect'. Learners should also be able to enlarge the text using browser zoom to make it easier to see without losing any of the content or functionality on the page. Another requirement is that they should be able to adjust the spacing between text as for many people with visual impairments this can have more of an impact on readability than simply enlarging the text.

Hearing impairments

Assistive technology for all hearing impairments

People who are deaf or hard of hearing use a range of assistive devices. These generally fall into two categories. The first category contains devices which help amplify hearing and are often known as assistive listening devices (ALDs). These devices vary depending on the hearing condition. They include hearing aids, bone conduction hearing devices and a variety of implants.[21] The second category includes alerting devices which translate audio signals such as notification sounds into visual or tactile ones. The devices in both these categories do not need to be specifically accommodated by content authors. Captions, transcripts and sign language, however, are forms of assistive technology which need to be considered.

Making content accessible for all hearing impairments

Captions are a key requirement for people who are deaf or hard of hearing. Captions need to be provided for all prerecorded content and any live content if this is included in the learning resource. They should be synchronized with the action and be descriptive, ie contain the important information that learners with hearing impairments will miss. This could include details such as who is speaking, important background noises and sound effects. Providing descriptive transcripts is important since the speed of captions can sometimes make it difficult for people to read them. Another key requirement for learners with hearing impairments is to make sure that if any sound effects are used, such as a buzzer when the learner makes an error or a tone when a topic is completed, this information is also conveyed in text. Allowing learners to stop audio or control the volume is another important consideration.

In addition to these requirements, there are some best-practice WCAG AAA recommendations which support people with hearing impairments. The first is to provide a sign language alternative for videos. This accommodates people whose first language is sign language and who may find it difficult to process the information in captions or a written transcript. Another important AAA recommendation is to make sure that any background audio for audio-only tracks is not distracting. This normally refers to music playing in the background when people are speaking. The level of the background noise should be low enough not to cause interference or learners should be able to turn it off. Although the WCAG recommendation refers specifically to audio-only content, it is considered good practice for videos with background audio tracks. This is an important consideration as so many people with different types of hearing impairments struggle to process content if there is distracting background audio.

Motor impairments

Assistive technology for motor impairments

In a digital context, motor impairments include any conditions which limit people's ability to interact with computer hardware or mobile devices. For example, people with motor impairments which affect manual dexterity may find it difficult or impossible to use a standard mouse on a desktop, a trackpad on a laptop, or finger gestures on a mobile device. There is, however, a wide variety of assistive devices and software which give people alternative ways to interact with digital content.

KEYBOARDS

Although the keyboard is a standard way to input data, it can also be considered a form of assistive technology. This is the case where someone predominantly uses a keyboard to navigate and input data. In this book I refer to learners who use keyboards in this way as 'keyboard users'.

ADAPTIVE KEYBOARDS

Keyboards can be adapted in various ways to help people with motor impairments. This can be something as simple as the shape, as is the case with ergonomic keyboards. These are designed to minimize muscle strain, normally by allowing users to type with hands at a slight angle. Other adaptive keyboards have accommodations such as raised areas in between keys which let people place their hands on the keyboard and then run their fingers along the raised areas to the correct key. They can also have separate numeric pads, larger keys or high-contrast keys as with high-visibility keyboards. Adaptive keyboards include specialized keyboards such as braille or chording keyboards. Chording keyboards have only a few keys which are pressed in combination, like the chords on a piano, to create letters, numbers and other characters. Onscreen keyboards are another form of adaptive keyboard or keyboard interface. These are often used in conjunction with word completion technology, which makes it easier and faster to enter data.

INTERACTING WITH KEYBOARDS

There are many devices and technologies which allow people to interact with keyboards. These include mouth sticks and head wands, which are rods held either in the mouth or strapped to the head and which are used to operate standard or onscreen keyboards. Eye-tracking technology which uses a camera to analyse the movement of the user's eyes can also be used to allow people to interact with onscreen keyboards.

SWITCHES

A wide variety of devices comes under the umbrella term switches. These can vary from mechanical buttons which are placed according to the range of movement available to the user, for example next to the head or on the arm of a mobility device such as a wheelchair, to sip and puff switches activated by inhaling (ie sipping) or exhaling (ie puffing), and cheek sensor switches activated by movement. Switches can also be activated by bite, footplates or handle bar-like grasps. The actions of switches are interpreted by specialist software on the computer, allowing the user to both input data and navigate content.

VOICE RECOGNITION

Voice or speech recognition software allows users to use a microphone and voice commands to input text and to perform mouse actions such as opening a file or printing. Many of us are already familiar with similar technology in the form of mainstream voice assistants such as Apple's Siri, Microsoft's Cortana and Google Assistant. The software used in assistive technology is more sophisticated and has the capability of being trained to recognize a user's voice. This is particularly important for conditions which might make speech less clear and also those that can sometimes lead to changes in a voice during the course of a day. A specific requirement needed for voice recognition is to make sure that the accessible name of buttons matches the visible name. Not using single character key shortcuts is another important consideration as this can interfere with voice recognition commands.

Making content accessible for all motor impairments

The range of assistive technology available for people with motor impairments can make it bewildering to know how to ensure learning resources are compatible. The good news is that the requirements which make learning content accessible for keyboard users should also ensure that it can accommodate the software and devices that we have covered.

The most important consideration is that all interactive items in the eLearning resource must be operable with a keyboard. Learners must be able to use keys such as the 'Tab' or 'Arrow' keys to select or 'move focus' to interactive items and must be able to operate them once they are selected or 'have focus'. This includes navigation items and links, and is particularly important for input items such as radio buttons and check boxes which are often used in quizzes and assessments in eLearning resources. Multi-media players must also be operable with a keyboard. It is important that as well as being able to move focus to and operate interactive items, keyboard users must be able to move focus away from them. If they can't, this leads to what is known as a 'keyboard trap'. It effectively means that the learner is trapped and can't access the rest of the content in the eLearning resource. A visible focus indicator such as a dotted line or a border around interactive items which have focus from the keyboard is also important since many keyboard users are visual. Visible focus indicators help keyboard users orientate themselves on the page but are also vital to let learners know that they have selected an item before activating it. All of these requirements are generally controlled by the functionality of the authoring tool.

Content authors are responsible for ensuring that the focus order of interactive items on a page is logical for keyboard users. With some tools they have the ability to control the appearance of the focus indicator, which can be helpful to ensure there is good contrast between the indicator and interactive items. Another accommodation content authors may need to provide is a mechanism whereby keyboard users can skip repeated blocks of content such as menus repeated on every page of the learning resource. This can sometimes be provided automatically by the authoring tool, but if it is not, it is the responsibility of the content author. An additional consideration to be aware of for learners with motor impairments which affect dexterity is just how much extra time and effort can be needed to interact with digital content. It is therefore important to have a clear and consistent layout which makes things easy to find and best practice is to avoid any interactions or activities which have time limits imposed. Another recommendation is to use inclusive language, ie use 'Select' instead of 'Click', which assumes that everyone is using a mouse, or 'Tap', which assumes everyone is using finger gestures on a mobile device.

If content is mobile compatible, there are some specific requirements which accommodate learners with mobility impairments. The first is that for any interactions which need learners to carry out complex gestures such as a two-finger pinch to zoom, a single point of contact alternative is provided. Another is to stop learners accidentally activating interactive items by triggering functionality on the up-event rather than the down-event. The up-event is when learners release their finger, the pointer or the mouse click. The down-event is when they press their finger, the pointer or the mouse click down. A final consideration is to make sure that learners can disable functionality which is triggered by movement, such as shaking or tilting a device to undo an action, and that the same functionality can be activated using standard controls such as a button or a link.

Cognitive impairments

Assistive technology for cognitive impairments

Much of the assistive technology which makes digital content more accessible to people with cognitive impairments helps with reading, writing and concentration issues. It is most commonly provided by third-party software packages. These programs can, for example, allow users to change the spacing between text, the colour and size of the text or the font itself. They can also let learners mask part of the screen to help reduce distractions, and highlight or underline text to keep focus. Other common functionality includes helping users to spell by using predictive text or symbols.

Making content accessible for all cognitive impairments

Ensuring that third-party software can work reliably with learning content is normally dependent on the underlying code of the authoring tool. There are, however, many other measures which content authors can take to make content more accessible for learners with cognitive impairments. One key requirement is to provide transcripts for audio-only and video content. Not only does this allow learners to take advantage of the features offered by assistive technology when interpreting the text, it also allows them to take the time they need to process and make sense of the content. Other requirements include making sure that navigation is clear and consistent and that instructions are easy to understand and not ambiguous in any way. Some WCAG standards also benefit people with cognitive impairments by helping learners avoid making mistakes and supporting them with error suggestions if they do. One particularly important standard for learning content is that learners are given the opportunity to reverse, check and correct or confirm data which is submitted in test responses.

Another important consideration involves moving content. This can be distracting for learners who have difficulties with concentration or focus. It should be avoided unless learners are able to control the movement. Any content which starts automatically should also be avoided, although this is a recommendation rather than a requirement. A final consideration is content which flashes rather than moves. This should be avoided unless it falls below the required thresholds, otherwise it can cause seizures for learners with photosensitive epilepsy. Other recommendations include making sure that the language used throughout the learning resource is straightforward and clear. It is also helpful to provide explanations for any complex vocabulary or abbreviations. In addition, there are many recommendations around the font and formatting of the text. These include choosing a readable font, left aligning text, ensuring that there is enough space between lines of text and avoiding text in all caps.

Summary

- Understanding assistive technology and how it can help people encourages content authors to take the extra time and effort needed to make learning content accessible.

- It is important not to make assumptions about how people with disabilities use assistive technology.

- Assistive technology users have many overlapping needs and disabilities. They also have a wide range of technological skills and abilities.

- When designing accessible content it is important to consider learners with visual, hearing, motor and cognitive impairments.

- Each of these categories has specific requirements and recommendations which have a positive impact on assistive technology users and other learners with impairments.

Endnotes

[1] Hendren, S (2014) All technology is assistive, 16 October, https://www.wired.com/2014/10/all-technology-is-assistive/ (archived at https://perma.cc/6MDH-9BE4)

2   https://www.microsoft.com/en-us/ai/seeing-ai (archived at https://perma.cc/Q2AM-8FGG)

3   https://www.blindsquare.com/ (archived at https://perma.cc/2N27-H5XQ)

4   https://www.microsoft.com/en-us/research/product/soundscape/ (archived at https://perma.cc/2ZBG-E4GH)

5   WebAIM (Updated 2017) Designing for screen reader compatibility, 21 April, https://webaim.org/techniques/screenreader/ (archived at https://perma.cc/U9XB-B5R4)

6   W3C (Updated 2016) Web accessibility perspectives videos (online video), https://www.w3.org/WAI/perspective-videos/ (archived at https://perma.cc/58NL-ZRXF)

7   Pacercenter (Updated 2014) Assistive technology in action (online video), https://www.youtube.com/playlist?list=PLMe9zDtTPTVe62Gb6b9Dkk_IPBUTGQHoD (archived at https://perma.cc/AA7G-3G3G)

8   https://www.nvaccess.org/ (archived at https://perma.cc/DF5U-QG3Y)

9   https://www.freedomscientific.com/products/software/jaws/ (archived at https://perma.cc/2XAS-AA95)

10 WebAIM (2019) Screen reader user survey #8 results, 27 September, https://webaim.org/projects/screenreadersurvey8/#used (archived at https://perma.cc/2VEN-2VQT)

11 https://www.nvaccess.org/ (archived at https://perma.cc/DF5U-QG3Y)

12 WebAIM (Updated 2017) Designing for screen reader compatibility, 21 April, https://webaim.org/techniques/screenreader/ (archived at https://perma.cc/U9XB-B5R4)

13 WebAIM (Updated 2020) Keyboard shortcuts for NVDA, 25 September, https://webaim.org/resources/shortcuts/nvda (archived at https://perma.cc/58JR-XEA4)

14 WebAIM (Updated 2020) Keyboard Shortcuts for JAWS, 28 September, https://webaim.org/resources/shortcuts/jaws (archived at https://perma.cc/K6B3-2HDX)

15 https://support.microsoft.com/en-us/office/use-the-speak-text-to-speech-feature-to-read-text-aloud-459e7704-a76d-4fe2-ab48-189d6b83333c (archived at https://perma.cc/7T5Y-AF86)

16 https://www.naturalreaders.com/ (archived at https://perma.cc/7DRC-7NFN)

17 https://www.clarosoftware.com/ (archived at https://perma.cc/7HNU-K2P8)

18 Kalbag, L (2017) Accessibility for Everyone, A Book Apart, New York

19 https://www.zoomtext.com/products/zoomtext-magnifierreader/ (archived at https://perma.cc/7CZV-8E3M)

20 https://yourdolphin.com/en-gb/products/individuals/supernova-magnifier (archived at https://perma.cc/9PY6-SM9Y)

21 HEARnet online, The interactive ear, https://hearnet.org.au/ (archived at https://perma.cc/LX37-E3ZA)

05

The case for digital accessibility

Introduction

My first formal experience of advocating for eLearning accessibility took place in front of a panel of judges at the Learning Technology Awards in 2018. My entry for the award was an eLearning induction course designed to keep international university students safe and well when they arrived on campus in the UK. I wanted to prove that it was possible to create an eLearning resource which was not only accessible but also good enough to be shortlisted for one of the most prestigious awards in the learning technologies field. Since I was a public sector instructional designer with little influence in the eLearning industry, I'd decided that this was one of the best ways of raising awareness about the importance of accessible learning content. I also wanted the opportunity to challenge the fact that accessibility was not one of the criteria for any of the organization's awards.

Although the judges were slightly bewildered by my presentation and its focus on accessibility, rather than the statistics about organizational impact and return on investment which was required, they nevertheless listened patiently. When it came to their follow-up questions, however, my arguments fell apart. The judges wanted evidence about how many students with access needs my eLearning course had helped. They also wanted to know how much time had been saved by staff as a result. Both very valid questions. They were understandably unimpressed that the university knew of only two students, one with a visual impairment and one who had a broken wrist, who had been able to complete the module independently without the support they would otherwise have needed. This out of a cohort of more than 1,500 students just didn't have the impact that I was trying to create.

Although I did manage to explain how important it was that accessibility should be included in the criteria for future awards, particularly in the public sector categories where it had just become a clear legal obligation, I knew that I'd failed in having any influence which might have led to meaningful change.

After my presentation, I was furious with myself for not having put forward a better case. My arguments had simply not been compelling enough to convince the judges that the benefits of accessible learning content extended beyond the specific experiences of two learners with impairments. I recognized that I needed a coherent and convincing argument which included the ethical, legal and business case for digital accessibility. I also needed a focus on how it could improve the learning experience for everyone, not just for disabled learners. Most importantly, I realized that I needed this case not only when I was standing in front of a panel of judges but all the time. I had already experienced countless examples of disinterest or scepticism about the importance of accessible learning content from colleagues, managers and senior leaders, so I knew that to make an impact I would need to be much better prepared. This chapter is the result of that realization. It gives the case for digital accessibility so that everyone has the arguments they need to be a more effective advocate.

The ethical case

Whenever I deliver training events to raise awareness about eLearning accessibility, I begin by asking people the reasons why they believe it is important to design inclusive learning content. The most common answers they give are that it is 'the right thing to do', or it is unethical to unnecessarily exclude people due to disabilities or impairments. While this case is underpinned by legislation in many countries, I believe the most compelling evidence to support this view is the United Nations Convention on the Rights of Persons with Disabilities. The CRPD promotes the idea that digital accessibility is a right and not a privilege. It is a legally binding and internationally recognized human rights treaty, which came into force in 2008 and has been ratified by 181 countries to date. Its chief function is to 'enable persons with disabilities to live independently and participate fully in all aspects of life'. Article nine of the convention states: 'Access to information, communications and other services, including electronic services, is a human right.'[1]

As the CRPD makes clear, an important aspect of the ethical case for digital accessibility centres on the argument that it promotes equality. Along with lack of digital skills, poor connectivity and limited access to equipment, inaccessible services all contribute to the inequality often referred to as the 'digital divide'. This concept first became popular in the mid-nineties when the US Department of Commerce released a research report on the widespread inequalities in national ICT access in the US.[2] While there have been improvements in access to digital technology in the States and globally since this report was released, the digital divide remains a significant factor in societal inequality.

It is interesting to consider the effect COVID 19 has had on this inequality more recently. While the pandemic has undoubtedly been responsible for intensifying the digital divide,[3] it has also succeeded in heightening awareness of the importance of digital accessibility. For many people, experiencing lockdowns made it evident for the first time how reliant we are on day-to-day digital services. It also made many of us more aware just how essential it is that disabled people, particularly those who are most vulnerable in our society, have equal access to those services. The switch to online learning at all levels of education, but particularly in higher education, has also had a huge impact. It has contributed to a growing realization that to be equitable, learning content needs to be accessible as the default.

The legal case

It has been estimated that 84% of countries have laws protecting the rights of people with disabilities.[4] As a result, the threat of litigation remains one of the most common reasons businesses and organizations make content accessible. It is worth being aware, therefore, of some of the key facts in the legal case for accessibility. Since legal requirements vary internationally, it is only possible to include a detailed analysis of the accessibility laws of two countries in this overview. I have chosen to focus on the UK and the US for two reasons. The first is because they both have broad anti-discrimination and specific digital accessibility laws, which is a common theme in accessibility legislation. The second is because they demonstrate the growing trend for the WCAG to be regarded as the definitive technical standards underpinning legal compliance. For further information on international accessibility laws in other countries, two recommended resources are W3C's Web Accessibility Laws & Policies site[5] and the IAAP's CPACC Body of Knowledge.[6]

Note: The information in this section is an overview only and should not be considered legal advice.

UK accessibility law overview

THE EQUALITY ACT 2010: KEY FACTS

- The Equality Act 2010[7] is the principal anti-discrimination law in the UK. As its name suggests, it was passed in 2010 and brought together over 116 separate pieces of legislation, including the Disability Discrimination Act of 1995,[8] which remains the legislation in Northern Ireland to date.

- The Equality Act 'provides a legal framework which protects individuals from unfair treatment and promotes a fair and more equal society'.[9]

- It states that every organization has an 'anticipatory duty' to make 'reasonable adjustments'. This means that 'an organisation cannot wait until a disabled person wants to use its services, but must think in advance (and on an ongoing basis) about what disabled people with a range of impairments might reasonably need'.[10]

THE EQUALITY ACT 2010: IMPACT

Despite this clear mandate for organizations to provide services for people with disabilities, there has been little litigation against companies for digital inaccessibility in the UK. One exception was the legal action taken in 2012 by the Royal National Institute of Blind People (RNIB) against Bmibaby over the inaccessibility of its website.[11] This is generally the only known example in the UK largely as a result of the fact that the majority of companies that are sued settle out of court. This means not only that the outcome is not legally binding but also that there is little publicity about digital inaccessibility, since anonymity is typically part of the settlement agreement. The legal driver for change in digital accessibility practice in the UK therefore has had an unfortunately limited effect. It has been described 'as low key and low impact, leading to a landscape of inaccessibility'.[12]

Another reason why the Equality Act has been less effective in ensuring digital accessibility is due to the ambiguity around 'reasonable adjustments'. Although W3C identifies the WCAG as the underlying guidelines for the Equality Act,[13] the fact that this is not explicitly stated is commonly identified as a key reason why there is much confusion and a lack of action around digital accessibility in the UK. This situation, however, is widely anticipated to change as a result of regulations introduced in 2018.

THE PUBLIC SECTOR BODIES (WEBSITES AND MOBILE APPLICATIONS) ACCESSIBILITY REGULATIONS 2018 (PSBAR): KEY FACTS

- The PSBAR[14] are the result of Directive (EU) 2016/2102 of the European Parliament and of the Council of 26 October 2016 on the accessibility of the websites and mobile applications of public sector bodies.[15]

- They became law in the UK on 23 September 2018 and took full effect from September 2020, with a June 2021 deadline for mobile applications.

- The PSBAR cover websites, intranets and extranets and any digital content held on them, including learning content, documents and presentations. They also apply to mobile applications.

- The regulations cover public sector bodies, including central and local government organizations, higher and further education institutions and the National Health Service (NHS). The legislation also applies to charities or non-governmental organizations (NGOs) which are mostly financed by public funding or provide services which are either essential to the public or aimed at disabled people.[16]

- The Government Digital Service is responsible for monitoring the regulations, while the Equality and Human Rights Commission in Great Britain and the Equality Commission in Northern Ireland enforce them.[17]

- The required standard to meet for the PSBAR is the European standard EN 301 549.[18] This is directly in line with WCAG 2.1 levels A and AA, although it recommends AAA as best practice.

- The legislation also requires organizations to produce an accessibility statement.[19]

THE PSBAR: IMPACT

The PSBAR are predicted to have a significant impact on digital accessibility in the UK public sector and beyond. The main reason is because the regulations clearly establish WCAG 2.1 level AA as the standard to meet for legal compliance. This is regarded by many accessibility experts to be a game changer. Another important point to be aware of is that the EU directive on which the PSBAR is based also applies to all member states of the European Union. Each of those countries has passed equivalent legislation, with flexibility only in the monitoring and enforcing of the regulations. This represents a significant strengthening of digital accessibility laws not only in the UK but in the majority of Europe.

US accessibility law overview

AMERICANS WITH DISABILITIES ACT (ADA) KEY FACTS

- The ADA is one of various state and federal laws which govern web accessibility in the US and requires businesses to make accommodations for people with disabilities.

- The legislation does not give specific regulations regarding web accessibility as when it was introduced in 1990, the internet was still a relatively new concept. Businesses that fall under ADA Title I or ADA Title III, however, must have a website that gives 'reasonable accessibility'[20] to people with disabilities.

- ADA Title I covers businesses with at least 15 full-time employees that operate for 20 or more weeks every year. ADA Title III covers businesses that are classed as places of 'public accommodations'. These are generally open to the public and include restaurants, movie theatres, schools and doctors' offices.[21]

ADA: IMPACT

The US has by far the highest number of lawsuits filed for digital inaccessibility worldwide. In 2018, this amounted to 2,258 ADA Title III website accessibility lawsuits filed in federal court. This was a 171% increase on the number in 2017. The number of cases decreased very slightly to 2,256 in 2019. While this suggests that the explosion of lawsuits is levelling out,[22] it is still a good indication of the potential power that legislation can have on enforcing digital accessibility. It is also worth being aware that the threat of legal action extends beyond the borders of the US. In 2018, for example, 11% of companies sued in the US were headquartered internationally, including in Italy, France, Japan and Brazil.[23]

SECTION 508 OF THE US REHABILITATION ACT OF 1973: KEY FACTS

- The Rehabilitation Act was introduced in 1973. Its purpose was to prevent disability discrimination for both employees and members of the public at federal agencies and organizations receiving federal funding.

- As a result of technological advances, Congress amended the act in 1998. Section 508[24] requires that federal agencies make all electronic and information technology accessible for people with disabilities equivalent to the access available to others.

- In 2017 the US Access Board updated the standards with a 'Section 508 refresh' to bring them in line with European standards and the WCAG.

- Although the WCAG version referred to in Section 508 is WCAG 2.0, 2020 findings by Usablenet show that WCAG 2.1 has become the prevailing standard, with over 75% of federal claims now referencing WCAG 2.1.[25]

SECTION 508: IMPACT

Rather than a focus on the number of cases as with the ADA, analysis of the impact of Section 508 highlights high-profile success cases. The most significant of these include National Federation for the Blind (NFB) v Small Business Association, Disability Rights Advocates (DRA) v UC Berkeley, National Federation for the Blind v Social Security Administration, and National Association for the Deaf v Harvard University & Massachusetts Institute of Technology.[26]

The business case

While it is admittedly a powerful driver, the drawback of the litigation argument is that it creates the perception that accessibility is a threat rather than an opportunity. If the only motivation for making content and products accessible is to avoid the risk of being sued, it is understandable that many businesses believe that investing the time and resources to make this happen is not worthwhile. If we consider instead all the benefits that accessibility offers, then it becomes clear why many market leaders regard it as 'mission critical' rather than just a 'nice to have'. In a crowded learning technology marketplace, businesses are becoming increasingly aware of the commercial benefits that can be gained from creating accessible products and content.

Increased revenue

According to research carried out in 2019, inclusive products can expand customer reach fourfold and impact the bottom line of organizations.[27] This makes perfect sense if we consider the 'purple pound', which is a popular term used to describe the spending power of disabled people and their families. It is estimated to be worth a staggering £247 billion in the UK,[28] $490 billion in the US[29] and over $8 trillion worldwide.[30]

Brand enhancement

The market reach of accessible products, however, extends beyond just disabled people and their families. It also includes customers who are influenced by brand and are increasingly looking to businesses to show a commitment to inclusion and to making a social impact. In an influential economic impact report published in 2016, Forrester found that 83% of private sector and 69% of public sector respondents believed that their brand directly benefitted from their accessibility strategy.[31] One of the most well-known examples of this in the UK is Barclays. With its declared ambition to become the most accessible company in the FTSE 100, Barclays acknowledges that a commitment to accessibility gives it 'a concrete competitive advantage'.[32]

There are many other examples of increasing engagement with disability inclusion and accessibility in the business sector. One important movement driving this change is the Valuable 500. This organization was launched by founder Caroline Casey at the World Economic Forum in 2019. It currently has the support of 235 global businesses with a combined revenue of $3.8 trillion and this number is steadily increasing.[33] The community includes many leading technology providers such as IBM, Microsoft, Sony and Cisco. I believe it is very likely that these will soon be joined by leading learning technology content and product providers who are waking up to the commercial benefits of digital accessibility.

Innovation

Another advantage of accessibility is that it has the power to help businesses think differently when they create products or learning content. There are many examples of how accessibility has the power to generate transformative innovation which benefits everyone. Examples such as the typewriter and telephone, email and text to speech were all created as a result of considering the needs of people with disabilities yet are now mainstream.[34] A more recent example is the blur functionality for video calls provided in Microsoft Teams. This feature was originally developed to support people with hearing impairments who rely on lip reading by eliminating any distracting background features or movement. This functionality is now routinely used, however, by a whole range of people who benefit from blurring their background on video calls, particularly when working remotely.

Since so many businesses are trying to make ever more inventive products, it's easy to see how innovation can be considered the 'lifeblood of most companies'.[35] Although the eLearning industry lags behind other technology sectors in its understanding of how accessibility can lead to innovation, I believe this is a situation which cannot fail to change.

The learning case

While the broader advantages of digital accessibility are relevant for our industry, it's also important to be aware of the benefits which apply specifically to learning content. This is particularly important because a common opinion in the eLearning profession still seems to be that accessibility is something which harms rather than enhances the learning experience. To challenge this assumption it's useful to be aware of two inclusive design models which have particular relevance for learning and technology.

Universal Design for Learning (UDL)

UDL is an educational approach which gives everyone equal access to learning by using flexible strategies which can be customized to a range of needs. It grew out of the universal design movement initiated by architect Ronald L Mace. In 1984, the Center for Applied Special Technology (CAST)[36] first applied the thinking behind universal design to an educational framework. UDL recognizes the 'individualistic nature of learners and their need to accommodate such differences in order to produce effective learning experiences'.[37] One of the three principles central to this methodology is that it gives learners multiple means of representation. With this principle UDL shows that accommodating accessibility needs also caters to the preferences of all learners and thus creates a better learning experience for everyone.

Inclusive design

Inclusive design is a methodology which emerged from the digital technologies industry in the seventies and eighties. It is centred on the belief that including designers with disabilities and encouraging a change in mindset that considers all aspects of human diversity improves the product or service for everyone. As stated in Microsoft's inclusive design toolkit, 'Everyone has abilities, and limits to those abilities. Designing for people with permanent disabilities actually results in designs that benefit people universally.'[38] Inclusive design demonstrates how, since we all have different abilities and needs, designing to accommodate people with disabilities means we can be sure we are making the learning experience inclusive and more effective for everyone.

Accessibility and usability

We learnt from the W3C definition in Chapter 2 that digital accessibility means that disabled people can 'equally perceive, understand, navigate, and interact with websites and tools'. W3C also provides a useful definition of usability. This states that 'usability is about designing products to be effective, efficient, and satisfying'.[39] It is important to be aware that in order to create successful learning content we need to design for the 'sweet spot' between accessibility and usability. Because if we limit our focus to one or the other, this can negatively impact the learning experience. Stripping out all the interactivity from our learning content because we believe that it can't be keyboard accessible, for example, damages the learner experience for the sake of accessibility. Creating a custom navigation which is beautifully designed and easy to use but which means that keyboard users have to repeatedly tab through all the headings before they can reach the main content on each page is an example of usability at the expense of accessibility. Ideally, accessibility and usability work together to make experiences that not only are compliant with standards but are truly usable and open to all.

The WCAG has many requirements which show this overlap between accessibility and usability in action. The following are some examples from WCAG 2.1 levels A and AA, but there are also more at level AAA:

1   Good colour contrast for text and interactive items.
2   Consistent navigation.
3   Captions and transcripts for audio and video content.
4   Learner ability to control audio.
5   Link text which clearly explains where learners will be taken.
6   Clear instructions and labels for input items.
7   Support to help identify and correct errors.
8   Control over time limits and moving content.

9 Consistent labelling for interactive items such as buttons.

10 Clear titles and headings to structure and signpost content.

Content author development

One final argument in the case for accessible learning content is that learning about accessibility and how to apply it makes better content authors. One of my favourite learning quotes comes from writer Alvin Toffler who said, 'The illiterate of the 21st century will not be those who cannot read and write, but those who cannot learn, unlearn, and relearn.'[40] I believe that designing for accessibility is the best possible way for content authors to unlearn and relearn everything they know about creating and developing learning content. One aspect of my job involves evaluating and auditing learning resources. This means that I've seen a wide range of examples, both good and bad. In my experience, learning content which is accessible is consistently better. I believe this is because designing accessibly encourages content authors to be more empathetic and considerate to all their learners' needs.

Industry perspectives

To finish this overview of the case for digital accessibility we focus on perspectives from industry-leading authoring tool and content providers. They provide fascinating insights into the opportunities that digital accessibility provides for driving business performance and improving the learning experience for everyone.

Perspective one – CourseArc

Since day one, accessibility has been a priority for us. Prior to starting CourseArc, we were frustrated with how hard it was to make accessible content. We found that it required a team of web developers and accessibility experts to get it right. CourseArc was developed to empower content creators to design accessible content on their own. The CourseArc platform prompts content creators to write alt attributes for images and transcripts for audio and videos. CourseArc also automatically generates alternate activities for interactive content that could be challenging to navigate on a keyboard and/or with a screen reader. When we develop new features, accessibility review and planning is built into our development process to ensure all new product features are compliant.

Accessibility is part of the fabric of CourseArc. We put it front and centre in our mission statement: 'CourseArc is a digital content authoring and management tool that enables easy creation of engaging, interactive, and accessible online courses.' Our goal is to empower content creators to craft a very engaging learning experience for all students. Our solution provides real benefits for all learners, regardless of disability. For example, we often get feedback from instructors that learners love our graphing content because they can toggle into both views (graph and table) and they use the transcripts to ensure they understand the meaning of videos. This reinforces our commitment to providing content that meets the needs of all learners.

We have been creating online content for many years, and by the time we started CourseArc, we knew how important it was from both a legal and ethical perspective to get accessibility right. Most organizations expect it, and we believe the web should be accessible to everyone in order to provide equal access and opportunity to people with disabilities. Our commitment to accessibility differentiates CourseArc from our competitors and aligns us with customers who assign a high value to accessible learning. Instead of products that are created as a band aid for broken content, CourseArc puts accessibility at the centre of our solution. Our customers are therefore able to create cohesive learning experiences that feel intentional to all learners instead of having accessibility be an afterthought in the process. As a result, many of our customers are exemplars in the online learning space. We are humbled and amazed by the quality content they produce for their learners using CourseArc. By aligning with our customers in this way, we create a dynamic that facilitates innovation and development in accordance with the larger mission.

Perspective two – dominKnow, Inc.

Accessibility has been at the heart of what we do at dominKnow since we released our first authoring software in 2001. Our commitment to inclusive design was initially driven by some of our earliest clients who required their content to be Section 508 compliant. Since then, we have developed our product with the goal of alignment with the latest technological and legal developments in accessibility. Not only is our current tool dominKnow | ONE an industry leader for accessibility, it is also unique in its commitment to ensuring that designing inclusive content is central to the content development workflow. We believe that accessibility shouldn't be onerous, or an afterthought, but instead an integral part to everything that content authors do when they use our software. Our mission at dominKnow is to 'provide authoring software for content development that empowers instructional designers, developers, and teams to create better learning experiences efficiently, together'. Accessibility is central to this mission because we believe inclusive content provides a better learning experience for everyone. We are passionate about the positive impact that learning can have on people in general, but we also recognize how vital it is to the strategic success of businesses and organizations. As a result, it makes sense to create learning experiences, from the start, which enable access regardless of any disabilities or impairments.

At dominKnow, we believe that accessibility is simply the 'right thing to do'. But we also recognize that it has a significant impact on our sales strategy, which in turn has enabled us to extend our market reach. Our early commitment and continual development to ensure that we are compliant to the latest accessibility requirements provide a tangible advantage when it comes to selling our authoring software and services. While the impact was initially mainly in government or public sector customers, it has now grown in demand across our entire client base. The ability to design inclusive content is no longer regarded as a 'nice to have' for authoring software but is now seen as a core requirement for many organizations. It seems that although inclusive design may have been overlooked in the past, it is now so fundamental to the diversity and inclusion agenda of many organizations that providing learning content which is not accessible to all learners is no longer an option moving forward.

Improving our brand reputation and the sales potential with new customers are some key results of our commitment to accessibility, but it also has an impact on existing clients. They are looking to meet the same objectives as our new prospects, but more immediately all organizations are also beginning to see greater impacts in terms of litigation. This is particularly true in the US where the adherence to existing laws has seen a significant growth in enforcement, thus resulting in more organizations seeking to implement this inclusive approach across all aspects of their organization. Our reputation, and customer relations, specifically those with training departments, have undoubtedly been enhanced when they realize that dominKnow I ONE enables them to easily create compliant accessible learning that meets the needs of all their clientele and any legal obligations they may have.

Perspective three – Elucidat

There has been a drive to make Elucidat learning accessible for several years, but we have really doubled down on this goal in the last 12 months. This has included working with a range of customers to understand the accessibility challenges they have, and making adjustments to our interactions and colour palette to ensure they can deliver fully accessible learning to their employees. We have also developed an internal mission statement and working practices to ensure design, delivery and testing are all underpinned by an accessibility-first approach. The Elucidat values are 'Learn, Care, Share'. Everyone who works on the Elucidat team lives and breathes these values every day. We are passionate about people-centred learning and being able to reach all employees in a workforce to enable them to perform their roles effectively. These beliefs mean we are 100% committed to our mission to enable learning which is accessible to the widest possible audience. A key motivator is a desire to do the right thing for learners.

This is also an incredibly important subject for our customers, many of whom are highly motivated to provide accessible digital learning to the full range of their employees. We work closely with customers to ensure they can successfully achieve their goals using the Elucidat platform and ensuring accessibility is an integral part of this. There is an increasing desire across our existing customer base to be able to provide digital learning in line with the Web Content Accessibility Guidelines. In many cases this is a legal obligation. By ensuring that our learning complies with WCAG we can expand the usage of Elucidat within the organizations we work with and embed our platform more deeply into their processes.

One of the first questions our sales team are asked by prospective customers is about accessibility, as organizations are searching for a tool which will enable them to deliver accessible digital training. So not only does a commitment to accessibility align with our values, it has a tangible impact on revenue in terms of the growth of existing customers and the acquisition of new ones. It also makes the team here feel good about the work they are producing and the impact we are having on learners in the organizations we work with.

Perspective four – Kineo

As a City & Guilds Group business we're part of a global organization, leading the way in skills development, technology and credentialing. Each part of the group has its own focus, but we're united by our purpose of helping people, organizations and economies develop their skills for growth. We aspire to make a difference and our people are motivated by a shared purpose and ambition to provide the best in skills development. Our core values of 'leadership, imagination and integrity' shape how we work and what we deliver. Diversity and inclusion are integral to those values and designing content which is accessible for all is an important aspect. To us, accessibility means ensuring that everyone can use our products – it's that simple. We also believe that it's about everyone, not just people with disabilities. Thinking about the widest use case when we design and develop eLearning helps us to ensure that everyone can access and learn the content we produce. At the core of our commitment to accessibility is our belief in human-centred design. This means that we go beyond just adhering to technical standards and focus on providing the best possible learning experience. Alongside WCAG standards, we recognize the importance of checking our eLearning from the learner's perspective to ensure it's simple, easy to understand and caters for all learning abilities.

A key way that we support accessibility at Kineo is through the Adapt authoring tool. We were one of the original creators of the tool and continue to play an integral part in its development. One of the key strengths of Adapt is that it is open source. As a result, it benefits from having a community of developers who are committed to maintaining and improving its accessibility. We support this community and continuously update the tool so that it remains at the forefront of rapid technological advances in the field. This not only ensures that Adapt remains a market leader in accessible authoring tools, but also that it is sustainable for the future.

At Kineo we see accessibility not just as an ethical responsibility but also as a key strategic tool for driving business and market share. While it has always been a priority for many of our biggest clients, we are now seeing a shift in attitudes to inclusive design across the industry. Whereas in the past accessibility was regarded by many as an additional benefit, it is now increasingly seen as a core requirement of the products and services that we offer. There is a noticeable increase in awareness in accessibility in procurement procedures, with many potential customers now actively seeking out information about our accessibility credentials. Kineo's longstanding commitment to inclusive design undoubtedly gives us a competitive advantage in the current market. We believe that it will continue to do so as the demand for accessible learning products and services grows in the future.

Summary

- One of the strongest arguments for digital accessibility is that it is a human right. This means that it is unethical and inequitable to deprive people of their right to access content and to learn.

- Digital accessibility laws vary internationally, although the WCAG are increasingly considered the definitive technical guidelines to meet in order to be legally compliant.

- There are many business benefits to be gained from creating accessible products and content. These include increased revenue and market reach, and brand and innovation enhancement.

- The benefits of accessibility for learning content are illustrated by inclusive models such as Universal Design for Learning and Inclusive Design.

- Designing for both accessibility and usability leads to better learning experiences for everyone.

- Current industry perspectives acknowledge the importance of accessibility and the positive impact that it has on learners and businesses both now and in the future.

Endnotes

[1] United Nations, Convention on the Rights of Persons with Disabilities (CRPD), https://www.un.org/development/desa/disabilities/convention-on-the-rights-of-persons-with-disabilities.html (archived at https://perma.cc/NUX2-VMHL)

[2] Schweitzer, E J (Updated 2015) Digital divide, 23 November, https://www.britannica.com/topic/digital-divide (archived at https://perma.cc/7FB2-9SHV)

[3] Holmes, H and Burgess, G (2020) 'Pay the wi-fi or feed the children': Coronavirus has intensified the UK's digital divide, https://www.cam.ac.uk/stories/digitaldivide (archived at https://perma.cc/YXR4-2X8K)

[4] Cahill, J (2020) Introduction to digital accessibility, AbilityNet training (online video), https://abilitynet.org.uk/training/introduction-digital-accessibility-recording-1194 (archived at https://perma.cc/FH2K-UJWJ)

[5] Mueller, M, Jolly, R and Eggert, E (Updated 2018) Web accessibility laws & policies, 21 March, https://www.w3.org/WAI/policies/ (archived at https://perma.cc/C2AF-YGWQ)

[6] IAAP (2020) Body of knowledge for the certified professional in accessibility core competencies, https://www.accessibilityassociation.org/files/IAAP_CPACC_BOK_March2020.pdf (archived at https://perma.cc/LWQ4-XBWC)

7   Legislation.gov.uk, Equality Act 2010, https://www.legislation.gov.uk/ukpga/2010/15/contents (archived at https://perma.cc/7VBV-5279)

8   Legislation.gov.uk, Disability Discrimination Act 1995, https://www.legislation.gov.uk/ukpga/1995/50/contents (archived at https://perma.cc/FK7X-3ANY)

9   Equality and Human Rights Commission (Updated 2019) An introduction to the Equality Act, 19 June, https://www.equalityhumanrights.com/en/equality-act-2010/what-equality-act (archived at https://perma.cc/6LNV-V4ZU)

10   Equality and Human Rights Commission (Updated 2019) Using a service: Reasonable adjustments for disabled people, 2 December, https://www.equalityhumanrights.com/en/multipage-guide/using-service-reasonable-adjustments-disabled-people (archived at https://perma.cc/TEG5-XBGG)

11   May Young, N (2012) RNIB launches legal action over accessibility of bmibaby website, 30 January, https://www.civilsociety.co.uk/news/rnib-launches-legal-action-over-accessibility-of-bmibaby-website.html (archived at https://perma.cc/B944-4T4Z)

12   Christopherson, R (2019) How to give legal teeth to digital accessibility – New York vs Norway, 10 January, https://www.abilitynet.org.uk/news-blogs/how-give-legal-teeth-digital-accessibility-new-york-vs-norway (archived at https://perma.cc/7AGK-LG67)

13   Mueller, M, Jolly, R and Eggert, E (Updated 2018) Web accessibility laws & policies, 21 March, https://www.w3.org/WAI/policies/ (archived at https://perma.cc/C2AF-YGWQ)

14   Legislation.gov.uk, The Public Sector Bodies (Websites and Mobile Applications) (No. 2) Accessibility Regulations 2018, 23 September 2018, https://www.legislation.gov.uk/uksi/2018/952/made (archived at https://perma.cc/92BL-HDCR)

15   EUR-Lex, Directive (EU) 2016/2102 of the European Parliament and of the Council of 26 October 2016 on the accessibility of the websites and mobile applications of public sector bodies, https://eur-lex.europa.eu/legal-content/EN/TXT/?uri=CELEX%3A32016L2102 (archived at https://perma.cc/Y37D-FCN6)

16   GOV.UK (Updated 2020) Understanding accessibility requirements for public sector bodies, 23 September, https://www.gov.uk/guidance/accessibility-requirements-for-public-sector-websites-and-apps (archived at https://perma.cc/8DYG-3M2Q)

17   GOV.UK (2020) Public sector website and mobile application accessibility monitoring, 20 August, https://www.gov.uk/guidance/public-sector-website-and-mobile-application-accessibility-monitoring (archived at https://perma.cc/5SUW-4B5N)

18   ETSI, Accessibility requirements for ICT products and services, https://www.etsi.org/deliver/etsi_en/301500_301599/301549/02.01.02_60/en_301549v020102p.pdf (archived at https://perma.cc/DGC8-QYQB)

19 Legislation.gov.uk (2018) Accessibility statement, 23 September, https://www.legislation.gov.uk/uksi/2018/952/regulation/8/made (archived at https://perma.cc/R2S5-B4EC)

20 Reciteme, ADA Web Accessibility Law, https://reciteme.com/about-us/accessibility-legislation/ada-web-accessibility-law (archived at https://perma.cc/5ZJA-SC6F)

21 ADA.gov, Public Accommodations and Commercial Facilities (Title III), https://www.ada.gov/ada_title_III.htm (archived at https://perma.cc/9VY2-DEF2)

22 Launey, K and Vu, M (2020) The curve has flattened for federal website accessibility lawsuits, 29 April, https://www.adatitleiii.com/2020/04/the-curve-has-flattened-for-federal-website-accessibility-lawsuits/ (archived at https://perma.cc/WMX4-ESD3)

23 Taylor, J (2018) The 2018 web accessibility lawsuit recap report, 26 December, https://blog.usablenet.com/2018-ada-web-accessibility-lawsuit-recap-report (archived at https://perma.cc/77Q5-F83M)

24 Section 508.gov (Updated 2020) IT Accessibility Laws and Policies Section 508 of the Rehabilitation Act of 1973, https://www.section508.gov/manage/laws-and-policies (archived at https://perma.cc/7HQL-8LVB)

25 Taylor, J (2020) App and web accessibility lawsuits – what's new in 2020, 7 July, https://blog.usablenet.com/web-accessibility-lawsuits-whats-new-in-2020 (archived at https://perma.cc/A6EK-8CZ5)

26 Enamorado, S (2019) Quick guide to Section 508 & 504 accessibility lawsuits, 2 July, https://www.3playmedia.com/2019/02/22/quick-guide-section-508-504-lawsuits/ (archived at https://perma.cc/8LNM-AEKA)

27 Centre for Inclusive Design (2019) The benefit of designing for everyone – a research report on the importance of inclusive design, https://g3ict.org/publication/the-benefit-of-designing-for-everyone-a-research-report-on-the-importance-of-inclusive-design (archived at https://perma.cc/W3YC-FT5K)

28 Botterill, S (2019) Businesses are missing out on the purple pound, says Scope, 20 November, https://abilitynet.org.uk/news-blogs/businesses-are-missing-out-purple-pound-says-scope (archived at https://perma.cc/2ZY5-5C8A)

29 Yin, M, Shaewiz, D, Overton, C and Smith, D (2018) A hidden market: The purchasing power of working-age adults with disabilities, https://www.air.org/system/files/downloads/report/Hidden-Market-Spending-Power-of-People-with-Disabilities-April-2018.pdf (archived at https://perma.cc/W7K2-YP5X)

30 Return on Disability (2016) 2016 annual report – the global economics of disability, https://www.academia.edu/38995163/RETURN_ON_DISABILITY_Translate_Different_Into_Value_2016_Annual_Report_The_Global_Economics_of_Disability (archived at https://perma.cc/CB5G-FU26)

31 Forrester (2016) Assessing the value of accessible technologies for organizations, A total economic impact study, https://blogs.microsoft.com/uploads/prod/

sites/73/2018/10/5bc08e8059d68-5bc08e8059d6bMicrosoft-TEI-Accessibility-Study_Edited_FINAL-v2.pdf.pdf (archived at https://perma.cc/U5RG-92JC)

32 Management Today (2017) A mission to become the most accessible FTSE 100 company, 17 July, https://www.managementtoday.co.uk/mission-become-accessible-ftse-100-company/reputation-matters/article/1437662 (archived at https://perma.cc/6RWT-596T)

33 The Valuable 500 (2020) The leaders of the inclusion revolution summary report, https://www.thevaluable500.com/wp-content/uploads/2020/01/The-Leaders-of-The-Inclusion-Revolution-2019-Summary-Report.pdf (archived at https://perma.cc/Q6L2-RQT6)

34 Rush, S (2018) The business case for digital accessibility, 9 November, https://www.w3.org/WAI/business-case/ (archived at https://perma.cc/6TQT-LAJE)

35 Hassell, J (2019) *Inclusive Design for Organisations, Including your missing 20% by embedding web and mobile accessibility*, Rethink Press, Gorleston-on-Sea

36 CAST, About Universal Design for Learning, http://www.cast.org/our-work/about-udl.html#.X183aWhKjcs (archived at https://perma.cc/G88E-RVD4)

37 Knowbly (2020) Universal Design for Learning: The intersection of flexibility and specificity, 16 April, https://www.knowbly.com/post/t-universal-design-for-learning-the-intersection-of-flexibility-and-specificity (archived at https://perma.cc/9YVC-W4JN)

38 Microsoft Inclusive Design Toolkit, https://www.microsoft.com/design/inclusive/ (archived at https://perma.cc/Y8D7-8YQL)

39 Lawton Henry, S, Abou-Zahara, S and White, K (Updated 2016) Accessibility, usability, and inclusion, https://www.w3.org/WAI/fundamentals/accessibility-usability-inclusion/ (archived at https://perma.cc/R259-9GAN)

40 Subramanian, C (2016) Alvin Toffler: What he got right – and wrong, BBC News, 1 July, https://www.bbc.co.uk/news/world-us-canada-36675260 (archived at https://perma.cc/G28Z-78GV)

Accessibility frameworks

06

The WCAG (Web Content Accessibility Guidelines) framework

Introduction

The WCAG framework is structured in the same way as the full guidelines created by the World Wide Web Consortium (W3C). This structure groups the standards into the four POUR principles which are Perceivable, Operable, Understandable and Robust. They are further broken down into subdivisions for each principle known as guidelines. The WCAG framework can be useful when developing content, but many people find it is better suited to testing for conformance or for formulating an accessibility statement. The framework has some useful additional features designed to make applying accessibility easier. The first is the inclusion of the key exceptions relevant for each standard. This can help to save you time, as not every one of the standards will apply to the content you are designing. Each of the standards in the framework also has a quick reference icon set which indicates what it applies to in an eLearning context (see Table 6.1). Another feature of the framework is the ability to cross reference full explanations in Part Three of the book. This is a useful safety net if you're not quite sure what the summary given in the framework means. It also allows you the opportunity to explore each of the WCAG standards in more detail and to reference further resources if you want to extend your knowledge or carry out additional research.

Note: The explanations given in this chapter are interpretations of WCAG standards and do not guarantee that content will be fully compliant with legal regulations. For further guidance and the full W3C wording for each

TABLE 6.1

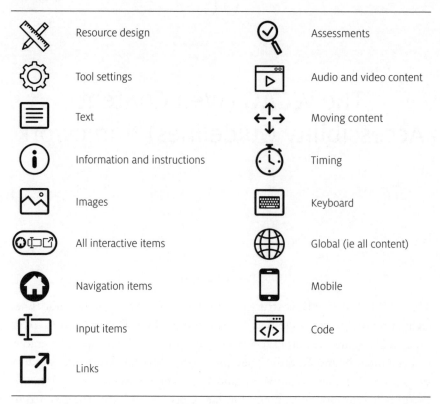

	Resource design		Assessments
	Tool settings		Audio and video content
	Text		Moving content
	Information and instructions		Timing
	Images		Keyboard
	All interactive items		Global (ie all content)
	Navigation items		Mobile
	Input items		Code
	Links		

of the standards, see: How to Meet WCAG (quick reference).[1] The wording used for the principle and guidelines headings and subheadings is from W3C and is copyright. Copyright © 2019 W3C® (MIT,[2] ERCIM,[3] Keio,[4] Beihang[5]).

Principle 1 – Perceivable

Information and user interface components must be presentable to users in ways they can perceive.

Guideline 1.1 – Text Alternatives

Provide text alternatives for any non-text content so that it can be changed into other forms people need, such as large print, braille, speech, symbols or simpler language.

1.1.1 NON-TEXT CONTENT – LEVEL A

Provide an alternative text description for visual items such as images which add meaning, or interactive items so that they can be recognized by assistive technology. Also provide alternative text which allows assistive technology such as screen readers to announce audio or video content before it begins playing. Finally, make sure that assistive technology ignores any visual items that do not add meaning such as images used only for decoration or spacing.

Exceptions:

- Images which are part of a test. You can provide a simple descriptive label instead of a full image description so that it does not give learners the answer.

- Images which create a 'sensory experience', such as a work of art. You can provide alternative text which explains what the content is rather than trying to describe it fully.

- Images which are fully described in a caption.

Guideline 1.2 – Time-based Media

Provide alternatives for time-based media.

1.2.1 AUDIO-ONLY AND VIDEO-ONLY (PRERECORDED) – LEVEL A

Provide an alternative way for learners to access the information in pre-recorded audio-only content such as podcasts, or prerecorded video-only content such as silent animations. You can do this by providing a text transcript which contains all the information learners need to understand the audio-only or video-only content. For video-only content, another option is to provide an audio description track which describes everything that happens in the video.

Exceptions:

- The audio-only content or video-only content is provided as an alternative for text and it is made clear to learners that this is the case.

- Video-only content which is used for decoration.

1.2.2 CAPTIONS (PRERECORDED) – LEVEL A

For prerecorded videos which have sound, provide synchronized captions, ie text which appears on screen at the same time as people speak. As well as providing the words that are said, captions should identify who is speaking and describe any important sound effects.

Exception:

- The video is provided as an alternative for text and it is made clear to learners that this is the case.

1.2.3 AUDIO DESCRIPTION OR MEDIA ALTERNATIVE (PRERECORDED) – LEVEL A

For prerecorded videos which have sound, provide either audio description or a text transcript (media alternative). These should give all the information non-visual learners need to understand the video. This could include the action taking place, the expressions of characters, scene changes, etc. Transcripts should also provide all the words which are said in the video and identify who is speaking.

Exceptions:

- The video is provided as an alternative for text and it is made clear to learners that this is the case.
- Videos which have all the information conveyed in spoken word, eg a 'talking head' video.
- Videos of presentations, as long as the presenter explains all the visual information contained in the slides, eg images, charts or tables.

1.2.4 CAPTIONS (LIVE) – LEVEL AA

For live presentations with audio content such as webinars or lectures, provide synchronized captions, ie text which appears on screen at the same time as people speak.

1.2.5 AUDIO DESCRIPTION (PRERECORDED) – LEVEL AA

Provide audio description for prerecorded videos that have sound. The audio description should give all the information non-visual learners need to understand the video. This could include the action taking place, the expressions of characters, scene changes, etc.

Exceptions:

- Videos which have all the information conveyed in spoken word, eg a 'talking head' video.

- Videos of presentations as long as the presenter explains all the visual information contained in the slides, eg images, charts or tables.

Guideline 1.3 – Adaptable

Create content that can be presented in different ways (for example, simpler layout) without losing information or structure.

1.3.1 INFO AND RELATIONSHIPS – LEVEL A

Make sure that assistive technology can interpret structures such as headings, lists, tables, input fields and page regions. This is normally done through the underlying code of the tool. If this isn't possible, use text to give the same information.

1.3.2 MEANINGFUL SEQUENCE – LEVEL A

Make sure that all content which adds meaning in the eLearning resource is structured in a logical linear order so that it makes sense and is easy to navigate for assistive technology users.

1.3.3 SENSORY CHARACTERISTICS – LEVEL A

Make sure that instructions and information do not rely only on visual cues such as shape, colour, size or location. Also make sure that instructions and information do not rely only on auditory cues, such as sounds, to tell learners if they have made a mistake.

1.3.4 ORIENTATION – LEVEL AA
Added in 2.1

Make sure that learners can choose either portrait or landscape view, ie either vertical or horizontal view, for the eLearning resource.

Exception:

- A particular orientation for the eLearning resource is essential, eg a simulation that uses virtual reality.

1.3.5 IDENTIFY INPUT PURPOSE – LEVEL AA
Added in 2.1

Make sure that any input fields which collect personal data are correctly coded so that assistive technology users can understand the purpose of those fields.

Guideline 1.4 – Distinguishable

Make it easier for users to see and hear content, including separating fore-ground from background.

1.4.1 USE OF COLOUR – LEVEL A

Make sure you use devices such as icons, patterns, formatting or text to supplement colour in the eLearning resource. You need to do this when you are giving learners information or explaining what action they need to take.

It's also important when you are asking learners for a response to a question or when they need to see a visual element clearly such as the lines in a graph.

1.4.2 AUDIO CONTROL – LEVEL A

For any audio content in the eLearning resource which starts automatically and lasts longer than three seconds, make sure that learners can pause or stop the audio. Another option is to allow them to adjust the volume, but this must be with a control which does not affect the overall volume of the rest of the audio content in the eLearning resource.

1.4.3 CONTRAST (MINIMUM) – LEVEL AA

For any text and the background it appears on, choose colours that have a contrast ratio of at least 4.5:1. This applies to 'normal' size text which W3C defines as 17 point or smaller for regular text and 13 point or smaller for bold text. 'Large' text, ie 18 point or larger for regular text and 14 point or larger for bold text, has a contrast ratio requirement of at least 3:1.

Exceptions:

- Text or images of text which are incidental. This includes text in deactivated interactive items such as disabled buttons, text which is deliberately not visible, text in decorative images and text in images which is not important to convey meaning.
- Text which is included in a logo or a brand name.

1.4.4 RESIZE TEXT – LEVEL AA

Make sure that visual learners can enlarge the text up to 200% and still carry out all the functions on a page and see all its content. They should be able to do this with standard functionality, such as using a browser to zoom in, as well as with assistive technology.

Exceptions:

- Captions, since they are often created to a fixed size.

- Text within images since it does not scale very well and often pixelates and becomes difficult to read.

1.4.5 IMAGES OF TEXT – LEVEL AA

Use onscreen text rather than images of text to convey information as long as the authoring tool allows you to achieve the visual presentation you need. This standard applies unless learners can customize the text in the image or the visual presentation of the text is essential such as an image of a logo.

Exception:

- The image is used only for decoration and understanding any text in the image is not important to the meaning of the content.

1.4.10 REFLOW – LEVEL AA
Added in 2.1

Make sure that when eLearning resources are enlarged to 400% using browser zoom, the content reflows so that horizontal scrolling is not needed. Visual learners should still be able to carry out all the functions of the page and see all its content without having to use a horizontal scroll bar.

Exception:

- Any content such as complex images and data tables which would not make sense if it was reflowed.

1.4.11 NON-TEXT CONTRAST LEVEL – AA
Added in 2.1

For interactive items choose colours which have a contrast ratio of at least 3:1 against the colour of the background they appear on, or items they appear next to. This also applies to important visual elements essential to understanding such as the lines in a graph.

Exceptions:

- Interactive items which are inactive such as a disabled 'Back' button, or if the user agent such as the web browser determines the appearance of the interactive item.

- Visual elements if a particular presentation is essential to the information being conveyed, eg a medical diagram which uses specific biological colours, a heatmap or a screenshot of a website.

1.4.12 TEXT SPACING – LEVEL AA
Added in 2.1

If the authoring tool uses a markup language such as HTML, make sure that visual learners can change the spacing between text, and that they can still see all the content and carry out all the functions of a page. This applies to spacing between lines of text, paragraphs, words and letters.

Exceptions:

- Captions which are embedded in the video frame instead of being provided as a separate caption file.

- Text in images.

1.4.13 CONTENT ON HOVER OR FOCUS – LEVEL AA
Added in 2.1

Make sure content such as tooltips or sub-menus which appear or 'pop up' when learners hover over or move keyboard focus to interactive items can be dismissed. Also make sure that if learners need to interact with pop-up content, it doesn't disappear until they have finished interacting with it. Finally, if the content appears only on hover, make sure that learners can move the cursor away from the item that triggered the pop-up content to the content itself.

Principle 2 – Operable

User interface components and navigation must be operable.

Guideline 2.1 – Keyboard Accessible

Make all functionality available from a keyboard.

2.1.1 KEYBOARD – LEVEL A

Make sure that all functionality in the eLearning resource is usable with a keyboard or keyboard interface. This includes all interactive items and audio and video player controls. Also make sure that 'keystrokes', ie pressing the keys, do not have any time constraints.

Exception:

- Functionality which depends on the path of the user's movements, eg a handwriting tool or a freehand painting or drawing program.

2.1.2 NO KEYBOARD TRAP – LEVEL A

Make sure that learners who navigate using a keyboard or keyboard interface can move away from all content that receives focus in the eLearning resource. Also make sure that this can be achieved using standard keyboard keys such as the 'Tab' or 'Arrow' keys, or that learners are made aware if they need to use non-standard keys.

2.1.4 CHARACTER KEY SHORTCUTS – LEVEL A
Added in 2.1

Avoid assigning keyboard shortcuts which use only a single letter, punctuation, number or symbol character key. If they do, make sure that the shortcut can be modified by adding another key, can be turned off, or for interactive items is active only when it receives focus.

Guideline 2.2 – Enough Time

Give users enough time to read and use content.

2.2.1 TIMING ADJUSTABLE – LEVEL A

   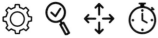

Do not set time limits for any activities in the eLearning resource unless learners can turn them off, adjust or extend them. This applies to the length of time learners have to complete quiz questions, the amount of time content remains on the page, etc. Also make sure that learners have control over any content which moves, scrolls or updates automatically as this also effectively imposes a time limit.

Exceptions:

- Activities where the timing is essential, eg the steps in a simulation of a real activity which need to be completed in a fixed amount of time.

- Real-time events such as an online auction (eg eBay) where extending a time limit would disadvantage participants, or a live online broadcast of the audio or video feed from a meeting or event.

2.2.2 PAUSE, STOP, HIDE – LEVEL A

Make sure learners can pause, stop or hide any content that starts automatically, moves, scrolls or blinks for longer than five seconds and appears alongside other content. The same must also be true for content that automatically updates and appears alongside other content.

Exceptions:

- Animations such as a progress bar which needs to move in order to show that it hasn't frozen or broken.

- Standalone content which is not presented alongside other content, eg an animation which appears alone on a page while a video is being downloaded.

- Moving, scrolling, blinking or automatically updating content which is essential, eg automatically updating financial information on a stocks and shares website.

Guideline 2.3 – Seizures and Physical Reactions

Do not design content in a way that is known to cause seizures or physical reactions.

2.3.1 THREE FLASHES OR BELOW THRESHOLD – LEVEL A

In order to prevent seizures do not include any content which flashes more than three times per second unless the flashes are small enough or dim enough to fall below the required thresholds. If the flashes contain very little of the colour red, they may also fall below the required threshold.

Guideline 2.4 – Navigable

Provide ways to help users navigate, find content and determine where they are.

2.4.1 BYPASS BLOCKS – LEVEL A

Make sure learners who navigate using a keyboard or keyboard interface can skip blocks of content repeated over multiple pages and move directly to the main content of a page. In eLearning resources this most often applies to navigation items such as menus which are repeated on multiple pages.

Exception:

- Small, repeated sections of content such as individual words, phrases or single links.

2.4.2 PAGE TITLED – LEVEL A

Give each page in the eLearning resource a descriptive title which explains the topic or purpose of the page.

2.4.3 FOCUS ORDER – LEVEL A

Make sure that when learners navigate using a keyboard or keyboard interface, they move through interactive items in a logical linear order.

Exception:

- Interactive items which do not need a logical sequence to be understood, eg a random series of links in a word cloud.

2.4.4 LINK PURPOSE (IN CONTEXT) – LEVEL A

Make sure that learners know where they will be taken when they select a link. You can do this either by using information in the link text itself or by adding information in the text surrounding the link. Underlying code should also be used so that assistive technology users know where links will take them.

Exception:

- Ambiguous links if they are deliberate, eg to create the element of surprise in a game.

2.4.5 MULTIPLE WAYS – LEVEL AA

Give learners more than one way to navigate content in eLearning resources. For example, provide a 'Home' icon, a menu and a search facility.

Exception:

- Content which is part of a process and which needs to be followed in sequence, eg content which is step locked due to a required learner journey.

2.4.6 HEADINGS AND LABELS – LEVEL AA

Make sure that any page headings describe the topic or purpose of the page and section headings explain the topic or purpose of the text that follows.

Also make sure that the labels provided for interactive items make it clear what the purpose of the item is.

2.4.7 FOCUS VISIBLE – LEVEL AA

Make sure that when learners navigate using a keyboard or keyboard interface there is a visible focus indicator for interactive items. This means there is a visible sign to show that these items have been selected. This could be with a change in the appearance of a button or a coloured border around a link, etc.

Guideline 2.5 – Input Modalities

Make it easier for users to operate functionality through various inputs beyond the keyboard.

2.5.1 POINTER GESTURES – LEVEL A
Added in 2.1

For any interactions which need learners to carry out complex gestures, provide an alternative simple gesture which needs only a single point of contact. Complex gestures include 'multipoint' gestures which need two fingers, such as a two-finger pinch to zoom, and 'path-based' gestures where the path that the finger takes is important, such as a touch and drag interaction to pan.

2.5.2 POINTER CANCELLATION – LEVEL A
Added in 2.1

Stop learners accidentally activating interactive items by triggering functionality on the up-event rather than the down-event unless they can undo or reverse the action. The up-event is when learners release their finger, the pointer or the mouse click. The down-event is when they press their finger, the pointer or the mouse click down.

Exception:

- Any functionality in which the down-event is an essential interaction such as selecting the letters on an onscreen keyboard.

2.5.3 LABEL IN NAME – LEVEL A
Added in 2.1

Make sure that interactive items which have a visible label such as the text on buttons also have the same accessible name which can be recognized by assistive technology.

2.5.4 MOTION ACTUATION – LEVEL A
Added in 2.1

Make sure that learners can disable functionality which is triggered by movement such as shaking or tilting a device to undo an action. Also make sure that the same functionality can be activated using standard controls such as a button or a link.

Principle 3 – Understandable

Information and the operation of the user interface must be understandable.

Guideline 3.1 – Readable

Make text content readable and understandable.

3.1.1 LANGUAGE OF PAGE – LEVEL A

Identify the main text language used in the eLearning resource so that assistive technology can correctly pronounce and display the language.

3.1.2 LANGUAGE OF PARTS – LEVEL AA

Identify the language of text used in individual passages or phrases if this is different from the main text language used in the eLearning resource.

Exceptions:

- Proper nouns.
- Technical terms in another language.
- Words in another language which are commonly used and understood in the default language.
- Words in an unknown language.

Guideline 3.2 – Predictable

Make web pages appear and operate in predictable ways.

3.2.1 ON FOCUS – LEVEL A

When learners move the focus to interactive items, make sure this does not cause anything unexpected to happen such as a new window opening without warning.

3.2.2 ON INPUT – LEVEL A

Make sure when learners interact with input items such as entering data into a data entry field or selecting a radio button, this doesn't cause anything unexpected to happen unless learners are warned what to expect before it happens.

3.2.3 CONSISTENT NAVIGATION – LEVEL AA

Make sure that navigation items such as 'Home' icons or links to other pages which are repeated throughout the eLearning resource appear in the same order in the layout.

Exception:

- Navigation controls which can be moved by learners, eg using assistive technology or setting preferences.

3.2.4 CONSISTENT IDENTIFICATION – LEVEL AA

Make sure that if interactive items with the same function have a visible label, eg the text or icon on a button, the visible label remains the same throughout the eLearning resource. Also make sure that the accessible name for interactive items with the same function remains consistent.

Guideline 3.3 – Input Assistance

Help users avoid and correct mistakes.

3.3.1 ERROR IDENTIFICATION – LEVEL A

If learners make a mistake when they interact with input items such as radio buttons or data entry fields, make sure it is clear which input item the error applies to. Also make sure that the error is described to learners using text.

3.3.2 LABELS OR INSTRUCTIONS – LEVEL A

When learners interact with input items such as radio buttons or data entry fields, make sure they are given instructions or labels which explain what they need to do. Also make sure that they are given information about how any data they need to enter should be formatted and whether it is mandatory.

3.3.3 ERROR SUGGESTION – LEVEL AA

Give learners suggestions to help them correct any mistakes they make when they interact with input items such as radio buttons or data entry fields.

Exception:

- Suggestions which could invalidate the purpose of the interaction, eg by giving away the correct answer to a quiz question in a mandatory compliance training assessment.

3.3.4 ERROR PREVENTION (LEGAL, FINANCIAL, DATA) – LEVEL AA

When learners input any information using input items such as data entry fields or check boxes, make sure they can reverse, check and correct or confirm their data before they submit it. This applies if the interaction has legal or financial implications. It also applies if the interaction changes or deletes information held in data storage systems and if the interaction submits test responses.

Principle 4 – Robust

Content must be robust enough that it can be interpreted by a wide variety of user agents, including assistive technologies.

Guideline 4.1 – Compatible

Maximize compatibility with current and future user agents, including assistive technologies.

4.1.1 PARSING – LEVEL A

If the authoring tool uses a markup language such as HTML, make sure that the code doesn't cause any issues for assistive technology. This can happen if there are errors in the code such as when elements are missing complete start and end tags.

4.1.2 NAME, ROLE, VALUE – LEVEL A

Make sure that all interactive items have an accessible name and role and that the state of items, eg whether they are expanded or collapsed, is communicated to assistive technology.

4.1.3 STATUS MESSAGES – LEVEL AA

Added in 2.1

If the authoring tool uses a markup language such as HTML, make sure that assistive technology can recognize and announce status messages. This applies to status messages which appear on a page but do not receive keyboard focus.

Endnotes

1   W3C Web Accessibility Initiative (2019) How to Meet WCAG (quick reference), 4 October, https://www.w3.org/WAI/WCAG21/quickref/ (archived at https://perma.cc/LWF9-R5U7)

2   https://www.csail.mit.edu/ (archived at https://perma.cc/DA8Q-WP6W)

3   https://www.ercim.eu/ (archived at https://perma.cc/9XZQ-WM5P)

4   https://www.keio.ac.jp/en/ (archived at https://perma.cc/U58Q-ZQAE)

5   https://ev.buaa.edu.cn/ (archived at https://perma.cc/CCL3-NZCD)

07

The eLa (eLearning accessibility) framework

Introduction

The eLa (eLearning accessibility) framework covers all the 50 WCAG 2.1 level A and AA standards. Instead of following the W3C structure, however, the framework divides the WCAG into six steps, each of which is relevant to a particular eLearning theme or subject area. The framework is structured so that these categories are considered in a contextual order that is logical for designing and developing learning content using any authoring tool. This allows you to dip in and out to find the standards and recommendations relevant for a particular subject area. It does mean, however, that standards can be repeated several times due to their relevance to different contexts.

Just as with the WCAG framework, the eLa framework contains exceptions and allows you to cross reference full explanations in Part Three if you need further support. However, the exceptions detailed in this framework are those relevant to the context in which the standards appear. Another important feature is that in addition to the level A and AA standards, the eLearning accessibility framework contains advisory guidelines. These recommendations are taken from the advanced AAA level standards, supplementary material from W3C and other sources such as style guides from the British Dyslexia Association. They are included either because they are considered best practice or because they are particularly relevant to learning content. This makes the eLa framework a resource which helps you to improve the learner experience as well as meeting the requirements of a set of strict technical guidelines. Since they are recommendations, any

FIGURE 7.1   The eLa (eLearning accessibility) framework

Step 6
Mobile and code

Step 1
Resource design and
tool settings

Step 5
Keyboard and
global content

eLa
eLearning
accessibility
framework

Design   Develop   Test   Update

Step 2
Text, information and
instructions and images

Step 4
Audio & video content,
moving content and timing

Step 3
Interactive items
and assessments

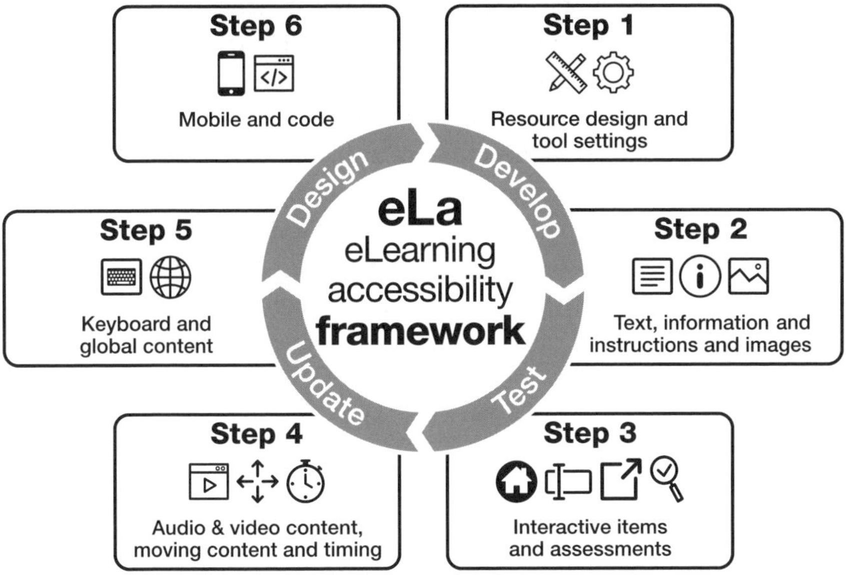

The six steps of the eLearning accessibility framework which are important when designing, developing, testing and updating accessible learning content.

exceptions for AAA standards are not included in the framework. They can be found by cross referencing Chapter 12 WCAG 2.1 level AAA accessibility standards.

Although the eLa framework is by necessity structured in this book in a linear order, it is important to be aware that the principles are just as relevant when you test or make any ongoing updates to your content. This is why the framework is represented as a cyclical process in Figure 7.1.

The first step of the eLa framework contains standards you need to consider when designing and setting up your eLearning project. The next step includes standards concerned with text, any information or instructions you give to learners, and images. The third step contains interactive icons. These are subdivided into navigation items, input items and links. This step also contains standards which are important to consider when you are creating any assessments for your learners. The fourth step focuses on standards around multimedia content such as audio and visual resources and also includes considerations which apply to moving content and timing constraints. Standards which are crucial for people who use keyboards or keyboard interfaces, including screen reader users, are part of the fifth step. Also included in this step are standards which are relevant for all items in the eLearning resource. The final step includes standards which are particularly relevant if content is mobile compatible as well as standards which must be achieved using the underlying source code of the eLearning resource. These include any standards which need to be 'programmatically determined' or require the use of markup languages such as HTML.

As there are so many authoring tools available and they all work differently, this order is only a suggested way of applying the standards. You may find that it makes more sense to the way that you design, or to the way that your tool allows you to develop content, to tackle the WCAG standards in a different order. This is where the contextual groupings prove useful as you can address each step or category within the framework whenever it works best for you.

Note: The explanations given in this chapter are interpretations of WCAG standards and do not guarantee that content will be fully compliant with legal regulations. For further guidance and the full W3C wording for each of the standards, see: How to Meet WCAG (quick reference).[1] Any W3C wording used is copyright. Copyright © 2019 W3C® (MIT, ERCIM, Keio, Beihang).

Step 1 – Resource design and tool settings

Standards to consider when designing and setting up the eLearning resource.

eLa 1.1 Resource design

Standards to consider when setting up master pages, templates and design themes etc.

Note: If your tool allows you to set up custom navigation, all standards in **eLa 3.2 Navigation items** also apply.

TOPIC 1 – STRUCTURE AND NAVIGATION

eLa 1.1.1 Page titles

When designing the structure of the eLearning resource, give each page a descriptive title which explains the topic or purpose of the page.

(WCAG 2.4.2 Page Titled – Level A)

eLa 1.1.2 Descriptive headings

Make sure that any page headings describe the topic or purpose of the page.

(WCAG 2.4.6 Headings and Labels – Level AA)

eLa 1.1.3 Multiple ways to navigate

Give learners more than one way to navigate content in eLearning resources. For example, provide a 'Home' icon, a menu and a search facility.

Exception:

- Content which is part of a process which needs to be followed in sequence, eg content which is step locked due to a required learner journey.

(WCAG 2.4.5 Multiple Ways – Level AA)

eLa 1.1.4 Page location (Advisory)

Make sure learners can identify where the page they are on is located in the eLearning resource. This could be done with a breadcrumb trail or with an indicator that gives the page number and the total number of pages in the section, eg 3/14.

(WCAG 2.4.8 Location – Level AAA)

eLa 1.1.5 Glossary for unusual words and abbreviations (Advisory)

If the content has unusual, difficult or technical words or abbreviations, consider explaining them in a glossary added to the eLearning resource.

(WCAG 3.1.3 Unusual Words – Level AAA and 3.1.4 Abbreviations – Level AAA)

TOPIC 2 – COLOUR AND CONTRAST

eLa 1.1.6 Accessible design theme (Advisory)

Choose an accessible design or colour theme if this is available in your authoring tool.

eLa 1.1.7 Text and background contrast

For any text and the background it appears on, choose colours that have a contrast ratio of at least 4.5:1. This applies to 'normal' size text which W3C defines as 17 point or smaller for regular text and 13 point or smaller for bold text. 'Large' text, ie 18 point or larger for regular text and 14 point or larger for bold text, has a contrast ratio requirement of at least 3:1.

Exceptions:

- Text or images of text which are incidental. This includes text in deactivated interactive items such as disabled buttons, text which is deliberately not visible, text in decorative images and text in images which is not important to convey meaning.

- Text which is part of a logo or brand name.

(WCAG 1.4.3 Contrast (Minimum) – Level AA)

eLa 1.1.8 Enhanced text and background contrast (Advisory)

For any text and the background it appears on, choose colours which have a contrast ratio of at least 7:1. This applies to 'normal' size text which W3C defines as 17 point or smaller for regular text and 13 point or smaller for bold text. For 'large' text, ie 18 point or larger for regular text and 14 point or larger for bold text, the recommended contrast ratio is at least 4.5:1.

(WCAG 1.4.6 Contrast Enhanced – Level AAA)

eLa 1.1.9 Colour contrast for interactive items

For interactive items choose colours which have a contrast ratio of at least 3:1 against the colour of the background they appear on, or items they appear next to.

Exception:

- Interactive items which are inactive such as a disabled 'Back' button.

(WCAG 1.4.11 Non-text Contrast – Level AA)

TOPIC 3 – ASSISTIVE TECHNOLOGY

eLa 1.1.10 Alternative text on master pages and templates

Provide an alternative text description for visual items such as images which add meaning, or interactive items so that they can be recognized by assistive technology. Also make sure that assistive technology ignores any visual items that do not add meaning such as images used only for decoration or spacing.

(WCAG 1.1.1 Non-text Content – Level A)

eLa 1.1.11 Logical reading order

Make sure all content which adds meaning on master pages and templates is structured in a logical linear order so that it makes sense and is easy to navigate for assistive technology users.

(WCAG 1.3.2 Meaningful Sequence – Level A)

eLa 1.1.12 Logical focus order

Make sure that when learners navigate using a keyboard or keyboard interface, they move through interactive items in a logical linear order.

(WCAG 2.4.3 Focus Order – Level A)

TOPIC 4 – FORMATTING

eLa 1.1.13 Font type (Advisory)

Opinion is divided on the best-practice choice of fonts for accessibility, but a recommendation from the British Dyslexia Association is to choose sans-serif fonts such as Arial, Calibri or Tahoma.

eLa 1.1.14 Font size (Advisory)

Font size should be minimum 12–14 point or equivalent (eg 1–1.2 em/ 16–19 px).

Note: These are the most important standards to be aware of with regard to text on master pages and templates. Further recommendations for formatting text can be found in **eLa 2.1 Text – Topic 5 – Formatting.**

eLa 1.2 Tool settings

Standards which may need you to adjust tool settings when setting up or publishing the eLearning resource.

Note: Due to the variations in authoring tools it is not possible to provide a comprehensive set of standards which are applied using tool settings for each authoring tool. This list is intended to be a suggestion of some of the things you may need to consider and a reminder to check the accessibility features of the authoring tool you are using.

eLa 1.2.1 Tool accessibility settings (Advisory)

Activate any accessibility settings available in your authoring tool. You often need to do this at the start of the project, but with some tools this can be when selecting publishing settings.

eLa 1.2.2 Open orientation

Select any settings which allow learners to choose either portrait or landscape view, ie either vertical or horizontal view, for the eLearning resource.

Exception:

- A particular orientation for the eLearning resource is essential, eg a simulation which uses virtual reality.

(WCAG 1.3.4 Orientation – Level AA)

eLa 1.2.3 Adjustable time limits

Do not set time limits for any activities in the eLearning resource unless learners can turn them off, adjust or extend them.

(WCAG 2.2.1 Timing Adjustable – Level A)

eLa 1.2.4 Language of resource

Identify the main text language used in the eLearning resource so that assistive technology can correctly pronounce and display the language.

(WCAG 3.1.1 Language of Page – Level A)

eLa 1.2.5 Enlarge text to 200%
Choose tool or publishing settings which allow visual learners to enlarge the text up to 200% with browser zoom and still carry out all the functions on a page and see all its content.

(WCAG 1.4.4 Resize text – Level AA)

Step 2 – Text, information and instructions, and images

Standards which affect text, information and instructions for learners, and images.

eLa 2.1 Text

Standards which affect any kind of text, including standard body text, page titles, headings and text in images.

TOPIC 1 – STRUCTURE

eLa 2.1.1 Page titles
Give each page in the eLearning resource a descriptive title which explains the topic or purpose of the page.

(WCAG 2.4.2 Page Titled – Level A)

eLa 2.1.2 Descriptive headings
Make sure that any page headings describe the topic or purpose of the page and section headings explain the topic or purpose of the text that follows.

(WCAG 2.4.6 Headings and Labels – Level AA)

eLa 2.1.3 Section headings (Advisory)
Use section headings and subheadings to organize and give structure to content and to help learners process information and navigate.

(WCAG 2.4.10 Section Headings – Level AAA)

eLa 2.1.4 Text and background contrast

For any text and the background it appears on, choose colours that have a contrast ratio of at least 4.5:1. This applies to 'normal' size text which W3C defines as 17 point or smaller for regular text and 13 point or smaller for bold text. 'Large' text, ie 18 point or larger for regular text and 14 point or larger for bold text, has a contrast ratio requirement of at least 3:1.

Exceptions:

- Text or images of text which are incidental. This includes text in deactivated interactive items such as disabled buttons, text which is deliberately not visible, text in decorative images and text in images which is not important to convey meaning.

- Text which is part of a logo or brand name.

(WCAG 1.4.3 Contrast (Minimum) – Level AA)

eLa 2.1.5 Enhanced text and background contrast (Advisory)

For any text and the background it appears on, choose colours which have a contrast ratio of at least 7:1. This applies to 'normal' size text which W3C defines as 17 point or smaller for regular text and 13 point or smaller for bold text. For 'large' text, ie 18 point or larger for regular text and 14 point or larger for bold text, the recommended contrast ratio is at least 4.5:1.

(WCAG 1.4.6 Contrast Enhanced – Level AAA)

TOPIC 3 – LEARNER CONTROL

eLa 2.1.6 Enlarge text to 200%

Make sure that visual learners can enlarge the text up to 200% and still carry out all the functions on a page and see all its content. They should be able to do this with standard functionality such as using a browser to zoom in, as well as with assistive technology.

Exception:

- Captions, since they are often created to a fixed size.

(WCAG 1.4.4 Resize text – Level AA)

eLa 2.1.7 Text spacing

If the authoring tool uses a markup language such as HTML, make sure that visual learners can change the spacing between text and that they can still see all the content and carry out all the functions of a page. This applies to spacing between lines of text, paragraphs, words and letters.

Exceptions:

- Captions which are embedded in the video frame as opposed to being supplied as a separate caption file.

- Text in images.

(WCAG 1.4.12 Text Spacing – Level AA)

eLa 2.1.8 Images of text

Use onscreen text rather than images of text to convey information as long as the authoring tool allows you to achieve the visual presentation you need. This standard applies unless learners can customize the text in the image, eg change the font, colour or spacing, etc, or the visual presentation of the text is essential such as an image of a logo.

Exception:

- The image is used only for decoration and understanding any text in the image is not important to the meaning of the content.

(WCAG 1.4.5 Images of Text – Level AA)

TOPIC 4 – ASSISTIVE TECHNOLOGY

eLa 2.1.9 Headings, lists and tables

Make sure that assistive technology can interpret structures such as headings, lists and tables. This is normally done through the underlying code of the tool. If this isn't possible, use text to give the same information.

(WCAG 1.3.1 Info and Relationships – Level A)

eLa 2.1.10 Language of resource

Identify the main text language used in the eLearning resource so that assistive technology can correctly pronounce and display the language.

(WCAG 3.1.1 Language of Page – Level A)

eLa 2.1.11 Language of individual phrases

Identify the language of text used in individual passages or phrases if this is different from the main text language used in the eLearning resource.

Exception:

• Proper nouns, technical terms in another language and words in another language which are commonly used and understood in the default language.

(WCAG 3.1.2 Language of Parts – Level AA)

TOPIC 5 – FORMATTING

eLa 2.1.12 Font type (Advisory)

Opinion is divided on the best-practice choice of fonts for accessibility, but a recommendation from the British Dyslexia Association is to choose sans-serif fonts such as Arial, Calibri or Tahoma.

eLa 2.1.13 Font size (Advisory)

Font size should be minimum 12–14 point or equivalent (eg 1–1.2 em/ 16–19 px).

eLa 2.1.14 Line and paragraph spacing (Advisory)

Make sure there is enough space between lines of text and paragraphs. W3C recommends at least a space-and-a half between lines (ie the space is 150% larger than the default space between lines, or 1.5 in formatting options). For the space between paragraphs, 1.5 times the space between lines is recommended.

(WCAG 1.4.8 Visual Presentation – Level AAA)

eLa 2.1.15 Capital letters (Advisory)

Avoid text in all capital letters, eg 'WELCOME TO THE COURSE', especially in titles and sentences. Text in all capital letters is harder to read than text in standard upper and lower case letters, eg, 'Welcome to the course'.

eLa 2.1.16 Italics and underlining (Advisory)

Avoid underlining and italics as this can make the text appear to run together and cause crowding. Use bold for emphasis instead.

eLa 2.1.17 Text block alignment (Advisory)

Do not justify text to both left and right margins. For left to right languages such as English, text should be left aligned. This also means that text centred in a text block is not recommended.

(WCAG 1.4.8 Visual Presentation – Level AAA)

eLa 2.1.18 Text block width (Advisory)

Make sure the width of blocks of text is no longer than 80 characters.

(WCAG 1.4.8 Visual Presentation – Level AAA)

TOPIC 6 – PLAIN ENGLISH

eLa 2.1.19 Plain English (Advisory)

Use the simplest and clearest language suitable for the audience. The WCAG advanced standard recommends providing an easily readable alternative or supplementary content if language is too difficult to understand for someone with a lower secondary education reading level, ie with about nine years of education. This is therefore considered a recommended reading level to aim for if the content is standard, ie not technical or specialized for a particular field.

(WCAG 3.1.5 Reading Level – Level AAA)

eLa 2.2 Information and instructions

Standards to consider when you are giving information and instructions to learners.

TOPIC 1 – COLOUR AND SENSORY CUES

eLa 2.2.1 Supplement colour for information and instructions

Make sure you use devices such as icons, patterns, formatting or text to supplement colour when you are giving learners information and instructions or explaining what action they need to take. It's also important when you are asking learners for a response to a question.

(WCAG 1.4.1 Use of Color – Level A)

eLa 2.2.2 Sensory cues for information and instructions

Make sure that instructions and information do not rely only on visual cues such as shape, colour, size or location. Also make sure that instructions and information do not rely only on auditory cues, such as sounds, to tell learners if they have made a mistake.

(WCAG 1.3.3 Sensory Characteristics – Level A)

TOPIC 2 – INSTRUCTIONS

eLa 2.2.3 Inclusive language (Advisory)

In instructions which involve learner interaction, avoid language such as 'Click', 'Tap' or 'Hit'. Use 'Select' instead to include all learners and the different ways they may interact with the eLearning resource.

eLa 2.2.4 Instructions for input items

When learners interact with input items such as radio buttons or data entry fields, make sure they are given instructions or labels which explain what they need to do. Also make sure that they are given information about how any data they need to enter should be formatted and whether it is mandatory.

(WCAG 3.3.2 Labels or Instructions – Level A)

TOPIC 3 – POP-UP CONTENT AND MESSAGES

eLa 2.2.5 Pop-up content

Make sure information and instructions such as tooltips which appear or 'pop up' when learners hover over or move keyboard focus to interactive items can be dismissed. Also make sure that if learners need to interact with pop-up content, it doesn't disappear until they have finished interacting with it. Finally, if the content appears only on hover, make sure that learners can move the cursor away from the item that triggered the pop-up content to the content itself.

(WCAG 1.4.13 Content on Hover or Focus – Level AA)

eLa 2.2.6 Status messages

If the authoring tool uses a markup language such as HTML, make sure that assistive technology can recognize and announce status messages. This applies to status messages which appear on a page but do not receive keyboard focus.

(WCAG 4.1.3 Status Messages – Level AA)

eLa 2.2.7 Identify errors

If learners make a mistake when they interact with input items such as radio buttons or data entry fields, make sure it is clear which input item the error applies to. Also make sure that the error is described to learners using text.

(WCAG 3.3.1 Error Identification – Level A)

eLa 2.2.8 Suggest corrections for errors

Give learners suggestions to help them correct any mistakes they make when they interact with input items such as radio buttons or data entry fields.

Exception:

- Suggestions which could invalidate the purpose of the interaction, eg by giving away the correct answer to a quiz question in a mandatory compliance assessment.

(WCAG 3.3.3 Error Suggestion – Level AA)

eLa 2.3 Images

Standards which affect any kind of images. These could include images which add meaning to the eLearning resource, images used for decoration or spacing, images used for links, images of text and complex images such as charts, graphs and diagrams.

TOPIC 1 – ALTERNATIVE TEXT

eLa 2.3.1 Alternative text for images which convey meaning

Provide a descriptive text alternative for any images which add meaning to the eLearning resource. When writing alternative text, think about the context of each image and what information you are trying to convey by using it.

Exceptions:

- Images which are part of a test. You can provide a simple descriptive label instead of a full image description so that it does not give learners the answer.
- Images which create a 'sensory experience' such as a work of art. You can provide alternative text which explains what the content is rather than trying to describe it fully.
- Images which are fully described in a caption.

(WCAG 1.1.1 Non-text Content – Level A)

eLa 2.3.2 Alternative text for complex images

Provide alternative text for complex images such as charts, graphs and diagrams. This can be done by providing a short alternative text description of the image, eg 'Bar chart detailing cases of vision impairments', and then a further detailed description of the information provided in the chart or the original raw data used to make a graph, etc.

(WCAG 1.1.1 Non-text Content – Level A)

eLa 2.3.3 Alternative text for functional images

Provide alternative text for any images in the resource which are functional, eg behave like a button or a link. Make sure the alternative text explains the function of the image, ie what happens if it is selected.

(WCAG 1.1.1 Non-text Content – Level A)

eLa 2.3.4 No alternative text for decorative images

Stop assistive technology recognizing images which do not add meaning to the eLearning resource, eg if they are used only for decoration or for spacing.

(WCAG 1.1.1 Non-text Content – Level A)

TOPIC 2 – COLOUR AND IMAGES OF TEXT

eLa 2.3.5 Colour contrast for important visual elements

For important visual items essential to understanding such as the bars in a bar chart or the lines in a graph, choose colours which have a contrast ratio of at least 3:1 against the colour of the background they appear on, or items they appear next to.

Exception:

- Visual elements if a particular presentation is essential to the information being conveyed, eg a medical diagram which uses specific biological colours, a heatmap or a screenshot of a website.

(WCAG 1.4.11 Non-text Contrast – Level AA)

eLa 2.3.6 Supplement colour for visual elements

Make sure you use devices such as icons, patterns, formatting or text to supplement colour when learners need to see a visual element clearly, such as the bars in a bar chart or the lines in a graph.

(WCAG 1.4.1 Use of Color – Level A)

eLa 2.3.7 Images of text

Use onscreen text rather than images of text to convey information as long as the authoring tool allows you to achieve the visual presentation you need. This standard applies unless learners can customize the text in the image or the visual presentation of the text is essential such as an image of a logo.

Exception:

- The image is used only for decoration and understanding any text in the image is not important to the meaning of the content.

(WCAG 1.4.5 Images of Text – Level AA)

Step 3 – Interactive items and assessments

Standards which affect any items which learners interact with. WCAG calls these 'user interface components' and defines them as 'a single control for a distinct function'. In the eLa framework, interactive items are subdivided into three categories: navigation items, input items and links. This step also covers the key requirements for assessments.

eLa 3.1 All interactive items

Standards which affect all interactive items, including navigation items, input items and links.

TOPIC 1 – APPEARANCE AND BEHAVIOUR

eLa 3.1.1 Colour contrast for interactive items
For interactive items choose colours which have a contrast ratio of at least 3:1 against the colour of the background they appear or items they appear next to.

Exception:

• Interactive items which are inactive such as a disabled 'Back' button.

(WCAG 1.4.11 Non-text Contrast – Level AA)

eLa 3.1.2 Target size (Advisory)
Make sure that interactive items are large enough to select easily. The size of the target should be at least 44 × 44 CSS pixels (9 mm square on most mobile devices).

(WCAG 2.5.5 Target Size – Level AAA)

eLa 3.1.3 Pop-up content
Make sure content such as tooltips or submenus which appear or 'pop up' when learners hover over or move keyboard focus to interactive items can be dismissed. Also make sure that if learners need to interact with pop-up content, it doesn't disappear until they have finished interacting with it. Finally, if the content appears only on hover, make sure that learners can move the cursor away from the item that triggered the pop-up content to the content itself.

(WCAG 1.4.13 Content on Hover or Focus – Level AA)

eLa 3.1.4 Unexpected events on focus
When learners move the focus to interactive items, make sure this does not cause anything unexpected to happen such as a new window opening without warning.

(WCAG 3.2.1 On Focus – Level A)

eLa 3.1.5 Trigger functionality

Stop learners accidentally activating interactive items by triggering functionality on the up-event rather than the down-event unless they can undo or reverse the action. The up-event is when learners release their finger, the pointer or the mouse click. The down-event is when they press their finger, the pointer or the mouse click down.

Exception:

• Any functionality in which the down-event is an essential interaction such as selecting the letters on an onscreen keyboard.

(WCAG 2.5.2 Pointer Cancellation – Level A)

TOPIC 2 – LABELS

eLa 3.1.6 Descriptive labels

Make sure that the labels provided for interactive items are descriptive, ie make it clear what the purpose of the item is. For example, a button with the label 'Start course'.

(WCAG 2.4.6 Headings and Labels – Level AA)

eLa 3.1.7 Matching visible label and accessible name

Make sure that interactive items which have a visible label such as the text on buttons have the same accessible name which can be recognized by assistive technology.

(WCAG 2.5.3 Label in Name – Level A)

eLa 3.1.8 Consistent visible label and accessible name

Make sure that if interactive items with the same function have a visible label, eg the text or icon on a button, the visible label remains the same throughout the eLearning resource. Also make sure that the accessible name for interactive items with the same function remains consistent.

(WCAG 3.2.4 Consistent Identification – Level AA)

TOPIC 3 – ASSISTIVE TECHNOLOGY

eLa 3.1.9 Keyboard accessible

Make sure that all interactive items in the eLearning resource are usable with a keyboard or keyboard interface. Also make sure that 'keystrokes', ie pressing the keys, do not have any time constraints.

(WCAG 2.1.1 Keyboard – Level A)

eLa 3.1.10 No keyboard trap

Make sure that learners who navigate using a keyboard or keyboard interface can move away from all content that receives focus in the eLearning resource. Also make sure this can be achieved using standard keyboard keys such as the 'Tab' or 'Arrow' keys, or that learners are made aware if they need to use non-standard keys.

(WCAG 2.1.2 No Keyboard Trap – Level A)

eLa 3.1.11 Visible focus indicator

Make sure that when learners navigate using a keyboard or keyboard interface there is a visible focus indicator for interactive items. This means there is a visible sign to show that these items have been selected. This could be with a change in the appearance of a button or a coloured border around a link, etc.

(WCAG 2.4.7 Focus Visible – Level AA)

eLa 3.1.12 Logical focus order

Make sure that when learners navigate using a keyboard or keyboard interface, they move through interactive items in a logical linear order.

Exception:

- Interactive items which do not need a logical sequence to be understood, eg a random series of links in a word cloud.

(WCAG 2.4.3 Focus Order – Level A)

eLa 3.1.13 Alternative text for interactive items

Make sure interactive items which are not automatically recognized by assistive technology have alternative text which describes their purpose. Many authoring tools ensure that assistive technology can recognize interactive items. If you create these manually, however, eg a bespoke button instead of one created by the authoring tool, you often need to add alternative text.

(WCAG 1.1.1 Non-text Content – Level A)

eLa 3.1.14 Name, role and value

Make sure that all interactive items have an accessible name and role and that the state of items, eg whether they are expanded or collapsed, is communicated to assistive technology.

(WCAG 4.1.2 Name, Role, Value – Level A)

eLa 3.2 Navigation items

These are standards which affect interactive items used specifically for navigating eLearning resources. They include items such as 'Home' or 'Hamburger' icons, menus, a search facility and tags, interactive page numbers, 'Forward' and 'Back' arrows, a breadcrumb trail, links to other pages, etc.

Note: All standards in **eLa 3.1 All interactive items** also apply.

eLa 3.2.1 Multiple ways to navigate

Give learners more than one way to navigate content in eLearning resources. For example, provide a 'Home' icon, a menu and a search facility.

Exception:

- Content which is part of a process that needs to be followed in sequence, eg content that is step locked due to a required learner journey.

(WCAG 2.4.5 Multiple Ways – Level AA)

eLa 3.2.2 Consistent order in layout

Make sure that navigation items such as 'Home' icons or links to other pages which are repeated throughout the eLearning resource appear in the same order in the layout.

Exception:

- Navigation controls which can be moved by learners, eg using assistive technology or setting preferences.

(WCAG 3.2.3 Consistent Navigation – Level AA)

eLa 3.2.3 Skip repeated blocks of content

Make sure learners who navigate using a keyboard or keyboard interface can skip blocks of content repeated over multiple pages and move directly to the main content of a page. In eLearning resources this most often applies to navigation items such as menus which are repeated on multiple pages.

Exception:

- Small, repeated sections of content such as individual words, phrases or single links.

(WCAG 2.4.1 Bypass Blocks – Level A)

eLa 3.3 Input items

Standards which affect interactive items that receive input from learners. This input can be as simple as selecting an item in order to trigger an action. Examples include a 'Submit' button which submits quiz answers and a dial, slider or toggle, etc. Input items also include interactive items that require learners to input a value. Examples include radio buttons and check boxes and text entry or number entry fields.

Note: All standards in **eLa 3.1 All interactive items** also apply.

eLa 3.3.1 Instructions for input items

When learners interact with input items such as radio buttons or data entry fields, make sure they are given instructions or labels that explain what they need to do. Also make sure they are given information about how any data they need to enter should be formatted and whether it is mandatory.

(WCAG 3.3.2 Labels or Instructions – Level A)

eLa 3.3.2 Unexpected events on input

Make sure when learners interact with input items such as entering data into a data entry field or selecting a radio button, this doesn't cause anything unexpected to happen unless you warn learners what to expect before it happens.

(WCAG 3.2.2 On Input – Level A)

eLa 3.3.3 Identify errors

If learners make a mistake when they interact with input items such as radio buttons or data entry fields, make sure it is clear which item the error applies to. Also make sure that the error is described to learners using text.

(WCAG 3.3.1 Error Identification – Level A)

eLa 3.3.4 Suggest corrections for errors

Give learners suggestions to help them correct any mistakes they make when they interact with input items such as radio buttons or data entry fields.

Exception:

- Suggestions which could invalidate the purpose of the interaction, eg by giving away the correct answer to a quiz question in a mandatory compliance assessment.

(WCAG 3.3.3 Error Suggestion – Level AA)

eLa 3.3.5 Error prevention

When learners input any information using input items such as data entry fields or check boxes, make sure they can reverse, check and correct or confirm their data before they submit it. This applies if the interaction has legal or financial implications. It also applies if the interaction changes or deletes information held in data storage systems and if the interaction submits test responses.

(WCAG 3.3.4 Error Prevention (Legal, Financial, Data) – Level AA)

eLa 3.3.6 Input fields which collect personal data

Make sure that any input fields which collect personal data are correctly coded so that assistive technology users can understand the purpose of these fields.

(WCAG 1.3.5 Identify Input Purpose – Level AA)

eLa 3.4 Links

Standards that affect interactive links which take learners to another destination such as text links and images used as links.

Note: All standards in **eLa 3.1 All interactive items** also apply.

eLa 3.4.1 Link destination from link and additional information

Make sure that learners know where they will be taken when they select a link. You can do this either by using information in the link text itself or by adding information in the text surrounding the link. Underlying code should also be used so that assistive technology users know where links will take them.

Exception:

• Ambiguous links if they are deliberate, eg to create the element of surprise in a game.

(WCAG 2.4.4 Link purpose (In Context) – Level A)

eLa 3.4.2 Link destination from link alone (Advisory)

Make sure learners know where they will be taken when they select a link just from the link text itself rather than from the link text and additional information.

(WCAG 2.4.9 Link Purpose (Link Only) – Level AAA)

eLa 3.4.3 Colour for links

Don't use colour alone to show that text is a link. For example, use a formatting device such as underlining to make sure that learners can easily recognize that this is the case.

(WCAG 1.4.1 Use of Color – Level A)

eLa 3.5 Assessments

Key standards which affect learner assessments such as quizzes, tests and knowledge checks. Assessments in eLearning resources can involve a wide range of methods and interactions. They can vary from complex activities such as branching scenarios and interactive videos to more straightforward activities such as multiple choice or true or false questions. As a result, this section focuses only on key general requirements for assessments.

TOPIC 1 – INSTRUCTIONS

eLa 3.5.1 Supplement colour for information and instructions
Make sure you use devices such as icons, patterns, formatting or text to supplement colour when you are giving learners instructions for assessments.

(WCAG 1.4.1 Use of Color – Level A)

eLa 3.5.2 Sensory cues for information and instructions
Make sure that instructions and feedback do not rely only on visual cues such as shape, colour, size or location. Also make sure that they do not rely only on auditory cues, such as sounds to tell learners if they have made a mistake.

(WCAG 1.3.3 Sensory Characteristics – Level A)

eLa 3.5.3 Instructions for input items
When learners interact with input items such as radio buttons or data entry fields, make sure they are given instructions or labels that explain what they need to do. Also make sure that they are given information about how any data they need to enter should be formatted and whether it is mandatory.

(WCAG 3.3.2 Labels or Instructions – Level A)

eLa 3.5.4 Inclusive language (Advisory)
In instructions for assessments that involve learner interaction, avoid language such as 'Click', 'Tap' or 'Hit'. Use 'Select' instead, to include all learners and the different ways they may interact with the eLearning resource.

eLa 3.5.5 Clear instructions (Advisory)

Make sure the language you use in instructions and quiz questions for assessments is clear and unambiguous. Don't try to trip up or trick learners, eg by using double negatives.

TOPIC 2 – TIMING AND ERRORS

eLa 3.5.6 Adjustable time limits

Do not set time limits for assessment activities unless learners can turn them off, adjust or extend them.

Exception:

- Activities where it is essential to test the timing, eg the steps in a simulation of a real activity which need to be completed in a fixed amount of time.

(WCAG 2.2.1 Timing Adjustable – Level A)

eLa 3.5.7 No time limits (Advisory)

Do not set time limits for assessment activities.

(WCAG 2.2.3 No Timing – Level AAA)

eLa 3.5.8 Identify errors

If learners make a mistake when they interact with input items such as radio buttons or data entry fields, make sure it is clear which input item the error applies to. Also make sure that the error is described to learners using text.

(WCAG 3.3.1 Error Identification – Level A)

eLa 3.5.9 Suggest corrections for errors

Give learners suggestions to help them correct any mistakes they make when they interact with input items such as radio buttons or data entry fields.

Exception:

- Suggestions which could invalidate the purpose of the interaction, eg by giving away the correct answer to a quiz question in a mandatory compliance assessment.

(WCAG 3.3.3 Error Suggestion – Level A)

eLa 3.5.10 Feedback for errors (Advisory)

Unless the assessment is a mandatory compliance test, give learners feedback on incorrect answers. Make sure that the feedback appears for every incorrect answer and has a clear and consistent layout.

eLa 3.5.11 Error prevention for information input

When learners input any information using input items such as data entry fields or check boxes, make sure they can reverse, check and correct or confirm their data before they submit it. This applies if the interaction submits test responses.

(WCAG 3.3.4 Error Prevention (Legal, Financial, Data) – Level AA)

Step 4 – Audio and video content, moving content and timing

Standards which affect audio and video content, any moving content and timing limits.

eLa 4.1 Audio and video content

Standards which affect audio and video content in the eLearning resource. This includes audio-only content such as podcasts, video-only content such as silent animations, videos with sound and live presentations such as webinars.

TOPIC 1 – CAPTIONS AND AUDIO DESCRIPTION

eLa 4.1.1 Alternatives for audio-only and video-only content

Provide an alternative way for learners to access the information in prerecorded audio-only content such as podcasts, or prerecorded video-only content such as silent animations. You can do this by providing a text transcript which contains all the information learners need to understand the audio-only or video-only content. For video-only content, another option is to provide an audio description track which describes everything that happens in the video.

Exceptions:

- The audio-only content or video-only content is provided as an alternative for text and it is made clear to learners that this is the case.
- Video-only content which is used for decoration.

(WCAG 1.2.1 Audio-only and Video-only (Prerecorded) – Level A)

eLa 4.1.2 Captions for prerecorded videos

For prerecorded videos which have sound, provide synchronized captions, ie text which appears on screen at the same time as people speak. As well as providing the words that are said, captions should identify who is speaking and describe any important sound effects.

Exception:

- The video is provided as an alternative for text and it is made clear to learners that this is the case.

(WCAG 1.2.2 Captions (Prerecorded) – Level A)

eLa 4.1.3 Captions for live presentations

For live presentations with audio content such as webinars or lectures, provide synchronized captions, ie text which appears on screen at the same time as people speak.

(WCAG 1.2.4 Captions (Live) – Level AA)

eLa 4.1.4 Audio description for prerecorded videos

Provide audio description for prerecorded videos that have sound. The audio description should give all the information non-visual learners need to understand the video. This could include the action taking place, the expressions of characters, scene changes, etc.

Exceptions:

- Videos which have all the information conveyed in spoken word, eg a 'talking head' video.
- Videos of presentations as long as the presenter explains all the visual information contained in the slides, eg images, charts or tables.

(WCAG 1.2.5 Audio Description (Prerecorded) – Level AA)

eLa 4.1.5 Extended audio description for prerecorded videos (Advisory)

This standard refers to prerecorded videos with sound which do not have long enough pauses between the dialogue and the action to add audio description. If this is the case, edit the video to manually extend the existing pauses, or to add further pauses so that the background descriptive information can be added. This means that the video content pauses temporarily while the narrator continues describing the important visual details.

(WCAG 1.2.7 Extended Audio Description (Prerecorded) – Level AAA)

TOPIC 2 – TRANSCRIPTS AND SIGN LANGUAGE

eLa 4.1.6 Audio description or transcript for prerecorded videos

For prerecorded videos which have sound, provide audio description or a text transcript. These should give all the information non-visual learners need to understand the video. This could include the action taking place, the expressions of characters, scene changes, etc. Transcripts should also provide all the words said in the video and identify who is speaking.

Exceptions:

- The video is provided as an alternative for text and it is made clear to learners that this is the case.
- Videos which have all the information conveyed in spoken word, eg a 'talking head' video.
- Videos of presentations, as long as the presenter explains all the visual information contained in the slides, eg images, charts or tables.

(WCAG 1.2.3 Audio Description or Media Alternative (Prerecorded) – Level A)

eLa 4.1.7 Transcript for prerecorded videos (Advisory)

For prerecorded videos with sound, provide a text transcript. This should give all the information non-visual learners need to understand the video. This could include the action taking place, the expressions of characters, scene changes, etc. Transcripts should also provide all the words which are said in the video and identify who is speaking. Accessibility experts strongly recommend providing transcripts for all prerecorded videos with sound even if audio description has been provided. This is because transcripts accommodate a wider range of accessibility needs than audio description.

(WCAG 1.2.8 Media Alternative (Prerecorded) – Level AAA)

eLa 4.1.8 Sign language for prerecorded videos (Advisory)
Provide sign language interpretation for all prerecorded videos with sound. Sign language provides expression, intonation and emotion and therefore gives a much closer equivalent to the video than just captions.

(WCAG 1.2.6 Sign Language (Prerecorded) – Level AAA)

TOPIC 3 – ASSISTIVE TECHNOLOGY

eLa 4.1.9 Alternative text for audio or video content
Provide alternative text which allows screen readers to announce audio or video content before it begins playing.

(WCAG 1.1.1 Non-text Content – Level A)

eLa 4.1.10 Keyboard accessible player controls
Make sure that audio and video player controls are usable with a keyboard or keyboard interface.

(WCAG 2.1.1 Keyboard – Level A)

eLa 4.1.11 No keyboard trap for player controls
Make sure that learners who navigate using a keyboard or keyboard interface can move focus away from all audio and video player controls in the eLearning resource. Also make sure this can be achieved using standard keyboard keys such as the 'Tab' or 'Arrow' keys, or that learners are made aware if they need to use non-standard keys.

(WCAG 2.1.2 No Keyboard Trap – Level A)

TOPIC 4 – LEARNER CONTROL

eLa 4.1.12 Audio Control
For any audio content in the eLearning resource which starts automatically and lasts longer than three seconds, make sure that learners can pause or stop the audio. Another option is to allow them to adjust the volume, but this must be with a control which does not affect the overall volume of the rest of the audio content in the eLearning resource.

(WCAG 1.4.2 Audio Control – Level A)

eLa 4.1.13 Audio narration (Advisory)

Audio narration where a narrator reads aloud the content of slides can cause accessibility issues. For example, if the narrator reads the onscreen text this can be distracting for some learners as it may be faster or slower than they would naturally read content. A solution to this is to provide the learner with a mechanism to switch off the audio narration. This can cause issues, however, if the narrator provides information which supplements or is different to the onscreen text. Learners risk missing information if they turn off the narration due to preference or because it interferes with the output of a screen reader.

eLa 4.1.14 Audio-only content with background audio (Advisory)

For prerecorded audio-only content which has speech in the foreground and background audio, such as music, make sure the learner can switch off the background sounds. Another option is to make sure that the background audio is approximately four times quieter than the foreground audio, ie 20 decibels lower.

Note: Although this recommendation refers specifically to audio-only content, it is also good practice for videos which have speech in the foreground and background audio.

(WCAG. 1.4.7 Low or No Background Audio – Level AAA)

eLa 4.2 Moving content

Standards which affect anything that moves in the eLearning resource. This includes animated GIFs, moving text, image carousels, flashing buttons, etc.

eLa 4.2.1 Adjustable time limits

Do not set time limits for any activities in the eLearning resource, such as the length of time content remains on the page, unless learners can turn them off, adjust or extend them. Make sure that learners have control over any content that moves, updates or scrolls automatically as this also effectively imposes a time limit.

(WCAG 2.2.1 Timing Adjustable – Level A)

eLa 4.2.2 Automatically moving and updating content

Make sure learners can pause, stop or hide any content that starts automatically, moves, scrolls or blinks for longer than five seconds and appears alongside other content. The same must also be true for content that automatically updates and appears alongside other content.

Exceptions:

- Animations such as a progress bar which needs to move in order to show that it hasn't frozen or broken.

- Standalone content which is not presented alongside other content, eg an animation which appears alone on a page while a video is being downloaded.

(WCAG 2.2.2 Pause, Stop, Hide – Level A)

eLa 4.2.3 Flashing content to required thresholds

In order to prevent seizures, do not include any content which flashes more than three times per second unless the flashes are small enough or dim enough to fall below the required thresholds. If the flashes contain very little of the colour red, they may also fall below the required threshold.

(WCAG 2.3.1 Three Flashes or Below Threshold – Level A)

eLa 4.2.4 No flashing content (Advisory)

In order to prevent seizures do not include any content which flashes more than three times per second.

(WCAG 2.3.2 Three Flashes – Level AAA)

eLa 4.3 Timing

Standards which affect the amount of time that learners have to complete tasks.

eLa 4.3.1 Adjustable time limits

Do not set time limits for any activities in the eLearning resource unless learners can turn them off, adjust or extend them. This applies to the length of time learners have to complete quiz questions or to the amount of time content remains on the page, etc. Also make sure that learners have control over any content that moves, scrolls or updates automatically as this also effectively imposes a time limit.

Exceptions:

- Activities where the timing is essential, eg the steps in a simulation of a real activity which need to be completed in a fixed amount of time.
- Real-time events such as an online broadcast of the audio or video feed from a meeting or event.

(WCAG 2.2.1 Timing Adjustable – Level A)

eLa 4.3.2 No time limits (Advisory)
Do not set time limits for any activity or let any content move or scroll automatically.

(WCAG 2.2.3 No Timing – Level AAA)

eLa 4.3.3 No time constraints for keystrokes
Make sure that 'keystrokes', ie pressing the keys, do not have any time constraints.

(WCAG 2.1.1 Keyboard – Level A)

Step 5 – Keyboard and global content

Standards which allow keyboard-only and screen reader users to navigate and interact with the eLearning resource and standards which affect all content in the resource.

eLa 5.1 Keyboard

Standards which allow keyboard and keyboard interface users to navigate and interact with the eLearning resource.

Note: These standards also apply to screen reader users since they use the keyboard to navigate and interact with online content.

eLa 5.1.1 Keyboard accessible

Make sure that all functionality in the eLearning resource is usable with a keyboard or keyboard interface. This includes all interactive items and audio and video player controls. Also make sure that 'keystrokes', ie pressing the keys, do not have any time constraints.

(WCAG 2.1.1 Keyboard – Level A)

eLa 5.1.2 No keyboard trap

Make sure that learners who navigate using a keyboard or keyboard interface can move away from all content that receives focus in the eLearning resource. Also make sure this can be achieved using standard keyboard keys such as the 'Tab' or 'Arrow' keys, or that learners are made aware if they need to use non-standard keys.

(WCAG 2.1.2 No Keyboard Trap – Level A)

eLa 5.1.3 Visible focus indicator

Make sure that when learners navigate using a keyboard or keyboard interface there is a visible focus indicator for interactive items. This means there is a visible sign to show that these items have been selected. This could be with a change in the appearance of a button or a coloured border around a link, etc.

(WCAG 2.4.7 Focus Visible – Level AA)

eLa 5.1.4 Logical focus order

Make sure that when learners navigate using a keyboard or keyboard interface, they move through interactive items in a logical linear order.

Exception:

- Interactive items which do not need a logical sequence to be understood, eg a random series of links in a word cloud.

(WCAG 2.4.3 Focus Order – Level A)

eLa 5.1.5 Skip repeated blocks of content

Make sure learners who navigate using a keyboard or keyboard interface can skip blocks of content repeated over multiple pages and move directly to the main content of a page. In eLearning resources this most often applies to navigation items such as menus which are repeated on multiple pages.

Exception:

- Small, repeated sections of content such as individual words, phrases or single links.

(WCAG 2.4.1 Bypass Blocks – Level A)

eLa 5.1.6 Single character key shortcuts

Avoid assigning keyboard shortcuts which use only a single letter, punctuation, number or symbol character key. If they do, make sure that the shortcut can be modified by adding another key, can be turned off, or for interactive items is active only when it receives focus.

(WCAG 2.1.4 Character Key Shortcuts – Level A)

eLa 5.2 Global

Standards which affect all content in the eLearning resource.

eLa 5.2.1 Logical reading order

Make sure that all content which adds meaning in the eLearning resource is structured in a logical linear order so that it makes sense and is easy to navigate for assistive technology users.

(WCAG 1.3.2 Meaningful Sequence – Level A)

eLa 5.2.2 Content reflow

Make sure that when eLearning resources are enlarged to 400% using browser zoom, the content reflows so that horizontal scrolling is not needed. Visual learners should still be able to carry out all the functions of the page and see all its content without having to use a horizontal scroll bar.

Exception:

- Any content such as complex images and data tables, etc which would not make sense if it were reflowed.

(WCAG 1.4.10 Reflow – Level AA)

Step 6 – Mobile and code

Standards which apply to eLearning content on mobile devices or to the underlying source code of the eLearning resource.

eLa 6.1 Mobile

Key standards for mobile accessibility.

Note: While many of the WCAG standards are applicable to mobile content, this step focuses on a few which are key. For further information on mobile accessibility, a useful resource is Mobile Accessibility at W3C.[2]

eLa 6.1.1 Open orientation

Make sure that learners can choose either portrait or landscape view, ie either vertical or horizontal view, for the eLearning resource.

Exception:

- A particular orientation for the eLearning resource is essential, eg a simulation which uses virtual reality.

(WCAG 1.3.4 Orientation – Level AA)

eLa 6.1.2 Complex gestures

For any interactions which need learners to carry out complex gestures, provide an alternative simple gesture which needs only a single point of contact. Complex gestures include 'multipoint' gestures which need two fingers, such as a two-finger pinch to zoom, and 'path-based' gestures where the path that the finger takes is important, such as a touch and drag inter-action to pan.

Exception:

- Complex gestures which are essential such as in a game.

(WCAG 2.5.1 Pointer Gestures – Level A)

eLa 6.1.3 Trigger functionality

Stop learners accidentally activating interactive items by triggering function-ality on the up-event rather than the down-event unless they can undo or reverse the action. The up-event is when learners release their finger, the pointer or the mouse click. The down-event is when they press their finger, the pointer or the mouse click down.

Exception:

- Any functionality in the down-event is an essential interaction such as selecting the letters on an onscreen keyboard.

(WCAG 2.5.2 Pointer Cancellation – Level A)

eLa 6.1.4 Motion activated functionality

Make sure that learners can disable functionality which is triggered by movement such as shaking or tilting a device to undo an action. Also make sure that the same functionality can be activated using standard controls such as a button or a link.

(WCAG 2.5.4 Motion Actuation – Level A)

eLa 6.2 Code

Standards which W3C states must be achieved using the underlying source code of the eLearning resource.

Note: These include any standards which need to be 'programmatically determined' or require the use of markup languages such as HTML.

eLa 6.2.1 Content structure

Make sure that assistive technology can interpret structures such as head-ings, lists, tables, input fields and page regions. This is normally done through the underlying code of the tool. If this isn't possible, use text to give the same information.

(WCAG 1.3.1 Info and Relationships – Level A)

eLa 6.2.2 Logical reading order

Make sure that all content which adds meaning in the eLearning resource is structured in a logical linear order so that it makes sense and is easy to navigate for assistive technology users.

(WCAG 1.3.2 Meaningful Sequence – Level A)

eLa 6.2.3 Input fields which collect personal data

Make sure that any input fields which collect personal data are correctly coded so that assistive technology users can understand the purpose of those fields.

(WCAG 1.3.5 Identify Input Purpose – Level AA)

eLa 6.2.4 Text spacing

If the authoring tool uses a markup language such as HTML, make sure that visual learners can change the spacing between text, and that they can still see all the content and carry out all the functions of a page. This applies to spacing between lines of text, paragraphs, words and letters.

Exceptions:

- Captions which are embedded in the video frame as opposed to being supplied as a separate caption file.
- Text in images.

(WCAG 1.4.12 Text Spacing – Level AA)

eLa 6.2.5 Link destination

Use underlying code to make sure that assistive technology users know where links will take them.

Exception:

- Ambiguous links if they are deliberate, eg to create the element of surprise in a game.

(WCAG 2.4.4 Link purpose (In Context) – Level A)

eLa 6.2.6 Language of resource

Identify the main text language used in the eLearning resource so that assistive technology can correctly pronounce and display the language.

(WCAG 3.1.1 Language of Page – Level A)

eLa 6.2.7 Language of individual phrases

Identify the language of text used in individual passages or phrases if this is different from the main text language used in the eLearning resource.

Exception:

- Proper nouns, technical terms in another language and words in another language which are commonly used and understood in the default language.

(WCAG 3.1.2 Language of Parts – Level AA)

eLa 6.2.8 Coding errors

If the authoring tool uses a markup language such as HTML, make sure the code doesn't cause any issues for assistive technology. This can happen if there are errors in the code such as when elements are missing complete start and end tags.

(WCAG 4.1.1 Parsing – Level A)

eLa 6.2.9 Name, role and value

Make sure that all interactive items have an accessible name and role and that the state of items, eg whether they are expanded or collapsed, is communicated to assistive technology.

(WCAG 4.1.2 Name, Role, Value – Level A)

eLa 6.2.10 Status messages

If the authoring tool uses a markup language such as HTML, make sure that assistive technology can recognize and announce status messages. This applies to status messages which appear on a page but do not receive keyboard focus.

(WCAG 4.1.3 Status Messages – Level AA)

Endnotes

1   W3C Web Accessibility Initiative. (2019) How to Meet WCAG (quick reference), 4 October, https://www.w3.org/WAI/WCAG21/quickref/ (archived at https://perma.cc/LWF9-R5U7)

2   Lawton Henry, S and Brewer, J (Updated 2020) Mobile Accessibility at W3C, 20 November, https://www.w3.org/WAI/standards-guidelines/mobile/ (archived at https://perma.cc/5CLT-UMES)

PART THREE

WCAG 2.1 level A and AA accessibility standards

08

Perceivable

1.1.1 Non-Text Content – Level A

Provide an alternative text description for visual items such as images which add meaning, or interactive items so that they can be recognized by assistive technology. Also provide alternative text which allows assistive technology such as screen readers to announce audio or video content before it begins playing. Finally, make sure that assistive technology ignores any visual items that do not add meaning such as images used only for decoration or spacing.

Key information

This standard applies to more than just images; it also includes interactive items and audio and video content. Providing alternative text for these items is one of the most important things you can do to improve the accessibility of eLearning resources. This is because it allows everyone to have an equivalent learning experience. For example, it allows non-visual learners who use screen readers to be aware of audio or video content before it begins playing and to receive the same information about images through text as visual learners receive through the image itself. Using alternative text correctly also ensures that screen reader users have a good user experience. For example, it makes sure that screen readers do not read out the alternative text or file name for images which are used only for decoration. Imagine how time consuming and frustrating it would be to have to listen to the description of images that add nothing to the meaning of the resource.

Alternative text is also important for people who use other forms of assistive technology. Not only is alternative text recognized and voiced by screen readers, it can also be converted into formats such as braille or symbols. In addition, making sure that you label buttons and interactive items with alternative text means that people who use voice recognition software can operate those buttons with a voice command. People who use screen magnifiers also benefit from alternative text for images. This is because when screen magnifiers enlarge content, they show only a portion of the screen at a time. This can be confusing and time consuming when trying to interpret images. As a result people who use screen magnifiers which have screen reader capability may find it more efficient to use the alternative text to find out the meaning of an image.

How to conform

1 **Images that convey meaning**. Provide alternative text for any images that add meaning to the eLearning resource. When writing alternative text, think about the context of each image and what information you are trying to convey by using it. Most authoring tools allow you to add this, either when you add an image to the tool's asset library or when you add an image to a page. If your authoring tool does not have this functionality, another option is to give the full description of the image in a caption.

2 **Complex images**. Provide alternative text for complex images such as charts, graphs and diagrams. This can be done by giving a short alternative text description of the image, eg 'Bar chart detailing cases of vision impairments', and then a further detailed description of the information provided in the chart. Another option is to provide the information in a different format such as the data from a pie chart in an accessible table or the original raw data used to make a graph. Often the alternative information is given via a link to another layer or page. If this is the case, make sure that the link is easy to find and is accessible.

3 **Functional images**. Provide alternative text for any images in the resource which are functional, eg behave like a button or a link. Make sure the alternative text explains the function of the image, ie what happens if it is selected.

4 **Images of logos**. Provide alternative text for logos that are added to the resource as an image. Make sure this includes the brand name and any other text which is included in the image of the logo.

5 **Decorative images**. Stop assistive technology from recognizing images that do not add meaning to the eLearning resource, for instance if they are used only for decoration or for spacing. A basic way to check whether an image is decorative is to imagine that it has been removed from the page. If people can still learn everything they need to from the page without the image, then it is decorative and doesn't need alternative text.

6 **Interactive items**. Many authoring tools automatically provide a way that assistive technology can recognize interactive items such as navigation controls, buttons or links. If you create these manually, however, eg if you create a button using a rectangle shape with text on top, or you use an image of a button because you want to duplicate a button style from a legacy course, you often need to add alternative text manually. The alternative text must describe the purpose of the interactive item.

7 **Audio and video content**. Provide alternative text to allow assistive technology to identify audio or video content before it begins playing, eg 'Vice-Chancellor's speech to the university.'

8 CAPTCHA. If the eLearning resource has a CAPTCHA to prove that learners are human, alternative text can cause a problem because it means that the CAPTCHA can be operated by a 'Web robot'. Instead provide an alternative such as an audio version for non-visual learners which announces the numbers and letters that learners must enter into a field.

Exceptions

- You do not need to add full alternative text for an image that is part of a test. You can provide a simple descriptive label instead so that it does not give learners the answer.

- Content which is used because it creates a sensory experience, such as looking at a work of art, can be difficult to describe. If this is the case, you can provide alternative text which explains what the content is rather than trying to describe it fully.

- You do not need to add alternative text if you have given a full description of the image in a caption.

Best practice for alternative text for images

Keep alternative text concise. The character limit varies between tools, but a good working recommendation is a maximum of two or three sentences or about 250 characters.

Don't use the alternative text to explain what the item is, eg 'image of' or 'screenshot of'. Assistive technology automatically provides this information.

Don't provide information in the alternative text which is already in the surrounding text.

Use standard punctuation such as commas and full stops. Avoid using non-standard punctuation such as colons or exclamation marks because some screen readers may voice these depending on the settings that the screen reader user has selected.

Why?

Learners who benefit from this standard include:

- people who are blind or have low vision and use screen readers to voice the alternative text or convert it into braille;
- people who have low vision and use a screen magnifier with screen reader capability. They may find it easier to use the screen reader to voice the alternative text rather than trying to interpret an image of which they can see only a portion of at a time;
- people who have motor impairments and use speech recognition software to navigate. They can use the alternative text to operate a button or a linked image with a voice command;
- people affected by situational impairments, eg someone who has a slow internet connection and who may not be able to download images. They will normally be able to see the alternative text displayed on the page if this is the case.

Examples

FIGURE 8.1   Alternative text for images that convey meaning (dominKnow | ONE)

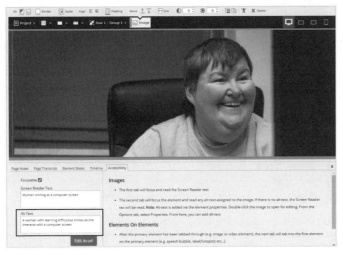

An image added to a resource using the dominKnow | ONE authoring tool. The image has been chosen because it shows the enjoyment that someone with learning difficulties experiences when she interacts with online content. As a result, the image does have meaning and the content author has therefore provided alternative text. This can be seen in the Alt Text field and reads 'A woman with learning difficulties smiles as she interacts with a computer screen'. The dominKnow | ONE authoring tool allows you to add a description of the image when it is first uploaded, which ensures that accessibility is part of the standard workflow. It also has an Accessibility tab which provides further information about how to design inclusively.

SOURCE Reproduced with permission of dominKnow, Inc.

FIGURE 8.2   Alternative text for complex images (CourseArc)

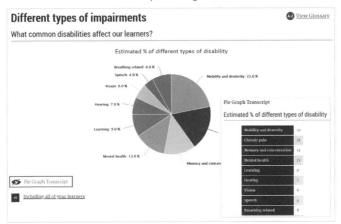

A pie chart created using the CourseArc authoring tool with an automatically generated Pie Graph Transcript link below. The link opens another layer shown in the insert with the data of the pie chart presented in an accessible table format.

SOURCE Reproduced with permission of CourseArc

FIGURE 8.3   Alternative text for decorative images (Lectora Online)

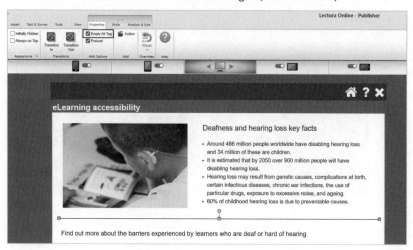

The Properties tab in the Lectora Online authoring tool showing the selected Empty Alt Tag field. This prevents a screen reader from announcing alternative text for the line image used to break up the content on the slide.

SOURCE Reproduced with permission of eLearning Brothers

FIGURE 8.4   Alternative text for interactive items (Articulate Storyline)

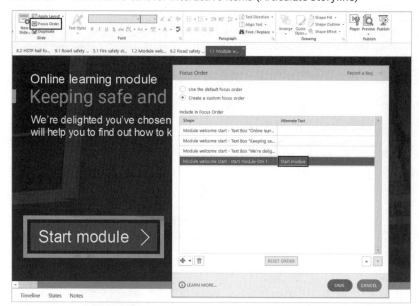

Alternative text for a 'Start module' button added in the Focus Order panel in the Articulate Storyline authoring tool. This button was created manually instead of using the pre-built button functionality of the tool. As a result alternative text has been added in the Alternate Text field for the button so that it can be recognized and announced by assistive technology.

SOURCE ©Articulate Global, Inc. Used with permission, all other rights reserved

How to test

1 Use a screen reader to voice all the content in the eLearning resource. Check that the alternative text for images allows you to have an equivalent learning experience to a visual learner. Also check that the alternative text allows you to interact with and navigate the content and that the screen reader announces any audio or video content before it begins playing.

2 Check that the screen reader does not announce the description or file name of any images which are used only for decoration or spacing, etc.

3 Make sure that alternative text for complex images is easy to find and that the information is provided in an accessible format.

Useful resources

- How to write better alt-text descriptions for accessibility[1]
  Practical guidance on improving alt text from Scope's Big Hack.

- Alternative text[2]
  Detailed alternative text guidance with practical examples from WebAIM.

- Image description[3]
  Best-practice guidelines and an image description training tool to develop skills in writing effective alternative text from Diagram Center.

- Web accessibility tutorials – Images Concepts[4]
  Guidance on alternative text from W3C.

- 1.1.1 Non-Text Content – Level A[5]
  W3C quick reference guide and further information for this standard.

1.2.1 Audio-Only and Video-Only (Prerecorded) – Level A

Provide an alternative way for learners to access the information in prerecorded audio-only content such as podcasts, or prerecorded video-only content such as silent animations. You can do this by providing a text transcript which contains all the information learners need to understand the audio-only or video-only content. For video-only content, another option is to provide an audio description track which describes everything that happens in the video.

Key information

This standard allows all learners to have an equivalent experience accessing the information in audio-only and video-only content. Audio-only content such as podcasts can be a barrier for people who are deaf or hard of hearing. Providing a text transcript allows them to access the information by reading the content rather than listening to it.

Video-only content such as a silent animation of how to use a fire extinguisher excludes people with visual impairments. Providing a text transcript which describes what happens in the silent video and which can be voiced by a screen reader or converted into braille allows everyone to access the information. Another way you can provide this information is to create an audio description track which describes what happens in the video.

How to conform

1 **Prerecorded audio-only content.** Provide a text transcript for audio-only content. Make sure it includes all spoken dialogue and any other important information such as who is speaking or sound effects.

2 **Prerecorded video-only content.** Provide either a text transcript, or an audio description track for video-only content. Make sure that the transcript or audio track describes all of the important visual information which takes place in the video.

Exceptions

- This standard applies unless the audio-only content or video-only content is provided as an alternative for text and it is made clear to learners that this is the case. For example, if you have a page with text describing a chemical reaction and a silent video demonstrating the same reaction, you don't need to add a transcript or an audio description track as long as you tell learners that the video content is an alternative for the text.

- You don't need to provide a transcript or audio description track if the video-only content is only for decoration, for example a video of the earth spinning in an eLearning resource about environmental issues.

Why?

Learners who benefit from transcripts for audio-only content such as a podast include:

- people who are deaf or hard of hearing who can read the content instead of listening to it;
- people who may find it easier to read rather than listen to content, eg second-language learners;
- people who prefer to read rather than listen to content;
- people with temporary hearing impairments, eg someone who has an ear infection which impacts their hearing;
- people affected by situational hearing impairments, eg someone who has a desktop computer with no sound capability.

Learners who benefit from transcripts or audio description tracks for video-only content such as a silent animation include:

- people who are blind or have low vision and use screen readers to voice the transcript;
- people who are deafblind and convert the transcript to braille;
- people who are blind or have low vision who can listen to an audio description track which describes everything that happens in video-only content.

Example

FIGURE 8.5   Audio description track (Evolve)

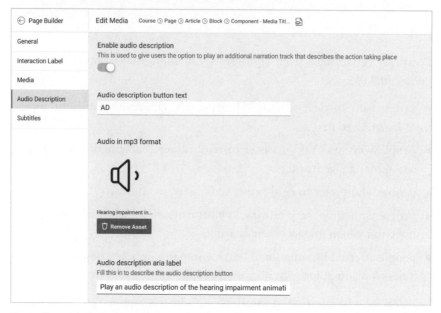

The media options in the Evolve authoring tool which allow you to add an audio description track.
SOURCE Reproduced with permission of Intellum UK Limited

How to test

1 Check that audio-only content has a transcript and that video-only content has either a transcript or an audio description track.

2 Check that the transcript conveys the same information as audio-only content.

3 Check that either the transcript or the audio description track convey the same information as video-only content.

4 Make sure that any links to transcripts or audio description tracks are easy to find.

5 Make sure the information provided in transcripts is in an accessible format.

Useful resources

- Transcripts on the web[6]
  Best-practice guidelines for creating transcripts from uiAccess.
- Podcast: Interview on WCAG 2[7]
  An example from the Web Accessibility Initiative (WAI) showing good practice for podcast transcripts.
- 1.2.1 Audio-Only and Video-Only (Prerecorded) (Level A)[8]
  W3C quick reference guide and further information for this standard.

1.2.2 Captions (Prerecorded) – Level A

For prerecorded videos which have sound, provide synchronized captions, ie text which appears on screen at the same time as people speak. As well as providing the words that are said, captions should identify who is speaking and describe any important sound effects.

Key information

Captions are needed so that people who are deaf or hard of hearing can understand video content. They need to appear at the same time that people are speaking in the video to make the content easier to understand. They also need to describe any sound effects which are important to understand, such as a phone ringing. Captions can be either open or closed. Open captions are always visible and cannot be switched off. They have the advantage that they cannot be missed, but some learners can find them distracting, particularly people with cognitive impairments who are sensitive to moving content or are easily distracted. Closed captions give learners more control as they can choose whether to view the captions or to switch them off.

Captions are sometimes called subtitles. In British English, subtitles normally mean onscreen text for people who can hear but who don't understand the language used in video content. While subtitles provide a translation of the speech, they don't identify who is speaking or include sound effects.

How you add captions to your eLearning resource depends on the capability of your authoring tool. Some tools allow you to add caption files to videos embedded in the eLearning resource. Others have a captioning option which allows you to manually create and edit captions within the tool. Many authoring tools also allow you to embed video content which is held on a video hosting platform (eg YouTube or Vimeo). If you use this method, make sure that the videos you embed have captions added. Hosting platforms normally give you the option to upload a caption file. Some sites add captions generated by machine speech recognition, known as 'auto captions'. The accuracy of auto captions depends on several factors such as the audio quality in the video and the clarity of the spoken language. You must always edit auto captions as they contain no punctuation and always have errors. Auto captions are not considered accurate enough to conform to this standard unless they are edited and are fully accurate.[9]

Note: The advanced standard **1.2.9 Audio-only (Live)** recommends that you provide synchronized captions or an alternative such as a transcript for audio-only content such as podcasts, radio plays or speeches. Another related advanced standard is **1.2.6 Sign Language (Prerecorded)**, which recommends that in addition to captions you provide sign language interpretation for all prerecorded videos with sound.

How to conform

Provide either open or closed captions for all non-live videos. Captions should be synchronized to the speech and any action happening in the video. They should include any words spoken, identify who is speaking and describe any sound effects that are important for understanding.

Exception

- This standard applies unless the video is provided as an alternative for text and it is made clear to learners that this is the case.

Why?

Learners who benefit from captions include:

- people who are deaf or hard of hearing who can read the captions and have an equivalent experience to those listening to the content;

- people who may find it easier to read and listen to content at the same time, eg second-language learners;

- people with temporary hearing impairments, eg someone who has Ménière's disease which temporarily impacts their hearing;

- people in noise-sensitive environments, eg someone watching a training video without headphones while commuting.

Examples

FIGURE 8.6   Upload a captions file for an embedded video (Lectora Online)

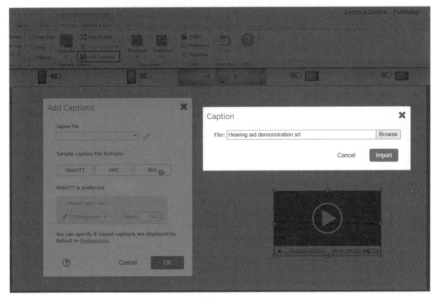

The Add Captions option in the Lectora Online authoring tool which allows you to upload different types of caption files for a video, eg WebVTT, SRT or XML.
SOURCE Reproduced with permission of eLearning Brothers

FIGURE 8.7   Manually add captions to an embedded video (Articulate Storyline)

The captioning tool in the Articulate Storyline authoring tool. The tool allows you to import a captions file, or to add and edit captions manually.
SOURCE ©Articulate Global, Inc. Used with permission, all other rights reserved

How to test

Check that all videos with sound have synchronized captions which identify who is speaking and describe any important sound effects.

Useful resources

- Ultimate guide to closed captioning[10]
  Comprehensive overview of closed captioning from 3Play Media.

- Captioning key[11]
  Guidelines and best practice for captioning educational videos from the Described and Captioned Media Program.

- BBC subtitle guidelines[12]
  Comprehensive style guide for subtitles/captions from the BBC.

- Make it accessible – captions, subtitles and transcripts[13]
  Aston University Technology Enhanced Learning blog with a video demonstration of creating captions and transcripts using YouTube's auto-captioning service.

- 1.2.2 Captions (Prerecorded) – Level A[14]

  W3C quick reference guide and further information for this standard.

1.2.3 Audio Description or Media Alternative (Prerecorded) – Level A

For prerecorded videos which have sound, provide either audio description or a text transcript (media alternative). These should give all the information non-visual learners need to understand the video. This could include the action taking place, the expressions of characters, scene changes, etc. Transcripts should provide all the words which are said in the video and identify who is speaking.

Key information

Learners who are blind or have low vision will be able to hear the words spoken in a video, but they won't be able to fully understand what is happening without additional background information. You can provide this information using a text transcript (media alternative). This effectively allows you to tell the story of what is happening and is similar to a script for a play or a movie. It allows you to provide important background information such as a description of the action taking place, eg 'Serita looks nervously at her watch as she waits for her job interview to start'. A text transcript should also contain all the dialogue spoken in the video and identify who is speaking. If the video contains any interaction, eg an information icon which learners can select in order to be taken to further information, then a transcript should provide the same functionality. This is normally done with a link. The most common way of providing a transcript is to add a link on the same page as the video resource. Tools with good accessibility features sometimes provide a transcript link automatically when you upload a video. Another option is to provide the transcript as a downloadable resource.

Audio description allows you to provide the extra information needed by non-visual learners. Most commonly this involves a narrator explaining the important visual details in the pauses between speech or action. This can normally be done with video-editing software, although some authoring tools may have this capability in the video-editing options available within the tool.

It is also possible to provide audio description that includes the words spoken and a description of important visual details in an audio description track which is separate from the video.

Note: Although this standard allows you to provide either a transcript or an audio description, the additional standard **1.2.5 Audio Description (Prerecorded)**, which is a level AA standard, requires that you provide audio description for all prerecorded videos with sound. This effectively means that at level A you can provide either audio description or a transcript whereas at level AA you must provide audio description.

Accessibility experts strongly recommend that you provide a transcript for all videos with sound even if you also provide audio description. This is because a transcript benefits many more learners than just those with visual impairments. For example, providing descriptive transcripts is essential for deafblind learners who use refreshable braille displays and who may not be able to hear or see the content. It is also a requirement of the advanced standard **1.2.8 Media Alternative (Prerecorded)**.

How to conform

1 Provide either a text transcript or audio description for prerecorded videos with sound.

2 If the video contains interaction, make sure that a transcript contains the same functionality.

3 Make sure that any links to transcripts or separate audio description tracks are easy to find.

4 Make sure that the information provided in transcripts is in an accessible format.

Exceptions

- This standard applies unless the video is provided as an alternative for text and it is made clear to learners that this is the case.

- You do not need to meet this standard if all the information in the video is conveyed through spoken words, eg if the video is a 'talking head', ie someone talking directly to the camera.

- If the video involves someone delivering a presentation, this is also exempt, as long as the presenter explains all the visual information contained in the slides, eg images, charts or tables.

Why?

1 Learners who benefit from audio description include:

   o people who are blind or have low vision. They will be able to understand the video due to the important visual details given in addition to the spoken words;

   o people affected by situational impairments, eg someone who has a damaged mobile phone screen and cannot see the video but can listen to it instead.

2 Learners who benefit from descriptive text transcripts include:

   o people who are blind or have low vision and use screen readers to read out transcripts. Most screen reader users set their assistive technology so that it reads much faster than an average human speaking voice. Providing a transcript therefore allows them to access the content much faster than if they were listening to a video with audio description;

   o people who read transcripts converted to braille;

   o people who find it easier to read transcripts than watch videos, eg people with some cognitive impairments who may have difficulty perceiving or understanding moving images;

   o second-language learners who may find it helpful to read transcripts of video content;

   o people who prefer to read transcripts than watch videos in certain situations, eg students who download course video transcripts and use them as study aids.

Example

FIGURE 8.8   Auto-generated transcript link for video (CourseArc)

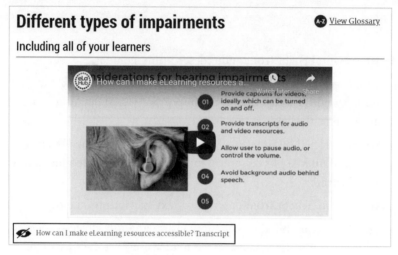

A video added to the CourseArc authoring tool which automatically generates a transcript link.
SOURCE Reproduced with permission of CourseArc

How to test

1 Check that videos with sound have either a text transcript or audio description.

2 Check that the text transcript or audio description contains all the visual details necessary for a non-visual learner to understand the video.

3 If the video contains interaction, check that a transcript contains the same functionality.

4 Make sure that links to transcripts, downloadable transcripts or separate audio description tracks are easy to find.

5 Make sure that the information provided in transcripts is in an accessible format.

Useful resources

• Captions, transcripts and audio descriptions[15]
A brief overview of captions, transcripts and audio description from WebAIM.

- Transcripts on the web[16]
  Best-practice guidelines on creating transcripts from uiAccess.
- Make it accessible – captions, subtitles and transcripts[17]
  Aston University Technology Enhanced Learning blog which includes a link to a tool that strips out timestamps from .srt files, which is useful for converting captions into a transcript.
- Inclusive Design Subject Matter Expert Series featuring Antoine Hunter.[18]
  An example of a video with audio description from Microsoft's Inclusive design toolkit
- The Ultimate Guide to Audio Description[19]
  A comprehensive guide to audio description from 3Play Media.
- 1.2.3 Audio Description or Media Alternative (Prerecorded) – Level A[20]
  W3C quick reference guide and further information for this standard.

1.2.4 Captions (Live) – Level AA

For live presentations with audio content such as webinars or lectures, provide synchronized captions, ie text which appears on screen at the same time as people speak.

Key information

Captions are needed so that people who are deaf or hard of hearing can understand live audio content in 'synchronized media', ie 'real-time' presentations. Live captions can be created manually in 'real time', ie at the same time as someone is speaking. This is normally a paid-for service and is done by a professional transcriber. Captions can also be automatically generated through artificial intelligence. Many video conferencing tools have the functionality to provide live captions either by allowing a live captioning service or by providing automatic captions.

Best practice for live captions is to identify who is speaking if there is more than one speaker and to identify any important sound effects such as a round of applause. For this reason, human transcribers are preferable to automatic captions, although the cost involved can be a barrier. Automatic captioning services have the advantage of being more cost effective or free, but they are not nearly as accurate as human transcribers. The accuracy of automatic captioning, however, is constantly improving with advances in technology.

Note: The advanced standard **1.2.9 Audio-only (Live)** recommends that you provide captions or an alternative such as a transcript for all live audio-only content such as podcasts, radio plays or speeches.

How to conform

If the eLearning resource allows you to provide live presentations with audio content, make sure that the content has synchronized captions.

Exception

- You do not need to provide live captions for two-way multimedia calls, eg for video conferencing calls.

Note: Live 'time-based media' is exempt from the UK Public Sector Bodies Accessibility Regulations.[21] This means that any live 'time-based media' in the UK public sector does not need synchronized captions to meet these requirements. 'Live is considered up to 14 days from when the content aired.'[22] After 14 days, however, the content is considered to be prerecorded and therefore needs to have captions under standard **1.2.2 Captions (Prerecorded)**.

Why?

Learners who benefit from captions include:

- people who are deaf or hard of hearing who can read the captions and have an equivalent experience to those listening to the content;
- people who may find it easier to read and listen to content at the same time, eg second-language learners;
- people affected by situational impairments, eg someone who is watching a webinar in an open-plan office but has no headphones.

How to test

Check that all live presentations with audio content have captions which appear at the same time as people are speaking.

Useful resources

- Real-time Captioning[23]
  WebAIM article on real-time captioning.
- Present Google slides with captions[24]
  An example of an automatic captioning service. Google Docs Help Centre article on presenting slides with captions.
- 1.2.4 Captions (Live) – Level AA[25]
  W3C quick reference guide and further information for this standard.

1.2.5 Audio Description (Prerecorded) – Level AA

Provide audio description for prerecorded videos that have sound. The audio description should give all the information non-visual learners need to understand the video. This could include the action taking place, the expressions of characters, scene changes, etc.

Key information

Learners who are blind or have low vision will be able to hear the words spoken in a video, but they won't be able to fully understand what is happening without additional background information. Audio description allows you to provide the extra information needed by non-visual learners. Most commonly this involves a narrator explaining the important visual details in the pauses between speech or action. This can normally be done with video-editing software, although some authoring tools may have this capability in the video-editing options available within the tool.

It is also possible to provide audio description that includes the words spoken and a description of important visual details in an audio description track which is separate from the video.

Note: Accessibility experts strongly recommend that you provide a transcript for all videos with sound even if you also provide audio description. This is because a transcript benefits many more learners than just those with visual impairments. It is also a recommendation of the advanced standard **1.2.8 Media Alternative (Prerecorded)**.

Another related advanced standard is **1.2.7 Extended Audio Description (Prerecorded)**. This recommends that if the pauses in the dialogue or action are not long enough to add visual information, these are manually extended or further pauses are added so that this information can be included. This means that the video content pauses temporarily while the narrator continues describing the important visual details.

How to conform

Provide audio description for prerecorded videos with sound.

Exceptions

- You do not need to meet this standard if all the information in the video is conveyed through spoken words, eg if the video is a 'talking head', ie someone talking directly to the camera.
- If the video involves someone delivering a presentation, this is also exempt, as long as the presenter explains all the visual information conveyed in the slides, eg images, charts or tables.

Why?

Learners who benefit from audio description include:

- people who are blind or have low vision. They will be able to understand the video due to the important visual details provided in addition to the spoken words;
- people affected by situational impairments, eg someone who has a damaged mobile phone screen and cannot see the video but can listen to the audio description instead.

How to test

1 Check that videos with sound have audio description.
2 Check that the audio description contains all the visual details necessary for non-visual learners to understand the video.
3 If the audio description is provided in a separate audio description track, make sure this is easy to find.

Useful resources

- Inclusive Design Subject Matter Expert Series featuring Antoine Hunter[26]
  An example of a video with audio description from Microsoft's inclusive design toolkit.
- Captions, Transcripts and Audio Descriptions[27]
  A brief overview of captions, transcripts and audio description from WebAIM.
- The Ultimate Guide to Audio Description[28]
  A comprehensive guide to audio description from 3Play Media.
- 1.2.5 Audio Description (Prerecorded) – Level AA[29]
  W3C quick reference guide and further information for this standard.

1.3.1 Info and Relationships – Level A

Make sure that assistive technology can interpret structures such as headings, lists, tables, input fields and page regions. This is normally done through the underlying code of the tool. If this isn't possible, use text to give the same information.

Key information

Learners often use visual cues to recognize structures such as headings, lists, tables, input fields and regions such as headers on a page. For example:

- Headings are shown using a larger font, spacing around the text and sometimes a different colour.
- Lists are shown using bullets or numbering.
- Input fields such as radio buttons have a label and are grouped together.
- Tables are shown using a grid. The information inside them is made easier to process and understand by using column and row headers.
- Header and footer regions are clearly visually distinct on a page and are separate from the main content.

If learners use assistive technology such as screen readers, the information which would normally be conveyed by visual cues needs to be communicated in other ways. This is often 'programmatically determined', ie achieved through the underlying code of the authoring tool using HTML markup elements. For example:

- Links use <a>.

- Headings use <h1> to <h6>.

- Lists use <ul> for unordered lists which display bullet points and <ol> for ordered lists which display numbers.

- Input fields such as radio buttons are given meaning and grouped using <fieldset> and <legend>.

- Tables use <table> and <th> for headers, <tr> for rows and <td> for cells.

- Page regions use elements such as <header> for the header section of a page, <nav> for a navigation menu and <main> to identify the main content of the page.

Some authoring tools automatically create accessible output if you use the correct inbuilt styles. For example, if you use the tool's bulleted list style, the underlying code of the tool includes the HTML element <ul> which tells assistive technology users that the information is presented in an unordered list. Another example is when you use the tool's automatic table style and the underlying code of the tool tells assistive technology users that the information on the page is presented in a tabular format. In the case of tables, you may also need to mark column and row headers to make it clear for assistive technology how to interpret the data in the table.

If your authoring tool is not coded so that assistive technology can interpret structures, you can provide the equivalent information in text. For example, if your authoring tool doesn't allow assistive technology to recognize and announce the headings in tables, you could provide a detailed text description of a table explaining the key points.

Best practice for heading levels

Many tools allow you to assign heading levels. Often these start at level 1 for the most important heading on the page and go through to level 6. If this is the case, make sure you use the headings in a logical hierarchical order.

An example of a best-practice hierarchical heading level structure is:

```
<h1>Main heading</h1>
    <h2>Sub-heading of h1</h2>
    <h2>Sub-heading of h1</h2>
        <h3>Sub-heading of h2</h3>
    <h2>Sub-heading of h1</h2>
        <h3>Sub-heading of h2</h3>
            <h4>Sub-heading of h3</h4>
    <h2>Sub-heading of h1</h2>
    <h2>Sub-heading of h1</h2>
```

Best practice is to have one heading level 1 on a page. The <h1> is important for assistive technology users because it essentially indicates where the main content starts.

The visual appearance of heading levels is also important if these can be modified by the content author. The size of the font is an important cue for visual learners and should follow a hierarchical structure. A heading level 3, for example, should not have a bigger font than a heading level 2.

How to conform

1 Make sure that assistive technology can interpret structures such as headings, lists, input fields, tables and page regions.
2 If your tool does not provide accessible code which can be interpreted by assistive technology, give this information in text format.

Why?

Learners who benefit from this standard include:

• people who use assistive technology and can correctly interpret structures;
• people who use assistive technology and will benefit from text which explains the purpose of any items or structures that can't be correctly interpreted by assistive technology due to tool limitations.

Examples

FIGURE 8.9   HTML source code for an unordered list (Xerte Online Toolkits)

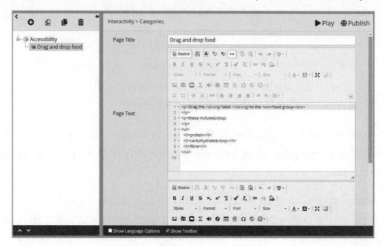

The source code option in Xerte Online Toolkits. This shows that by selecting the bulleted list option from the formatting menu, this automatically assigns the correct underlying code <ul> and <li> which tells assistive technology that the text is a bulleted list.

SOURCE Reproduced with permission of The Xerte Project

FIGURE 8.10   Assign table header properties (CourseArc)

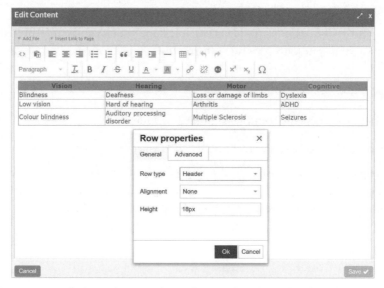

In the CourseArc authoring tool you can change the row properties to identify the header row in a table. This adds the correct HTML markup to the underlying code, which allows assistive technology to identify that the top row contains the column headings. This then allows screen readers to correctly interpret and voice the information in the table.

SOURCE Reproduced with permission of CourseArc

How to test

Check that a screen reader can interpret structures such as headings, lists, tables, input fields and page regions. If this is not the case, check that the same information is conveyed using text.

Note: This interpretation covers the basic requirements of this standard. As it also includes more detailed coding requirements, however, it is advisable to check that the eLearning resource conforms to all requirements of this standard with the support of an accessibility expert. Another option is to check with your authoring tool provider that the output of the tool conforms to this standard.

Useful resources

- Introduction to HTML[30]
  Introduction to the basics of HTML from MDN web docs.

- Web Accessibility Tutorials – Page Structure Concepts[31]
  Guidance from W3C on page structure concepts including page regions, labelling regions, headings and content structure.

- Semantic Structure: Regions, Headings, and Lists[32]
  Guidance from WebAIM on semantic structure, including regions, headings and lists.

- ARIA11: Using ARIA landmarks to identify regions of a page[33]
  Guidance from W3C Working Group on how to use ARIA landmarks to identify regions of a page.

- A First Review of Web Accessibility – Headings[34]
  Information from W3C about correct heading level hierarchy.

- Government Digital Service WCAG 2.1 Primer – 1.3.1. Info and relationships (A)[35]
  Information from the GDS about HTML requirements and common errors relating to this standard.

- 1.3.1 Info and Relationships – Level A[36]
  W3C quick reference guide and further information for this standard.

1.3.2 Meaningful Sequence – Level A

Make sure that all content which adds meaning in the eLearning resource is structured in a logical linear order so that it makes sense and is easy to navigate for assistive technology users.

Key information

When visual learners read a page, they can choose to view the content in any order that suits them. Very few people read an online page word by word, but instead use skimming and scanning skills to move around the page and find the content they want. Assistive technology, however, works by moving through content in a linear order. For English content the order begins in the top right-hand corner and moves down the page until it finishes in the bottom right. This is called the 'reading order' and is the order in which screen readers voice the content of a page.

If we think about the content on a typical eLearning resource page, a logical order could begin with a heading, then move to some introductory text. This could be followed by a subheading and a paragraph of body text and then maybe an image to illustrate an important learning point. The content order could then finish with navigation controls such as the 'Next' button, which allows learners to move on in the resource. Imagine how confusing and disorientating it would be if a screen reader read the body text first, then the heading text and then the subheading. Another common issue occurs when screen readers announce the alternative text for an image before the screen reader has read out the text. This means that learners have no context for the image or understanding of why it has been used when it is announced.

Authoring tools have various ways to make sure that content is ordered correctly and tool providers should give instructions on how this is possible. With some tools, just placing objects in the correct visual order on the page ensures that they have the correct reading order. Other authoring tools require you to take further action. Some common methods to ensure a correct reading order include:

1   Setting the correct focus or tab order for objects on a page.

2   Layering the objects on a page in the correct order.

3   Placing content blocks in the right order on the page.

How to conform

Make sure that content which adds meaning follows a logical linear reading order.

Why?

Learners who benefit from a logical reading order include:

- people who are blind or have low vision and use screen readers to voice content or convert it to braille;

- people who have cognitive impairments and may find it easier to access information using a screen reader rather than reading the content.

Examples

FIGURE 8.11   Set the correct focus order (Articulate Storyline)

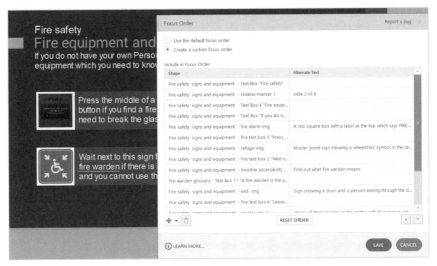

In the Articulate Storyline authoring tool the items you add to a slide automatically appear in the Focus Order list. The items appear in the order you add them to the page. You often need to create a custom focus order so you can rearrange the items so that they are announced in a logical order by a screen reader.

FIGURE 8.12   Place content blocks in the correct order (CourseArc)

In the CourseArc authoring tool content blocks must be placed in the correct sequence to make sure that the reading order is correct. This example shows how a text block is placed before an image block so that screen reader users receive some context from the text about the refreshable braille display before the alternative text for the image is announced.
SOURCE Reproduced with permission of CourseArc

How to test

Use a screen reader to voice all the content in the eLearning resource and check that it follows a logical linear reading order which makes sense.

Useful resources

- Designing for screen reader compatibility[37]
  WebAIM review of how screen readers work.

- What is the visual reading order?[38]
  CourseArc explanation of reading order for authoring tools which use content blocks.

- 1.3.2 Meaningful Sequence – Level A[39]
  W3C quick reference guide and further information for this standard.

1.3.3 Sensory Characteristics – Level A

Make sure that instructions and information do not rely only on visual cues such as shape, colour, size or location. Also make sure that instructions and information do not rely only on auditory cues, such as sounds to tell learners if they have made a mistake.

Key information

Clear and straightforward instructions are vital to the success of eLearning resources. If instructions rely only on one sense, such as vision or hearing, however, they exclude many learners. One of the best ways to make sense of this standard is to consider some examples which would cause issues and to explore why this is the case:

- **Colour.** 'Select the green option to continue.' This would cause a problem for someone who has a form of colour blindness which means that they cannot distinguish the colour green.

- **Visual location.** 'Select the button to the left of this paragraph to find out more.' This would cause a problem for someone with a visual impairment who could not see where the button was positioned on a page. A screen reader would announce where the button was depending on where it was positioned in the order of content on the page. Someone using a screen magnifier who was able to view only a portion of the page at a time could also have difficulty finding the button based on this instruction.

- **Shape.** 'Select the lozenge to see further options.' This could cause a problem for learners who may not understand what the shape described is. Even shapes which may be considered standard, such as a circle or a square, may not be easily recognized by people with cognitive impairments which affect visual perception. Instructions which tell learners how to respond to quiz questions with radio buttons or check boxes can be problematic in eLearning resources because content authors assume that learners can recognize shapes and understand what they mean. Some content authors assume that because radio buttons are generally round, learners will be able to recognize this and will know that only one correct option can be selected. A similar assumption is that learners will be able to recognize that because check boxes are generally square learners will know that multiple options can be selected. Not all learners, however, will be aware of these conventions nor will all be able to recognize the shape of the radio button or check box. As a result it is essential to be clear in instructions how many answer options learners need to select.

- **Sounds.** A chime sound to indicate that a section is complete. This would cause a problem for someone who was deaf or hard of hearing and could not hear the sound and so would not realize that they had completed the section.

Note: The purpose of this standard is not to discourage content authors from using visual or auditory cues, as these can be very helpful for learners. It just requires that they are not used alone. They need to be supplemented by other information so that they are inclusive for all learners.

How to conform

Avoid using instructions which rely only on visual or auditory cues. The best way to achieve this is to give learners more than one way to understand the instruction. For example:

- 'Select "More information" in the bottom right-hand corner of the slide to find out more about how our customers apply for a loan.' This instruction tells learners where the button is located, but it also gives the text description of the button, ie 'More information', so a screen reader user will also be able to recognize it.

- 'If you fill in a field incorrectly you will receive a red warning message and hear a warning sound.' This instruction shows how an auditory cue, ie the warning sound, can be supplemented with a visual clue, ie the warning message, so that learners with a hearing impairment can still make sense of the instruction.

Note: Since it is commonly understood that 'above' refers to content before and 'below' refers to content after, you can use 'above' and 'below' in instructions as long as the reading order of the page is correct. For example, if an instruction reads 'Select one of the options below', a screen reader user would understand that the options they need to select will be announced directly after the instruction they have just heard.

Why?

Learners who benefit from this standard include:

- people who are blind or have low vision and use screen readers. They will not be able to follow an instruction if it refers only to the visual location of something on a page;

- people who have low vision and use screen magnifiers. They can struggle to follow an instruction if it refers only to the location of something on a page as they typically view only a portion of the page at a time;

- people who are colour blind and have difficulty distinguishing certain colours;

- people who have cognitive impairments and may benefit from having textual as well as visual cues to make it easier for them to follow instructions;

- people who are deaf or hard of hearing and will not be able to understand instructions if they are based only on auditory cues.

How to test

1 Check that the eLearning resource contains no instructions or information which rely only on visual cues such as shape, colour, size or visual location to be understood.

2 Check that the eLearning resource contains no instructions or information which rely only on sound to be understood.

Useful resources

- Standards for Writing Accessibly[40]
  Article from A List Apart including guidance on how to write chronologically, not spatially.

- 1.3.3 Sensory Characteristics – Level A[41]
  W3C quick reference guide and further information for this standard.

1.3.4 Orientation – Level AA

Added in 2.1

Make sure that learners can choose either portrait or landscape view, ie either vertical or horizontal view, for the eLearning resource.

Key information

This standard helps learners with low vision who need to be able to enlarge the text and choose which orientation best supports this. It is also important for learners who may have their device mounted on a fixed holder, for example on a mobility aid such as a wheelchair. This can make it difficult or impossible to change the orientation of the device.

Some authoring tools allow the author to set and restrict the screen to either portrait or landscape view. This should be avoided unless a particular orientation is essential.

How to conform

Choose settings in the eLearning authoring tool which allow learners to view the resource in either portrait or landscape view.

Exception

- This standard applies unless a particular orientation is essential, eg for a simulated piano keyboard. This would need to be viewed in landscape view in order to simulate a real piano keyboard. Another example is a simulation which uses virtual reality.

Why?

Learners who benefit from this standard include:

- people who have low vision and need to be able to enlarge the text. They will be able to choose the orientation that works best for them, eg viewing the resource in landscape may make it easier to see the content when the text is enlarged;

- people who have devices mounted on fixed holders who cannot change the orientation of their device. They will be able to view the content using the orientation dictated by their device.

How to test

Check that the eLearning resource can be viewed in either portrait or landscape view.

Useful resources

- 1.3.4 Orientation – Level AA[42]
  W3C quick reference guide and further information for this standard.

1.3.5 Identify Input Purpose – Level AA

Added in 2.1

Make sure that any input fields which collect personal data are correctly coded so that assistive technology users can understand the purpose of those fields.

Key information

This standard applies only to input fields that collect certain types of personal data. These are listed in the W3C Input Purposes for User Interface Components list, which can be found in the Useful links section.

The purpose of this standard is to make sure that assistive technology can understand and convey what information needs to be entered into input fields that collect personal data. This needs to be programmatically determined, ie achieved through the underlying code of the authoring tool. Using the autocomplete attribute is the most supported way of meeting this standard. For example, the code for a field which collects a learner's first name would be as follows:

```
<label for="fname">First Name</label>
<input id="fname" type="text" autocomplete="given-name" ... >
```

Using the autocomplete attribute is important for learners with cognitive impairments who may struggle to process what information is required for a field. If the autocomplete attribute is used, these learners can use a browser plugin to replace the labels of the input fields with icons or other symbols. For example, the 'Date of Birth' label could be replaced with a symbol of a birthday cake.

Note: Although using the autocomplete attribute is the most supported way of achieving this standard, ensuring that learners can autocomplete these fields is not a requirement. If, for example, content authors wanted to disable the autocomplete functionality due to security concerns, this would be acceptable.

How to conform

Make sure that any input fields that collect personal data and qualify for this standard are correctly coded so that assistive technology users can understand the purpose of those fields.

Exceptions

- Any fields that collect personal data but are not in the W3C Input Purposes for User Interface Components list are exempt.
- The standard applies only if the underlying code of the tool supports this functionality.

Why?

Learners who benefit from this standard include:

- people who are blind or have low vision and use screen readers. They will be able to understand the purpose of input fields and how to fill them in correctly;
- people with cognitive impairments who may find it easier to replace text labels with icons or symbols to aid comprehension.

How to test

Check the underlying code to make sure that any input fields that collect personal data and qualify for this standard are correctly coded. If this is not possible, another option is to test this standard with the support of an accessibility expert, or to check with your authoring tool provider that the output of the tool conforms to this standard.

Useful resources

- Input Purposes for User Interface Components[43]
  List of applicable input purposes for interface components from W3C.

- Using HTML 5.2 autocomplete attributes[44]
  Information on using autocomplete attributes from W3C.

- How to turn off form autocompletion[45]
  Information from MDN web docs about how to disable the autocomplete function for a form.

- 1.3.5 Identify Input Purpose – Level AA[46]
  W3C quick reference guide and further information for this standard.

1.4.1 Use of Color – Level A

Make sure you use devices such as icons, patterns, formatting or text to supplement colour in the eLearning resource. You need to do this when you are giving learners information or explaining what action they need to take. It's also important when you are asking learners for a response to a question or when they need to see a visual element clearly such as the lines in a graph or links.

Key information

If you use only colour to communicate information, there is a risk that learners who are colour blind or have other difficulties perceiving colour may not understand what you are trying to convey. While many people are aware that red and green can cause problems, different forms of colour blindness affect a whole range of colours, including reds, greens, oranges, browns, purples, pinks, greys and blacks. This makes using colour alone to convey meaning problematic. Some common eLearning colour issue examples include:

- **Giving information.** Using very similar colours next to each other on a bar chart, eg showing UK sales in dark blue and US sales in dark purple.

- **Explaining what action learners need to take.** Showing that a topic in an eLearning module has been completed and the next topic can be started by changing the colour of a progress bar from amber to green. Another common example is using colour alone to show a link.

- **Giving feedback.** Showing that an answer given in a quiz is not correct by changing the text colour of the incorrect answer to red.

- **Asking learners to identify a visual element.** Distinguishing the lines on a graph by using only different coloured lines and not supplementing this with text.

How to conform

Always use additional methods to supplement the information conveyed by colour. For example:

- Use icons and text as well as colour to show if an answer is correct.

- Use pattern as well as colour on a chart. If the chart is a bar chart, good practice is also to use white space between the bars to make them easier to distinguish.

- Use a key or a text explanation to explain the meaning of a complex diagram which conveys information using colour.

- Use underlining as well as a different colour to show links.

Why?

Learners who benefit from this standard include:

- people who are colour blind. Colour blindness affects approximately 1 in 12 men (8%) and 1 in 200 women (0.5%) worldwide;[47]

- some older people, many of whom find it difficult to distinguish colour;
- people affected by situational impairments, eg learners who may be using limited colour or monochrome displays;
- people from different cultures who may associate colours with a different meaning. For example, while red for many people signifies an error, in some cultures it symbolizes good luck, celebration and happiness.

Example

FIGURE 8.13   Quiz feedback supplemented with icons and text (iSpring)

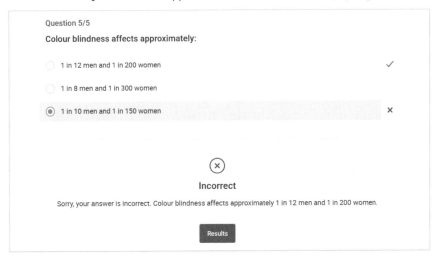

Quiz feedback in an eLearning resource created using the iSpring authoring tool. If the slide is viewed in colour, the tick icon next to the correct answer is green and the cross icon next to the incorrect answer is red. Learners can still understand which answers are correct and incorrect even if the slide is viewed in greyscale due to the cross and tick icons which have been used to supplement colour. This would not be the case, however, if the text of the correct answer changed to green and the text of the incorrect answer changed to red. Learners are given a further indication that their answer is not correct by the word 'Incorrect' which appears at the bottom of the feedback.
SOURCE Reproduced with permission of www.ispringsolutions.com (archived at https://perma.cc/2ZPC-5EAP)

How to test

Use a colour blind simulator or your screen display settings to change the eLearning resource to greyscale, then check that you can still understand all the content and follow all instructions.

Useful resources

- Types of colour blindness[48]
  Overview of the different types of colour blindness from Colour Blind
  Awareness.

- Improving the color accessibility for colour blind users[49]
  Article from *Smashing* magazine with many useful examples.

- Coblis colour blind simulator[50]
  Upload an image to see how it would look to people who have different
  types of colour blindness.

- NoCoffee vision simulator[51]
  Chrome extension which simulates different types of visual
  impairments, including colour blindness.

- 1.4.1 Use of Color – Level A[52]
  W3C quick reference guide and further information for this standard.

1.4.2 Audio Control – Level A

For any audio content in the eLearning resource which starts automatically
and lasts longer than three seconds, make sure that learners can pause or
stop the audio. Another option is to allow them to adjust the volume, but
this must be with a control that does not affect the overall volume of the rest
of the audio content in the eLearning resource.

Key information

This standard benefits people who use screen readers to voice the eLearning
content. If the resource contains other audio content such as a narrator
reading out the on screen text or the audio track of a video, this can interfere
with the output of the screen reader. This is why learners need to be able to
pause or stop the audio, or control the volume if it starts automatically and
lasts longer than three seconds. The volume control needs to be independent
of the normal audio control of the device which is being used. If it is not,

when screen reader users turn down the volume of the eLearning audio content, they will also turn down the volume of the screen reader.

Although it is not a requirement, this standard also recommends that any audio content in the eLearning resource does not start automatically ie does not 'autoplay'. This can be an issue for all learners, but it can be particularly distracting and even upsetting for learners with cognitive impairments such as autism spectrum disorder. Audio content which starts automatically presents further issues for screen reader users. If audio starts automatically it may play at the same time as the screen reader output. This can make it very difficult for the screen reader user to hear instructions on how to control or stop the audio playing in the eLearning resource. It is far better to design the play interaction so that learners have to start rather than stop any audio playing.

How to conform

1 Provide controls which let learners pause or stop any audio tracks or videos with sound which start automatically and last longer than three seconds. These could be inbuilt controls provided by your authoring tool or manual controls which you add to the resource.

2 Another option is to provide controls that let learners change the volume, including turning it down to zero. These controls must be independent of the normal audio controls in the system that learners are using.

3 Make sure that the pause or stop functionality or volume control you provide can be controlled by a keyboard as well as a mouse.

Why?

Learners who benefit from this standard include:

- people who are blind or have low vision and use screen readers. They will be able to stop the audio content or control the volume so that it does not interfere with their screen reader output;

- people with cognitive impairments who may find it difficult to concentrate on visual content when audio is playing benefit from being able to control the volume in a video with sound;

- people with cognitive impairments who may be sensitive to sound and unexpected events benefit from the recommendation to avoid content that autoplays;

- all learners benefit from the recommendation to avoid autoplaying content as this is poor user experience for everyone.

How to test

Check that you can pause, stop or control the volume for all audio content and videos with sound which start automatically and last longer than three seconds in the eLearning resource.

Useful resources

- Why Autoplay Is an Accessibility No-No[53]
  Article from the Bureau of Internet Accessibility.

- 1.4.2 Audio Control – Level A[54]
  W3C quick reference guide and further information for this standard.

1.4.3 Contrast (Minimum) – Level AA

For any text and the background it appears on, choose colours that have a contrast ratio of at least 4.5:1. This applies to 'normal' size text which W3C defines as 17 point or smaller for regular text and 13 point or smaller for bold text. 'Large' text, ie 18 point or larger for regular text and 14 point or larger for bold text, has a contrast ratio requirement of at least 3:1.

Key information

This standard is important for all visual learners, but it is vital for those who have low vision or who are colour blind. Contrast ratio is a measure of the difference between the brightness (or luminance) of two colours and is given as a value ranging from 1 to 21. White text on a white background has a contrast ratio of 1:1 for example, while black text on a white background has a contrast ratio of 21:1. The minimum WCAG contrast ratio for 'normal' size text and the background it appears on is 4.5:1 and applies both to text and images of text.

Authoring tools usually give colour values for text and background in the formatting options. If this functionality isn't available, you can use an online colour picking tool to find out the values. Once you know the values of the colours used, check contrast ratios using an online contrast checker. You will normally need to input the value of each colour using either:

- RGB (Red, Green, Blue) values, eg 0, 85, 125;
- Hex (Hexadecimal) or HTML values, eg #00557D;
- HSL (Hue, Saturation, Lightness) values, eg 199, 100%, 25%.

Contrast checkers give you the contrast ratio and let you know if your colour choices pass or fail WCAG standards. A good contrast checker will also have lightness sliders which allow you to darken or lighten the colours you have input until they pass WCAG requirements.

Note: The advanced standard **1.4.6 Contrast (Enhanced)** recommends that any text and the background it appears on has a contrast ratio of at least 7:1 for 'normal' size text and 4.5:1 for 'large' text. Another related requirement is standard **1.4.11 Non-text Contrast**. This refers to the contrast ratio between interactive items and visual elements essential to understanding such as the lines on a graph and the background they appear on or items they appear next to. The standard requires a contrast ratio of at least 3:1 for these items.

How to conform

1 For 'normal' size text, ie 17 point or smaller for regular text and 13 point or smaller for bold text, choose colours that have a contrast ratio of at least 4.5:1.

2 For 'large' text, ie 18 point or larger for regular text and 14 point or larger for bold text, choose colours that have a contrast ratio of at least 3:1.

3 This contrast ratio applies to any text in the eLearning resource, including body text, text in menus and sidebars.

4 This contrast ratio also applies to any text which appears in an image if it is essential for learners to be able to see it clearly so that they can understand what is being conveyed. For example, if the eLearning resource contains an image of a doctor's medical identity badge and learners need to be able to read the role of the doctor on the badge, the text and background have to comply to this standard.

Exceptions

The following text items have no contrast requirements:

- Text in any interactive item which is not active, eg a disabled 'Back' button.

- Text which is for decoration, eg an image which shows an extract of a legal document used to decorate a page rather than add meaning to it.

- Text which appears in an image but is not necessary to read due to other important visual content. For example, if a quiz question asked a learner to identify a hospital worker's role based on the uniform they were wearing, the text in an identity tag within the image would be exempt as learners would not need to be able to read it in order to answer the question.

- Text that is deliberately not visible. For example, text which is added to a resource to describe an image but which is included only for screen reader users and is not intended to be visible to visual learners.

- Text that is included in a logo or a brand name.

Other considerations

The following considerations are not specifically mentioned by this standard but are important for eLearning resources:

- As long as the contrast ratio on outline or halo effects is 4.5:1 the text will meet the requirements of this standard. Even if they do comply, however, these effects often make it difficult for people to read text.

- Using effects on backgrounds, such as using a background image, or a transparency or colour gradient, can also make it difficult to read text. There are contrast checkers which allow you to check text against a background image, or you can use a colour picker to test an area where the contrast is lowest.

- A common issue in eLearning resources is the contrast ratio between the text and the background colour on interactive items such as buttons. While content authors often check the contrast ratio for the 'Normal' state of the button, this must also be checked on all the other active states such as 'Hover'. Sometimes inbuilt buttons with default colour choices do not automatically meet this standard which means that the text or background colour needs to be adjusted.

Why?

Learners who benefit from good contrast include:

- people with low vision or who are colour blind and have difficulty reading text which doesn't have sufficient colour contrast with its background;

- some older people who commonly find it difficult to distinguish colour and need strong contrast to make it easier to read content;

- people with temporary visual impairments, eg someone who has been looking at a screen for a long time and has eye strain;

- people affected by situational impairments, eg someone using a device in bright sunlight or someone using an older display monitor with poor colour contrast.

Example

FIGURE 8.14   Contrast ratio on inbuilt button states (Articulate Storyline)

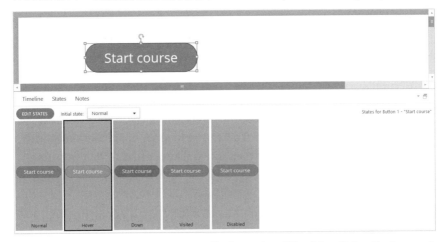

Ensuring a good contrast ratio between text and background on all the states of interactive items such as buttons is an important consideration in eLearning resources. For example, it is essential to check all the automatically created active states for inbuilt buttons. The contrast ratio for the 'Hover' state for this inbuilt button created using the Articulate Storyline tool fails the requirements of this standard which means that the text or background colour needs to be adjusted.

How to test

Use a colour contrast checker to check that the contrast ratio for the colours of the text and the background it appears on is at least 4.5:1 for 'normal' size text and 3:1 for 'large' text.

Useful resources

- Contrast and Color Accessibility[55]
  WebAIM guidance on WCAG contrast and colour requirements.

- Dyslexia friendly style guide[56]
  A style guide from the British Dyslexia Association which contains colour recommendations for learners with dyslexia.

- Colorcop colour picking tool[57]
  An example of a free colour picking tool for Windows. You can use the eyedropper to analyse the value of any colour used in your eLearning resource.

- WebAIM colour contrast checker[58]
  One of the most commonly used colour contrast checkers which shows whether colour choices pass or fail all WCAG criteria. It also has 'lightness sliders' which allow you to adjust colours until they meet requirements.

- Text on background image a11y (accessibility) check[59]
  An example of a tool which allows you to check the colour contrast ratio of text against an image. You can upload an image, set the colour and font size for the text and then move the text to different positions on the image to check whether it complies with WCAG requirements.

- 1.4.3 Contrast (Minimum) – Level AA[60]
  W3C quick reference guide and further information for this standard.

1.4.4 Resize Text – Level AA

Make sure that visual learners can enlarge the text up to 200% and still carry out all the functions on a page and see all its content. They should be able to do this with standard functionality, such as using a browser to zoom in, as well as with assistive technology.

Key information

Although visual learners benefit from being able to enlarge all content on a page, this standard refers specifically to text, since it is most critical for understanding. In some authoring tools this standard is achievable by default. In others you may need to adjust tool settings to ensure that the text in your eLearning resource can be enlarged to 200% without loss of functionality or content. Some authoring tools allow you to choose a publishing setting which locks the eLearning resource display to a particular size. This should be avoided as it prevents learners from being able to resize text.

Note: A similar standard **1.4.10 Reflow** was added to the WCAG in version 2.1. It requires that when learners resize content up to 400% using browser zoom, the content reflows so that horizontal scrolling is not needed. Visual learners should still be able to carry out all the functions of the page and see all its content without having to use both horizontal and vertical scroll bars.

How to conform

Make sure that you can enlarge the text in your eLearning resource by 200% using browser zoom, and that you can still carry out all the functions on a page and see all its content.

Exceptions

- Captions are exempt since they are often created to a fixed size.
- Text within images is exempt as it does not scale very well and often pixelates and becomes difficult to read.

Why?

Learners who benefit from this standard include:

- people with low vision who have difficulty reading small text;
- some older people who are often farsighted and have difficulty focusing on nearby objects and text;

- people with temporary visual impairments, eg someone who suffers from an allergy such as hay fever which affects their vision;

- people affected by situational impairments, eg someone who has lost their reading glasses.

How to test

Use the zoom function in a web browser to check that you can enlarge the text in your eLearning resource up to 200% without loss of content or functionality.

Useful resources

- 1.4.4 Resize Text – Level AA[61]
  W3C quick reference guide and further information for this standard.

1.4.5 Images of Text – Level AA

Use onscreen text rather than images of text to convey information as long as the authoring tool allows you to achieve the visual presentation you need. This standard applies unless learners can customize the text in the image or the visual presentation of the text is essential such as an image of a logo.

Key information

'Images of text' refer to text which is presented inside an image. This means it is added to the eLearning resource in an image format (eg JPEG, GIF, PNG) rather than by using the text functionality of the tool. Examples of text added as an image could include:

- a Venn diagram which contains text;

- headings added as images due to a particular decorative styling;

- an image of an email which contains text which is essential for learners to read;
- a quote on a decorative background;
- an infographic which contains important information in text.

Images of text cause a range of issues for learners with different types of impairments. One of the most important is that they prevent learners from customizing the text. The ability to customize text such as changing the font size, font or background colour, line spacing or alignment is important for learners with cognitive impairments such as dyslexia and for learners with low vision. Another issue which impacts learners with low vision who enlarge the text using browser settings or screen magnifiers, is that when text in an image is enlarged it often becomes pixelated and difficult to read. A final issue is that screen readers are not able to read out text which has been added as an image.

Note: The W3C definition of 'images of text' does not include text that is part of an image that 'contains significant other visual content'. Examples of such images include graphs, screenshots and diagrams which visually convey important information through more than just text.

How to conform

Use the text functionality of the authoring tool to add text rather than adding text as an image.

Exceptions

- If learners can customize the text in the image, eg change the font, size or colour, then the text is exempt.
- If the image is used only for decoration and understanding any text in the image is not important to the meaning of the content, eg an image of a historical letter used for decoration.
- If it is essential for the author to use a visual representation of the text which the text functionality of the authoring tool cannot achieve, this is exempt. For example, if an eLearning resource on graphic design needed to show an example of the Tahoma font but this was not an available font option in the authoring tool, using an image of text in the Tahoma font would be acceptable.

- If the image of text is part of a logo or brand identity, this is exempt as long as the text is made available in alternative text.

Note: The condition that images of text can be used if they are 'essential' means that this standard can sometimes be open to interpretation due to differing opinions about what is considered 'essential'. A pragmatic approach is to avoid images of text wherever possible. If an image is 'essential' and it is not possible to avoid using it, then provide any textual information conveyed in it by adding a descriptive text alternative. This could be provided by linking to the text description in an alternative location, or by adding it underneath the image etc.

Why?

Learners who benefit from this standard include:

- people who are blind or have low vision and use a screen reader to voice text or convert it to braille. Screen readers cannot recognize text within an image;
- people with low vision or cognitive impairments such as dyslexia who may find it easier to understand text if they can customise the font, size, background colour or spacing;
- people with cognitive impairments such as visual tracking problems who benefit from being able to adjust text alignment or the spacing between text;
- people affected by situational impairments, eg someone with a slow or unreliable internet connection. If a browser doesn't show or download images they will miss any information which is conveyed by using text in an image.

Example

FIGURE 8.15   Text added as an image (Evolve)

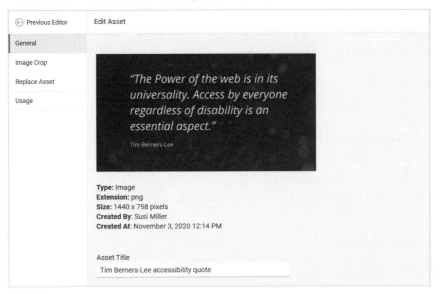

An example of text added as a PNG (Portable Network Graphics) using the Evolve authoring tool. This is a common practice in eLearning resources but causes issues both for screen reader users and for visual learners who rely on enlarging text as text added as an image can become pixelated and difficult to read when it is enlarged.
SOURCE Reproduced with permission of Intellum UK Limited

How to test

Check that no text in the eLearning resource has been added as an image unless learners are able to customize this text or adding the text as an image is essential. If it is essential to add text as an image, such as for a logo, make sure you provide alternative text so that it can be voiced by a screen reader.

Useful resources

- Images of Text[62]
  Web accessibility tutorial on images of text from the Web Accessibility Initiative.
- Why is it important for accessibility to use actual text instead of images of text?[63]
  Article on the importance of using text instead of an image of text from the Bureau of Internet Accessibility.

- 1.4.5 Images of Text – Level AA[64]
  W3C quick reference guide and further information for this standard.

1.4.10 Reflow – Level AA

Added in 2.1

Make sure that when eLearning resources are enlarged to 400% using browser zoom, the content reflows so that horizontal scrolling is not needed. Visual learners should still be able to carry out all the functions of the page and see all its content without having to use a horizontal scroll bar.

Key information

Reflow is one of the main principles of responsive design which allows pages to adapt to any screen size or device. Reflow refers to how the content on a page is presented differently when the size of the window in which it is displayed changes or when the content is enlarged using browser zoom. If content doesn't reflow when it is zoomed, learners have to use horizontal scroll bars to read the end of each line of text. As well as being awkward and time consuming, this often leads to problems such as learners losing their place when they return to the left margin of a page after scrolling to the right. Another common issue is learners missing navigation items because they can only be seen when the horizontal toolbar is used to scroll to the right of the page.

How to conform

Make sure that when learners resize content up to 400% (four times the default width and four times the default height) using browser zoom, the content reflows so that visual learners can carry out all the functions of the page and see all its content without having to use a horizontal scroll bar.

Exception

- Any content such as images and data tables which would not make sense if it was reflowed is exempt. For example, complex images such as maps, diagrams or tables cannot be reflowed as they would not make sense if the content was 'cut up' and vertically presented in one column. In this case, horizontal and vertical scroll bars are allowed.

Why?

Learners who benefit from this standard include:

- people with low vision who benefit from enlarging text. In addition to being able to see the text clearly, these learners need to be able to 'track', ie follow along lines of text and find navigation items;
- people with cognitive impairments which affect concentration who may find it difficult to use horizontal scroll bars and track text or to find navigation items;
- people with motor impairments who may find it difficult and even painful to repeatedly use scroll bars in order to fully access content;
- all learners, as using horizontal scrollbars to read text which does not reflow is a poor user experience for everyone.

How to test

Test the eLearning resource on a browser with the display set to 1280 pixels wide. Enlarge the resource to 400% using browser zoom functionality. Check that content reflows into a single column, that no text or interactive items are lost, and that this does not cause a horizontal scroll bar to appear.

Useful resources

- Responsive web design basics[65]
  Article from web.dev with information on how to create sites which respond to the needs and capabilities of the device they are viewed on.
- 1.4.10 Reflow – Level AA[66]
  W3C quick reference guide and further information for this standard.

1.4.11 Non-Text Contrast – Level AA

Added in 2.1

For interactive items choose colours which have a contrast ratio of at least 3:1 against the colour of the background they appear on, or items they appear next to. This also applies to important visual elements essential to understanding such as the lines in a graph.

Key information

This standard is important for all visual learners, but it is vital for those who have low vision or who are colour blind. Contrast ratio is a measure of the difference between the brightness (or luminance) of two colours and is given as a value ranging from 1 to 21. White items on a white background have a contrast ratio of 1:1, for example, while black items on a white background have a contrast ratio of 21:1. The minimum WCAG contrast ratio for this standard is 3:1.

W3C divides the items to which this standard applies into two categories, 'User Interface Components' and 'Graphical Objects'.

- **User Interface Components.** This refers to all interactive items such as navigation items, input items and links and their different states. It also applies to visual focus indicators which show when interactive items have focus. To pass this standard these items need to have a contrast ratio of at least 3:1 against both the colour that they appear on and colours that they appear next to. For example, link text which appears in a paragraph of text needs to have a contrast ratio of at least 3:1 against the background colour of the page and against the rest of the text in the paragraph.

- **Graphical Objects.** This refers to important visual elements which are essential for understanding such as the lines in a graph or the bars in a bar chart. It also applies to visual elements which are essential to see clearly in order to carry out functionality on the page, such as a search icon represented by a magnifying glass with no text. To pass this standard these items need to have a contrast ratio of at least 3:1 against both the colour that they appear on and colours that they appear next to. For example, the bars in a bar chart need to have a contrast ratio of at least

3:1 against the background colour of the chart, but also against each of the bars they are next to.

Authoring tools usually give colour values for interactive items and background in the formatting options. If this functionality isn't available, you can use an online colour picking tool to find out the values. Once you know the values of the colours used, check contrast ratios using an online contrast checker. You will normally need to input the value of each colour using either:

- RGB (Red, Green, Blue) values, eg 0, 85, 125;
- Hex (Hexadecimal) or HTML values, eg #00557D;
- HSL (Hue, Saturation, Lightness) values, eg 199, 100%, 25%;

Contrast checkers give you the contrast ratio and let you know if your colour choices pass or fail WCAG standards. A good contrast checker will also have lightness sliders which allow you to darken or lighten the colours you have chosen, until they pass WCAG requirements. Some contrast checkers also have a specific 'Graphical Objects and User Interface Components' option which checks specifically for this standard.

How to conform

Make sure that interactive items and important visual elements have a contrast ratio of at least 3:1 against the colour of the background they appear on or items they appear next to.

Exceptions

- For interactive items this standard does not apply if items are inactive such as a disabled 'Back' button, or if the user agent such as the web browser determines the appearance of the interactive item.
- For visual elements this standard does not apply if a particular presentation is essential to the information being conveyed, eg a medical diagram which uses specific biological colours, a heatmap or a screenshot of a website.

Contrast ratio for buttons with text

The contrast ratio for interactive objects such as buttons with text can be confusing. This is because there are two different requirements. For button text against button background the contrast ratio requirement is at least 4.5:1 for 'normal' size text. For the button background against the page background the contrast ratio requirement is at least 3:1.

FIGURE 8.16   Contrast ratio requirements for buttons with text

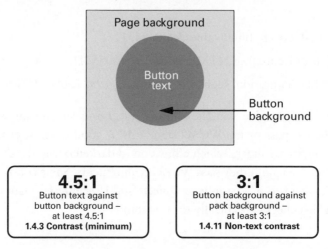

Diagram showing the two contrast ratio requirements for buttons with text.

Why?

Learners who benefit from this standard include:

- people with low vision or who are colour blind and have difficulty identifying items which do not contrast sufficiently with the background they appear on or items they appear next to;
- older people who commonly find it difficult to distinguish colour and need strong contrast to make it easier to identify interactive items and visual elements;
- people affected by situational impairments, eg someone who is using a monitor with poor colour contrast.

How to test

Check that interactive items and important visual elements have a contrast ratio of at least 3:1 against the colour of the background they appear on or items they appear next to.

Useful resources

- Contrast and Color Accessibility[67]
  WebAIM guidance on WCAG contrast and colour requirements.

- Understanding Success Criterion 1.4.11: Non-text contrast[68]
  Guidance from W3C with many helpful examples.

- Color Cop colour picking tool[69]
  An example of a free colour picking tool for Windows. You can use the eyedropper to analyse the value of any colour used in your eLearning resource.

- WebAIM colour contrast checker[70]
  One of the most commonly used colour contrast checkers. This contrast checker has a 'Graphical Objects and User Interface Components' option which checks specifically for this standard.

- Glitch.com contrast checker[71]
  A contrast checker which allows you to test both ratio requirements of buttons with text at the same time.

- 1.4.11 Non-Text Contrast – Level AA[72]
  W3C quick reference guide and further information for this standard.

1.4.12 Text Spacing – Level AA

Added in 2.1

If the authoring tool uses a markup language such as HTML, make sure that visual learners can change the spacing between text, and that they can still see all the content and carry out all the functions of a page. This applies to spacing between lines of text, paragraphs, words and letters.

Key information

This standard is important for people with low vision and cognitive impairments such as dyslexia who may find it easier to read text if they can customize the spacing between the lines of text, paragraphs, words and letters. Increasing the text spacing on a page to the requirements of this standard should be achievable without text or functionality being lost. A common issue when the text spacing is increased is that text disappears, or it becomes unreadable because it overlaps with other text. Visual examples of these issues can be found in the W3C Understanding text spacing article in the Useful resources section.

This standard is achieved with the underlying code of the authoring tool. It requires that the content is coded so that the containers that hold text are not fixed to a specified height and width parameter. If the size of containers is limited, then when the spacing between text is increased this can cause the text to spill over the container or to be truncated. Only some authoring tools allow this functionality, and some may be coded so that spacing between text in some parts of the resource such as menus or glossary can be adjusted while the spacing between text on the page cannot.

How to conform

Make sure that visual learners can see all the content and carry out all the functions of a page when they make **any or all** of the following adjustments to text spacing:

- **Lines.** Spacing between lines to at least 1.5 times the size of the font.
- **Paragraphs.** Spacing following paragraphs to at least 2 times the size of the font.
- **Words.** Spacing between words to at least 0.16 times the size of the font.
- **Letters.** Spacing between letters to at least 0.12 times the size of the font.

Exceptions

- Captions which are embedded in the video frame as opposed to being supplied as a separate caption file are exempt.
- Text in images is exempt.

- If any text used in the eLearning resource is in a language which does not have spacing between lines of text, paragraphs, words or letters, these properties are exempt.

Why?

Learners who benefit from this standard include:

- people who have low vision and may find it easier to read text if they can increase the spacing between paragraphs, lines of text, words and letters;
- people with cognitive impairments such as dyslexia who may benefit from more space between text elements, particularly if the form of dyslexia makes letters and words 'move around' on the page;
- people who have visual stress which causes visual distractions and discomfort and can make reading difficult and tiring, especially on a screen.

Example

FIGURE 8.17   Text spacing causes no loss of content or functionality (CourseArc)

An eLearning resource created with the CourseArc authoring tool viewed after using a browser extension to test this standard. The spacing between lines, paragraphs, letters and words all conforms to the required standards and there is no loss of content or functionality on the page.
SOURCE Reproduced with permission of CourseArc

How to test

Check the underlying code to make sure that the spacing between text, lines and paragraphs can be adjusted to the requirements of this standard without any issues. There is currently no recommended browser extension to test this, although there are experimental text spacing bookmarklets available. More information can be found in the Useful resources section.

If this is not possible, another option is to test this standard with the support of an accessibility expert, or to check with your authoring tool provider that the output of the tool conforms to this standard.

Useful resources

- Understanding Success Criterion 1.4.12: Text Spacing[73]
  W3C guidance with visual examples of some of the issues caused when text spacing is increased if this standard is not met.
- Accessibility Requirements for People with Low Vision[74]
  W3C guidance on spacing requirements for people with low vision.
- Text spacing bookmarklet[75]
  Information about the experimental bookmarklet used to test text spacing for this standard.
- 1.4.12 Text Spacing – Level AA[76]
  W3C quick reference guide and further information for this standard.

1.4.13 Content on Hover or Focus – Level AA

Added in 2.1

Make sure content such as tooltips or submenus which appear or 'pop up' when learners hover over or move keyboard focus to interactive items can be dismissed. Also make sure that if learners need to interact with pop-up content, it doesn't disappear until they have finished interacting with it. Finally, if the content appears only on hover, make sure that learners can move the cursor away from the item that triggered the pop-up content to the content itself.

Key information

Pop-up content displays information about an item on a page when learners hover over the item or when it receives keyboard focus. The normal behaviour of this content is that it appears after a short delay and disappears again when the mouse moves away from the item, when the item loses focus or when the 'Escape' key is pressed. A common example in eLearning resources is markers which appear on images and display more information when they are hovered over or receive focus.

Pop-up content can be very helpful but can also cause issues, particularly for users of assistive technology. Common issues include content appearing when learners haven't intended to trigger it or content appearing which makes it more difficult for learners to complete tasks because it obscures other content. Another common problem is content appearing without alerting learners so they are unaware that it has appeared. To prevent these issues, pop-up content needs to be either dismissible, hoverable or persistent.

- **Dismissible.** This means that learners can hide the pop-up content, usually with the 'Escape' key. This doesn't apply if the content is an error message. It also doesn't apply if the content doesn't obscure anything else on the page.

- **Hoverable.** This only applies to content which is triggered by the hover action of the mouse cursor. When the pop-up content appears it can sometimes be obscured by the cursor, especially if learners have enlarged the cursor to make it easier to see. Hoverable means that learners can move the cursor away from the original item which they hovered over to make the content appear to the pop-up content itself. It therefore allows learners to move the cursor so that it doesn't block the pop-up content.

- **Persistent.** This means that the content does not unexpectedly disappear. Content stays on the page until learners move the hover or focus away, manually dismiss the content, or it is no longer useful.

How to conform

Make sure that content that appears when learners hover or use the keyboard to focus on interactive items is either dismissible, hoverable or persistent.

Exception

- If the user agent such as the web browser determines the appearance of the pop up content it is exempt. A common example given by W3C is when a browser displays the HTML title attribute as a small tooltip.

Why?

Learners who benefit from this standard include:

- people with low vision who magnify content either via browser zoom or with screen magnifiers and who will find it easier to interact with pop-up content;
- people who increase the size of cursors using standard tool settings or assistive technology and will be able to view hoverable pop-up content without the cursor obscuring it;
- people with cognitive impairments who may benefit from having longer time to process and interact with pop-up content.

Examples

FIGURE 8.18   Dismissible pop-up content

A login page on an eLearning course showing the pop-up content which appears when learners hover over the 'Log in to course' button. This obscures the 'Register for course' button which appears underneath it. To conform to this standard, learners should be able to dismiss the pop-up content. This is normally done with the 'Escape' key.

FIGURE 8.19   Hoverable pop-up content

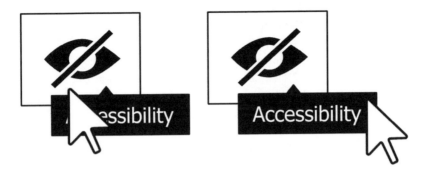

In the first image an enlarged mouse cursor obscures the pop-up content which appears when learners hover over the Accessibility icon. To conform to this standard, learners should be able to move the cursor away from the Accessibility icon to the pop-up content itself. This means that the pop-up content is not blocked by the cursor and is demonstrated in the second image.

How to test

Check that all content which appears automatically on hover or focus is either dismissible, hoverable, or persistent.

Useful resources

- Tooltip Guidelines[77]
  Guidelines from the Nielsen Norma Group with helpful explanations and examples.
- 1.4.13 Content on Hover or Focus – Level AA[78]
  W3C quick reference guide and further information for this standard.

Endnotes

[1] The Big Hack (2019) How to write better alt-text descriptions for accessibility [Blog] The Big Hack by SCOPE, 7 October, https://bighack.org/how-to-write-better-alt-text-descriptions-for-accessibility/ (archived at https://perma.cc/5Y2M-3TXB)

[2] WebAIM (Updated 2019) Alternative text, 14 October, https://webaim.org/techniques/alttext/ (archived at https://perma.cc/N6PN-2AJF)

3   Diagram Center (2019) Image description, http://diagramcenter.org/making-images-accessible.html (archived at https://perma.cc/VY2C-4TC9)

4   Eggert, E and Abou-Zahara, S (Updated 2019) Images concepts, 27 July, https://www.w3.org/WAI/tutorials/images/ (archived at https://perma.cc/FFP8-YS29)

5   W3C (Updated 2019), How to Meet WCAG (quick reference), 4 October, https://www.w3.org/WAI/WCAG21/quickref/#non-text-content (archived at https://perma.cc/U3HP-FL6J)

6   Lawton, S (2019) Transcripts on the web, http://www.uiaccess.com/transcripts/transcripts_on_the_web.html (archived at https://perma.cc/43CD-WYBN)

7   Web Accessibility Initiative (2006) Podcast transcript: Interview on WCAG 2, 6 July, https://www.w3.org/WAI/highlights/200606wcag2interview.html (archived at https://perma.cc/XFA9-JSL4)

8   W3C (Updated 2019) How to Meet WCAG (quick reference), 4 October, https://www.w3.org/WAI/WCAG21/quickref/#audio-only-and-video-only-prerecorded (archived at https://perma.cc/5KL5-9TLS)

9   Lawton, S (Updated 2021) Captions/Subtitles, https://www.w3.org/WAI/media/av/captions/#automatic-captions-are-not-sufficient (archived at https://perma.cc/DG5G-83ZV)

10   3Play Media, Ultimate guide to closed captioning, https://www.3playmedia.com/resources/popular-topics/closed-captioning/ (archived at https://perma.cc/HU2L-CEFH)

11   Described and Captioned Media Program, Caption Key, https://dcmp.org/learn/captioningkey (archived at https://perma.cc/H4K9-BWSB)

12   BBC (Updated 2019) Subtitle guidelines, http://bbc.github.io/subtitle-guidelines/ (archived at https://perma.cc/7PZD-M57B)

13   Cocklin, N (2018) Make it accessible – captions, subtitles and transcripts [Blog] Aston University TEL Support, 12 November, http://telsupport.tlc.aston.ac.uk/2018/11/12/make-it-accessible-captions-subtitles-and-transcripts/ (archived at https://perma.cc/LY5V-8YVL)

14   W3C (Updated 2019) How to Meet WCAG (quick reference), 4 October, https://www.w3.org/WAI/WCAG21/quickref/#captions-prerecorded (archived at https://perma.cc/2B3K-FL92)

15   WebAIM (Updated 2020) Captions, transcripts and audio descriptions, 1 July, https://webaim.org/techniques/captions/#captions (archived at https://perma.cc/A5BL-ME9M)

16   Lawton, S (2019) Transcripts on the web, http://www.uiaccess.com/transcripts/transcripts_on_the_web.html (archived at https://perma.cc/43CD-WYBN)

17   Cocklin, N (2018) Make it accessible – captions, subtitles and transcripts [Blog] Aston University TEL Support, 12 November, http://telsupport.tlc.aston.ac.uk/2018/11/12/make-it-accessible-captions-subtitles-and-transcripts/ (archived at https://perma.cc/LY5V-8YVL)

18 Microsoft (2016) Inclusive Design Subject Matter Expert Series featuring Antoine with audio description [Online video] 10 November, https://www.youtube.com/watch?v=-nGaDdfLXNg (archived at https://perma.cc/VK39-8QL7)

19 3Play Media, The ultimate guide to audio description, https://www.3playmedia.com/resources/popular-topics/audio-description/ (archived at https://perma.cc/V98C-YXLL)

20 W3C (Updated 2019) How to Meet WCAG (quick reference), 4 October, https://www.w3.org/WAI/WCAG21/quickref/#audio-description-or-media-alternative-prerecorded (archived at https://perma.cc/M2FL-EH83)

21 Legislation.gov.uk, The Public Sector Bodies (Websites and Mobile Applications) (No. 2) Accessibility Regulations 2018, 23 September 2018, https://www.legislation.gov.uk/uksi/2018/952/made (archived at https://perma.cc/92BL-HDCR)

22 Lexdis, PSBAR scope, https://www.lexdis.org.uk/digital-accessibility/digital-accessibility-regulations/psbar-scope/ (archived at https://perma.cc/JB45-3FH9)

23 WebAIM (Updated 2020) Real-time captioning, 13 May, https://webaim.org/techniques/captions/realtime (archived at https://perma.cc/7C3B-FLEV)

24 Google, Present slides with captions, https://support.google.com/docs/answer/9109474?p=slides_captions&visit_id=637199918585448394-2478133777&rd=1 (archived at https://perma.cc/VWN6-PE93)

25 W3C (Updated 2019) How to Meet WCAG (quick reference), 4 October, https://www.w3.org/WAI/WCAG21/quickref/#captions-live (archived at https://perma.cc/T4DG-79LB)

26 Microsoft (2016) Inclusive Design Subject Matter Expert Series featuring Antoine with audio description [Online video] 10 November, https://www.youtube.com/watch?v=-nGaDdfLXNg (archived at https://perma.cc/VK39-8QL7)

27 WebAIM (Updated 2020) Captions, transcript and audio descriptions, 1 July, https://webaim.org/techniques/captions/#captions (archived at https://perma.cc/A5BL-ME9M)

28 3Play Media, The ultimate guide to audio description, https://www.3playmedia.com/resources/popular-topics/audio-description/ (archived at https://perma.cc/V98C-YXLL)

29 W3C (Updated 2019) How to Meet WCAG (quick reference), 4 October, https://www.w3.org/WAI/WCAG21/quickref/#audio-description-prerecorded (archived at https://perma.cc/LR57-K7DH)

30 MDN contributors (Updated 2020) Introduction to HTML, 9 July, https://developer.mozilla.org/en-US/docs/Learn/HTML/Introduction_to_HTML (archived at https://perma.cc/NH2F-ERS8)

31 Eggert, E and Abou-Zahara, S (Updated 2019) Page structure concepts, 27 July, https://www.w3.org/WAI/tutorials/page-structure (archived at https://perma.cc/7LPC-EKLU)

[32] WebAIM (Updated 2020) Semantic structure: Regions, headings and lists, 1 May, https://webaim.org/techniques/semanticstructure/ (archived at https://perma.cc/9FJL-LVAT)

[33] W3C Working Group Note (2016) ARIA11: Using ARIA landmarks to identify regions of a page, https://www.w3.org/TR/WCAG20-TECHS/ARIA11.html (archived at https://perma.cc/6AN8-EUYL)

[34] Lawton Henry, S (Updated 2020) Easy checks – a first review of web accessibility – headings, 28 April, https://www.w3.org/WAI/test-evaluate/preliminary/#headings (archived at https://perma.cc/C7GK-KBM2)

[35] GOV.UK, WCAG 2.1 Primer 1.3.1. Info and relationships, https://alphagov.github.io/wcag-primer/all.html#1-3-1-info-and-relationships-a (archived at https://perma.cc/H3S4-97G8)

[36] W3C (Updated 2019) How to Meet WCAG (quick reference), 4 October, https://www.w3.org/WAI/WCAG21/quickref/#info-and-relationships (archived at https://perma.cc/AY39-8ZWT)

[37] WebAIM (2017) Designing for screen reader compatibility, 21 April, https://webaim.org/techniques/screenreader (archived at https://perma.cc/7RGG-7H6Q)

[38] CourseArc (Updated 2020) What is the visual reading order? 21 July, https://coursearc.freshdesk.com/support/solutions/articles/9000124976-what-is-the-visual-reading-order (archived at https://perma.cc/UHP7-WH3W)

[39] W3C (Updated 2019) How to Meet WCAG (quick reference), 4 October, https://www.w3.org/WAI/WCAG21/quickref/#meaningful-sequence (archived at https://perma.cc/FT89-KBM6)

[40] Metts, M, J and Welfle, A (2020) Standards for writing accessibly, A list apart, 23 January, https://alistapart.com/article/standards-for-writing-accessibly/ (archived at https://perma.cc/PU4B-JS4Q)

[41] W3C (Updated 2019) How to Meet WCAG (quick reference), 4 October, https://www.w3.org/WAI/WCAG21/quickref/#sensory-characteristics (archived at https://perma.cc/2VJT-KYWK)

[42] W3C (Updated 2019) How to Meet WCAG (quick reference), 4 October, https://www.w3.org/WAI/WCAG21/quickref/#orientation (archived at https://perma.cc/T5YZ-EB77)

[43] W3C, Input purposes for user interface components, https://www.w3.org/TR/WCAG21/#input-purposes (archived at https://perma.cc/Q5Q6-73CY)

[44] W3C, Using HTML 5.2 autocomplete attributes, https://www.w3.org/WAI/WCAG21/Techniques/html/H98 (archived at https://perma.cc/L3R9-9R39)

[45] MDN contributors (Updated 2020) How to turn off form autocompletion, 10 July, https://developer.mozilla.org/en-US/docs/Web/Security/Securing_your_site/Turning_off_form_autocompletion (archived at https://perma.cc/DU7E-7MQK)

46 W3C (Updated 2019) How to Meet WCAG (quick reference), 4 October, https://www.w3.org/WAI/WCAG21/quickref/#identify-input-purpose (archived at https://perma.cc/53CW-BV3H)

47 Colour Blind Awareness, Colour blindness, https://www.colourblindawareness.org/colour-blindness (archived at https://perma.cc/HX36-DWKB)

48 Colour Blind Awareness, Types of colour blindness, http://www.colourblindawareness.org/colour-blindness/types-of-colour-blindness (archived at https://perma.cc/56MS-KATT)

49 Silver, A (2016) Improving the color accessibility for color-blind users, *Smashing Magazine*, 21 June, https://www.smashingmagazine.com/2016/06/improving-color-accessibility-for-color-blind-users (archived at https://perma.cc/92P4-6AZ4)

50 Wickline, M and the Human-Computer Interaction Resource Network (2000) Coblis – color blindness simulator, Colblindor, https://www.color-blindness.com/coblis-color-blindness-simulator (archived at https://perma.cc/LSG5-ELZL)

51 Leventhal, A (Update 2016) NoCoffee vision simulator, Google Chrome Web Store, 8 March, https://chrome.google.com/webstore/detail/nocoffee/jjeeggmbnhckmgdhmgdckeigabjfbddl (archived at https://perma.cc/637V-8MNB)

52 W3C (Updated 2019) How to Meet WCAG (quick reference), 4 October, https://www.w3.org/WAI/WCAG21/quickref/#use-of-color (archived at https://perma.cc/TEW5-7NQ8)

53 Bureau of Internet Accessibility (2020) Why autoplay is an accessibility no-no [Blog] 21 September, https://www.boia.org/blog/why-autoplay-is-an-accessibility-no-no (archived at https://perma.cc/7X7N-JLZB)

54 W3C (Updated 2019) How to Meet WCAG (quick reference), 4 October, https://www.w3.org/WAI/WCAG21/quickref/#audio-control (archived at https://perma.cc/K2QA-EVUS)

55 WebAIM (2018) Contrast and color accessibility, 29 November, https://webaim.org/articles/contrast (archived at https://perma.cc/7L82-6MRF)

56 The British Dyslexia Association, Dyslexia friendly style guide, https://www.bdadyslexia.org.uk/advice/employers/creating-a-dyslexia-friendly-workplace/dyslexia-friendly-style-guide (archived at https://perma.cc/3F8H-XUQK)

57 Color Cop, A free multi-purpose color picker for Windows, http://colorcop.net (archived at https://perma.cc/6P92-TATK)

58 WebAIM Contrast Checker, https://webaim.org/resources/contrastchecker (archived at https://perma.cc/HFF7-5S2A)

59 Brandwood.com, Text on background image a11y check, http://www.brandwood.com/a11y (archived at https://perma.cc/8P45-24SV)

60 W3C (Updated 2019) How to Meet WCAG (quick reference), 4 October, https://www.w3.org/WAI/WCAG21/quickref/#contrast-minimum (archived at https://perma.cc/GJ5X-25LY)

[61]   W3C (Updated 2019) How to Meet WCAG (quick reference), 4 October,
https://www.w3.org/WAI/WCAG21/quickref/#resize-text (archived at
https://perma.cc/F8KS-YK9J)

[62]   Eggert, E and Abou-Zahara, S (Updated 2019) Images of text, 27 July,
https://www.w3.org/WAI/tutorials/images/textual (archived at https://perma.cc/
Q3D7-39FF)

[63]   Bureau of Internet Accessibility (2018) Why is it important for accessibility to
use actual text instead of images of text? 24 December, https://www.boia.org/
blog/why-is-it-important-for-accessibility-to-use-actual-text-instead-of-images-
of-text (archived at https://perma.cc/E5YL-QS6A)

[64]   W3C (Updated 2019) How to Meet WCAG (quick reference), 4 October,
https://www.w3.org/WAI/WCAG21/quickref/#images-of-text (archived at
https://perma.cc/2U7E-6R3R)

[65]   LePage, P and Andrew, R (Updated 2020) Responsive web design basics,
14 May, https://web.dev/responsive-web-design-basics/ (archived at
https://perma.cc/BL4W-ZV99)

[66]   W3C (Updated 2019) How to Meet WCAG (quick reference), 4 October,
https://www.w3.org/WAI/WCAG21/quickref/#reflow (archived at
https://perma.cc/WUT8-HT8M)

[67]   WebAIM (2018) Contrast and color accessibility, 29 November,
https://webaim.org/articles/contrast (archived at https://perma.cc/7L82-6MRF)

[68]   W3C, Understanding success criterion 1.4.11: Non-text contrast,
https://www.w3.org/WAI/WCAG21/Understanding/non-text-contrast.html
(archived at https://perma.cc/33YJ-MWXH)

[69]   Color Cop, A free multi-purpose color picker for Windows,
http://colorcop.net (archived at https://perma.cc/6P92-TATK)

[70]   WebAIM Contrast Checker, https://webaim.org/resources/contrastchecker
(archived at https://perma.cc/HFF7-5S2A)

[71]   House, D and Colley, N (2019) Contrast checker, https://contrast-checker.glitch.
me (archived at https://perma.cc/3GBN-YMMV)

[72]   W3C (Updated 2019) How to Meet WCAG (quick reference), 4 October,
https://www.w3.org/WAI/WCAG21/quickref/#non-text-contrast (archived at
https://perma.cc/Q75F-GL3K)

[73]   W3C, Understanding success criterion 1.4.12: Text spacing,
https://www.w3.org/WAI/WCAG21/Understanding/text-spacing.html (archived
at https://perma.cc/7JJB-MQ8W)

[74]   Allan, J, Kirkpatrick, A, and Henry, S L (2016) Accessibility requirements for
people with low vision, 17 March, https://www.w3.org/TR/low-vision-
needs/#spacing (archived at https://perma.cc/GK6L-C4SH)

[75]   Faulkner, S (Updated 2020) text spacing bookmarklet, 7 October,
https://codepen.io/stevef/pen/YLMqbo/ (archived at https://perma.cc/AU8L-
KBT3)

[76] W3C (Updated 2019) How to Meet WCAG (quick reference), 4 October, https://www.w3.org/WAI/WCAG21/quickref/#text-spacing (archived at https://perma.cc/L5NC-RMFY)

[77] Joyce, A (2019) Tooltip guidelines, 27 January, https://www.nngroup.com/articles/tooltip-guidelines/ (archived at https://perma.cc/3UVK-DKFK)

[78] W3C (Updated 2019) How to Meet WCAG (quick reference), 4 October, https://www.w3.org/WAI/WCAG21/quickref/#content-on-hover-or-focus (archived at https://perma.cc/F7UV-F4QL)

09

Operable

Note: The explanations given in this chapter are interpretations of WCAG standards and do not guarantee that content will be fully compliant with legal regulations. For further guidance and the full W3C wording for each of the standards, see: How to Meet WCAG (quick reference). Any W3C wording used is copyright. Copyright © 2019 W3C® (MIT, ERCIM, Keio, Beihang).

2.1.1 Keyboard – Level A

Make sure that all functionality in the eLearning resource is usable with a keyboard or keyboard interface. This includes all interactive items and audio and video player controls. Also make sure that 'keystrokes', ie pressing the keys, do not have any time constraints.

Key information

This is one of the most important accessibility standards to achieve because it ensures that learners with a wide range of impairments and assistive technology needs can navigate the content and activate all the functions in eLearning resources. Many people are not able to use a mouse and the onscreen mouse pointer. Instead they use a standard keyboard, an adapted keyboard or an equivalent keyboard interface such as an onscreen keyboard to navigate and interact with content.

Common keys used to navigate include:

- 'Tab'. This key is used to move through the items on the page. If the eLearning resource conforms to standard **2.4.7 Focus Visible**, each item will have a visible focus such as a coloured border so that you can see where the tab key takes you on the page. Some authoring tools are programmed so that each item on the page is selected when it is tabbed to. Most tools are programmed so that they behave like standard web content. This means that only interactive items such as navigation items, input items and links are selected when the 'Tab' key is used.

- 'Shift' and 'Tab'. These two keys together are used to move from the item which is currently in focus to the previous focusable item on the page.

- 'Enter' or 'Space bar'. Both of these keys activate the functionality of buttons. For example, once a 'Submit' button has been selected by using the 'Tab' key, the 'Enter' key or 'Space bar' will activate the button.

- 'Enter'. The 'Enter' key is used to activate links.

- 'Arrow' keys. The arrow keys are often used to navigate through the items in a quiz answer such as multiple choice or radio button items. They are also sometimes used to navigate through a list of options in a dropdown list or in a list of additional resources.

How to conform

1 Make sure that learners can navigate through all the content and complete every task in the eLearning resource with a keyboard.

2 Make sure there are no limits imposed on the time that learners have to push and release keyboard keys. The same applies to equivalent keyboard interfaces such as onscreen keyboards.

Exception

- Functionality which depends on the path of the user's movements, eg a handwriting tool or a freehand painting or drawing program, is exempt.

Note: The advanced standard **2.1.3 Keyboard (No Exception)** does not allow any exceptions which depend on the path of the user's movements.

eLearning interactions

Any interactions which need learners to use a mouse are not accessible. Common examples include matching drag and drop, sequence drag and drop, hotspots and word banks. Your authoring tool should provide a list of content types which are accessible and inaccessible for keyboard users. A good example comes from the open source H5P interactive content plugin, which provides a list detailing the accessibility of different inter-activity on its 'Recommendations and overviews of content types' page.[1]

There are various options for tackling interactions which are not key-board accessible in eLearning resources. One possibility is to provide a tran-script. This is often done in the case of hotspot interactions where the position of the hotspots is not essential for understanding, eg a map of Europe detailing population. The transcript provides a list of all the hot-spots and the associated text for each one. Another option is to provide a keyboard-accessible alternative. Some tools, for example, provide an order-ing dropdown activity instead of an ordering drag-and-drop activity. A final option is to consider creating bespoke interactions which mimic mouse-dependent interactions. One example is to as use animation paths to mimic drag-and-drop interactions in a keyboard-accessible quiz option such as multiple choice.

Why?

Learners who benefit from this standard include:

- people with motor impairments with limited dexterity who are not able to use a mouse and so navigate using a keyboard or keyboard interface;
- people who are blind and use screen readers which they operate with standard keyboard commands and additional screen reader-specific keyboard commands;
- people with low vision who may be able to see the mouse pointer but may have trouble tracking its movement and who may also use screen readers;
- people with chronic conditions such as Repetitive Strain Injury (RSI) who need to limit or avoid using a mouse and use a keyboard to navigate content;

- people with temporary motor impairments, eg someone who has a broken arm or wrist and cannot use a mouse;

- people who prefer to use the keyboard to navigate in certain situations. A common example is navigating using a keyboard when entering data into input fields.

Examples

FIGURE 9.1   Hotspot interaction alternative (Articulate Storyline)

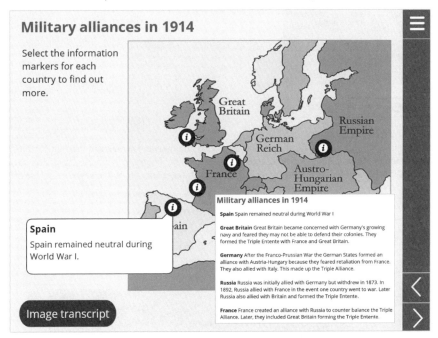

An example of a hotspot interaction created using the Articulate Storyline authoring tool. Since the placement of the hotspots is not essential for understanding the map, a transcript can be used to provide equivalent information. The image transcript shown in the insert contains all the information which a visual learner would see when they activate the hotspots.
SOURCE ©Articulate Global, Inc. Used with permission, all other rights reserved

FIGURE 9.2   Drag-and-drop multiple choice alternative (CourseArc)

Module 1

A-Z View Glossary

Types of impairments

Descriptions	Answers	Choices
Cognitive impairment		Tremors
Visual impairment		Dyslexia
Motor impairment		
Hearing impairment		

👁̸ Alternative Activity

Alternative Activity

Match up each description with a choice.

1. Cognitive impairment
   - ○ Tremors
   - ○ Colour blindness
   - ○ Deafness
   - ○ Dyslexia

CHECK ANSWER

Some authoring tools automatically provide accessible alternatives for drag-and-drop interactions. This example shows a drag-and-drop activity created in the CourseArc authoring tool. The tool automatically generates an Alternative Activity link which takes learners to the keyboard accessible multiple choice version, which is shown in the insert.
SOURCE Reproduced with permission of CourseArc

FIGURE 9.3   Drag-and-drop ordering alternative (iSpring)

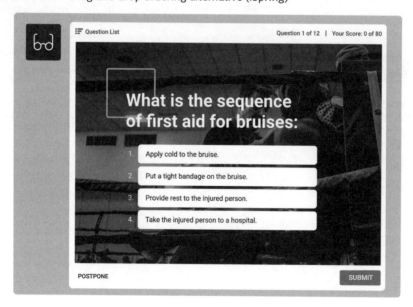

FIGURE 9.3   *continued*

Question 1 of 12   Your Score: 0 of 80

What is the sequence of first aid for bruises:

Apply cold to the bruise. | 4 ▾ |

Put a tight bandage on the bruise. | 2 ▾ |

Provide rest to the injured person. | 3 ▾ |

Take the injured person to a hospital. | 1 ▾ |

| POSTPONE | | SUBMIT |

▸ Question List

With some authoring tools you need to select an accessibility mode in order to provide a keyboard-accessible version of an interaction. This is the case with the iSpring authoring tool which provides an ordering dropdown activity instead of an ordering drag-and-drop activity in accessibility mode.

SOURCE Reproduced with permission of www.ispringsolutions.com (archived at https://perma.cc/2ZPC-5EAP)

FIGURE 9.4   Drag-and-drop simulation with animation paths (Articulate Storyline)

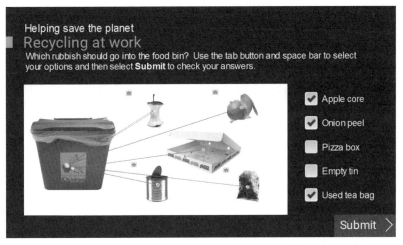

Helping save the planet
Recycling at work
Which rubbish should go into the food bin? Use the tab button and space bar to select your options and then select **Submit** to check your answers.

☑ Apple core

☑ Onion peel

☐ Pizza box

☐ Empty tin

☑ Used tea bag

Submit ❯

Finding your own alternatives for content which is not keyboard accessible is a great way to be creative and to develop your skills. One way of providing interactions which simulate drag-and-drop interactions, for example, is to use animation paths. Although many people who navigate using a keyboard do so because they are blind or have low vision and use a screen reader, many are also visual learners who use keyboard navigation due to limited dexterity. This example created using the Articulate Storyline authoring tool shows how you can add visual interest to a multiple choice activity by using animation paths to simulate a drag-and-drop interaction.

SOURCE ©Articulate Global, Inc. Used with permission, all other rights reserved

How to test

Navigate through the eLearning resource using only the keyboard. You can either use the basic functions detailed in the Key information section or use a complete guide to keyboard testing such as the one from WebAIM, which can be found in the Useful resources section.

Useful resources

- Keyboard Accessibility[2]
  WebAIM overview of keyboard accessibility including keyboard testing guidance.
- Keyboard Compatibility[3]
  W3C accessibility overview containing a video about keyboard accessibility.
- Using the tabindex attribute[4]
  Article from the Paciello Group explaining the HTML tabindex attribute used to manage keyboard focus.
- 2.1.1 Keyboard – Level A[5]
  W3C quick reference guide and further information for this standard.

2.1.2 No Keyboard Trap – Level A

Make sure that learners who navigate using a keyboard or keyboard interface can move away from all content that receives focus in the eLearning resource. Also make sure that this can be achieved using standard keyboard keys such as the 'Tab' or 'Arrow' keys, or that learners are made aware if they need to use non-standard keys.

Key information

Many people are not able to use a mouse and the onscreen mouse pointer. Instead they use a standard keyboard, an adapted keyboard or an equivalent keyboard interface such as an onscreen keyboard to navigate and interact with content. A keyboard trap describes the situation when learners can navigate to an item in the eLearning resource using the keyboard but cannot then move away from the selected item. They effectively become trapped and cannot move on to access the rest of the content. A common keyboard trap occurs with multimedia controls. This happens when it is possible for learners to use the 'Tab' key to select the player controls but the keyboard focus then gets stuck and they are not able to use the 'Tab' or 'Arrow' keys to move away.

How to conform

1 Check that learners can move away from all items in the eLearning resource that receive keyboard focus using standard keys, ie the 'Tab', 'Shift' and 'Tab' or 'Arrow' keys.

2 If non-standard keys are needed to move away from items, make sure this is explained to learners.

Why?

Learners who benefit from this standard include:

- people with motor impairments with limited dexterity who are not able to use a mouse and so navigate using a keyboard or keyboard interface;

- people who are blind and use screen readers which they operate with standard keyboard commands and additional screen reader-specific keyboard commands;

- people with low vision who may be able to see the mouse pointer but may have trouble tracking its movement and who may also use screen readers;

- people with chronic conditions such as RSI who need to limit or avoid using a mouse and use a keyboard to navigate content;

- people with temporary motor impairments, eg someone who has a broken arm or wrist and cannot use a mouse.

How to test

Navigate through the eLearning resource using only the keyboard. Make sure that you can move away from any selected item using only the 'Tab' or 'Arrow' keys on your keyboard. If other non-standard keys are needed to move away from a selected item, make sure this is explained to learners.

Useful resources

- Keyboard Accessibility[6]
  WebAIM overview of keyboard accessibility including keyboard testing guidance.
- Keyboard Compatibility[7]
  W3C accessibility overview containing a video about keyboard accessibility.
- 2.1.2 No Keyboard Trap – Level A[8]
  W3C quick reference guide and further information for this standard.

2.1.4 Character Key Shortcuts – Level A

Added in 2.1

Avoid assigning keyboard shortcuts which use only a single letter, punctuation, number or symbol character key. If they do, make sure that the shortcut can be modified by adding another key, can be turned off, or for interactive items is active only when it receives focus.

Key information

Many people use keyboard shortcuts to carry out online tasks, eg 'Ctrl + C' for copy and 'Ctrl + V' for paste. Many websites and social media sites also use shortcut keys. Twitter, for example, uses 'N' to create a new tweet, 'L' to like a tweet and 'T' to re-tweet. Some authoring tools allow you to set up keyboard shortcuts, ie assign specific functionality to a key. For example, you could program the 'N' key to take you to the next page of an eLearning resource. One issue which occurs as the result of assigning functionality to single keys, however, is that they can interfere with the keyboard shortcuts used by assistive technology. Screen reader users use keyboard shortcuts to navigate and interact with online content. These shortcuts can be pre-set or manually created. Pre-built shortcut keys used in the NVDA screen reader, for example, include 'K' which automatically jumps to links, 'G' for images and 'L' for lists.

Speech-input users also use keyboard shortcuts to navigate and interact with online content. If single character key shortcuts are used, this can cause issues because when speech-input users say a word which contains the single letter that has been programmed as a shortcut, this will activate the shortcut. A demonstration can be found in the Useful resources section. This shows how a user saying the word 'dead' when using speech input with a Google Docs document opens a Google drawing in a new window.[9]

Another common problem caused by single-character key shortcuts is that they can be accidently triggered by users with mobility impairments which affect dexterity, such as people who have tremors. This issue can be resolved by 'remapping', which requires another key such as 'Alt' or 'Ctrl' to be pressed in conjunction with the single-key shortcut. This makes it much more difficult for keyboard shortcuts to be activated by accident. Another way to avoid this issue is to simply give learners the ability to turn off single-character key shortcuts. Single-character key shortcuts which are active only when they receive focus, such as items in dropdown menus, are not an issue, however, because learners have already had to open the menu in order to allow the items to receive focus. They are therefore less likely to be accidentally triggered.

How to conform

Avoid assigning shortcuts to single-character keys including upper and lower case letters, punctuation, number or symbol keys unless at least one of the following conditions is met:

- Learners can turn off the shortcut.
- Learners can change or remap the shortcut so that it does not rely on a single key. This is done by adding another key which does not create a printable output, eg 'Alt' or 'Ctrl'. This needs to be pressed in combination with the single key for the shortcut to work.
- Shortcuts for interactive items are only active when they receive focus.

Why?

Learners who benefit from this standard include:

- people who use assistive technology such as screen readers or speech-input devices which use single-character keyboard shortcuts. The actions of the assistive technology keyboard shortcuts will not be disrupted by those programmed by the content author;
- people who have motor impairments which affect their dexterity. This standard makes it more difficult for them to trigger keyboard shortcuts by mistake.

Example

FIGURE 9.5   Keyboard shortcut for a button (Adobe Captivate)

A keyboard shortcut created for a 'Next' button in the Adobe Captivate tool. The shortcut in the example complies with this standard because the content author has chosen both 'Control' and the 'N' character for the shortcut. If they had chosen only the character 'N', the shortcut would fail this standard unless learners could turn off or remap the shortcut key.
SOURCE Reproduced with permission of Adobe Captivate

How to test

Check that all keyboard shortcuts in the eLearning resource do not use only a single letter, punctuation, number or symbol key unless the shortcut can be turned off, modified by adding another key or is active only when a component such as an item in a dropdown menu has focus.

Useful resources

- WCAG 2.1 – What is character key shortcuts[10]
  Article on character key shortcuts from Dig Inclusion.
- 2.1.4 Character Key Shortcuts – Level A[11]
  W3C quick reference guide and further information for this standard.

2.2.1 Timing Adjustable – Level A

Do not set time limits for any activities in the eLearning resource unless learners can turn them off, adjust or extend them. This applies to the length of time learners have to complete quiz questions or to the amount of time content remains on the page, etc. Also make sure that learners have control over any content which moves, scrolls or updates automatically as this effectively imposes a time limit.

Key information

This standard applies to time limits in activities such as filling in form fields, achieving a score on a game or completing a quiz. The problem with time limits is that they disadvantage users who have a range of impairments including visual, cognitive, hearing or motor impairments and who benefit from having more time to navigate and interact with content. This standard does allow time limits as long as the length of time needed to complete a task is adjustable, ie it can be controlled by learners.

The standard also applies to any animated, moving or scrolling content which automatically advances or updates. This is because this type of content effectively introduces a time limit on the learner's ability to interact with it. A common issue in eLearning occurs when content authors can control the amount of time that content remains on a page. The introductory page of a course, for example, could remain on the screen for 10 seconds before it automatically transitions to the next page of the course. Another frequent problem is animated text which flies onto the screen and then disappears more quickly than learners are able to read and process it. This can cause problems for assistive technology such as screen readers which often miss text that is animated as there is often not sufficient time to process and announce it. Moving content is allowed as long as there is an option for learners to control the movement or to access an alternative which does not have any timing constraints imposed. For example, learners could be given the option to override automatic transitions to the next page or could be directed to a static version of text rather than a page with animated text.

Note: The advanced standard **2.2.3 No Timing** recommends that no time limits are set even if learners can control them. The only exception is for real-time events such as webcasts, ie live online broadcasts of the audio or video feed from meetings or events. It also recommends that no content moves, updates or scrolls automatically.

How to conform

1 Either avoid imposing time limits for activities or give learners the ability to control the amount of time they have to complete them. Learners must be able to do one of the following:

   o Turn off the time limit.

   o Adjust the time limit so it is at least 10 times the length of the default setting.

   o Extend the time limit. Learners must be given at least 20 seconds to extend the time limit and this must be achievable with a simple action, eg pressing the space bar. They must also be able to extend the time limit at least 10 times.

2 Either avoid using animated, moving or scrolling content such as text or images which automatically advances or updates, or allow learners to control it.

Exceptions

- Activities where the timing is essential are exempt. An eLearning example could be a simulation of the technical steps needed to deactivate a power plant where learners need to become familiar with completing tasks in a fixed amount of time.

- Real-time events such as an online auction (eg eBay) where extending a time limit would disadvantage participants, or a live online broadcast of the audio or video feed from a meeting or event are also exempt.

- This standard does not apply to any time limits which are longer than 20 hours.

Why?

Learners who benefit from this standard include:

- people with cognitive or mobility impairments who may need more time to process content, input data and complete activities;

- people who are blind and use screen readers who may need more time to understand the layout of content or to operate controls;

- people who use screen readers and who may miss information such as text or alternative text for images if the content automatically moves or disappears before it has been announced by the screen reader;

- people with low vision and those who use screen magnifiers who may need more time to locate things on screen and to read text;

- people with cognitive impairments and some second language learners who may need more time to read text or process images before they automatically move or disappear;

- people who are deaf and communicate using sign language and may need more time to read information in text. For many sign language users, written English is a second language and takes longer to read and process;

- all learners, as having the ability to control time limits is good user experience for everyone.

Example

FIGURE 9.6   Quiz timing options (iSpring)

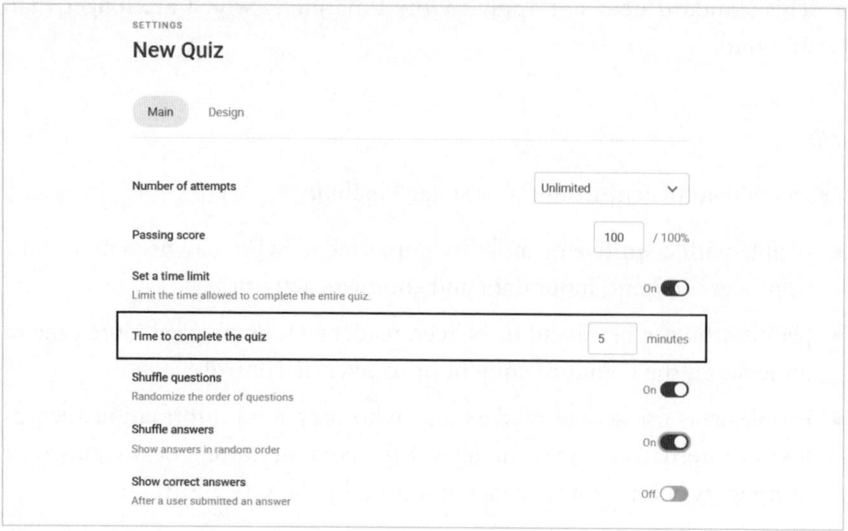

Quiz settings in the iSpring authoring tool. The content author has chosen to impose a 5-minute limit for completing the quiz. In order to pass this standard, time limits for quizzes should be used only if learners can turn off, adjust or extend them.
SOURCE Reproduced with permission of www.ispringsolutions.com (archived at https://perma.cc/2ZPC-5EAP)

How to test

1 Check that there are no time limits for activities unless learners can turn off, adjust or extend them.

2 Check that your eLearning resource does not contain any automatically moving text or other content which learners cannot control.

Useful resources

- 2.2.1 Timing Adjustable – Level A[12]
  W3C quick reference guide and further information for this standard.

2.2.2 Pause, Stop, Hide – Level A

Make sure learners can pause, stop or hide any content that starts automatically, moves, scrolls or blinks for longer than five seconds and appears alongside other content. The same must also be true for content that automatically updates and appears alongside other content.

Key information

Content that automatically moves, blinks or scrolls is commonly used in eLearning resources to add visual interest or draw learners' attention to items. An example of automatically moving content could be a looping animated GIF which repeatedly replays, an image carousel which continually moves to the next image or a marker which has pulse animation. Blinking content could be a start button which has an animation effect added to it. Scrolling content could be a scrolling panel with text which is programmed to scroll automatically. While any motion can add visual interest, it can also be distracting if it continues for too long. Moving content can cause particular problems for people with cognitive impairments such as attention deficit hyperactivity disorder (ADHD), who may find it difficult or even impossible to interact with the rest of the content on a page as a result of distracting movement. For learners with vestibular disorders, some moving content can lead to symptoms such as dizziness and nausea.

Automatically updating content such as news, weather information or social media feeds is a common feature of standard websites. In an eLearning context it could apply to a content curation feed. Again, movement caused by the updating content can be distracting and may make it difficult for learners to concentrate or to interact with the rest of the page.

Although this standard does allow moving, scrolling, flashing or automatically updating content as long as it can be controlled by learners, best practice is to avoid it.

Note: This standard refers specifically to blinking as opposed to flashing content. Blinking content causes a distraction, while flashing content can cause seizures. There are detailed technical specifications around what constitutes flashing content and these are covered by standard **2.3.1 Three Flashes or Below Threshold.**

How to conform

1 Make sure learners can pause, stop or hide any content which starts automatically and moves, scrolls or blinks for longer than 5 seconds.

2 Make sure learners can pause, stop or hide any automatically updating content or can control how frequently the content updates.

3 Make sure that any instructions on how to control content movement are clear and that any interactions are keyboard accessible.

Exceptions

• Animations such as a progress bar which needs to move in order to show that it hasn't frozen or broken are exempt.

• Standalone content which is not presented alongside other content is exempt. For example, an animation which appears alone on a page while a video is being downloaded.

• If the moving, scrolling, blinking or automatically updating content is essential to the activity, this is exempt, for example automatically updating financial information on a stocks and shares website.

Why?

Learners who benefit from this standard include:

• people who use screen readers and who may miss information such as text, or voiced alternative text for images if content automatically moves or disappears before it has been announced by a screen reader;

• people with cognitive impairments which affect concentration and attention such as attention deficit hyperactivity disorder (ADHD) who may find the movement of content distracting;

• people with cognitive impairments and some second language learners who may need more time to read text or process images before they automatically move or disappear;

• people affected by situational impairments which affect their ability to concentrate, for example people working from home in a noisy and stressful environment.

How to test

1 Check that learners can pause, stop or hide any content which starts automatically and moves, scrolls or blinks for longer than 5 seconds.

2 Check that learners can pause, stop or hide any automatically updating content or can control how frequently the content updates.

3 Check that any instructions on how to control content movement are clear and that interactions are keyboard accessible.

Useful resources

- 2.2.2 Pause, Stop, Hide – Level A[13]
  W3C quick reference guide and further information for this standard.

2.3.1 Three Flashes or Below Threshold – Level A

In order to prevent seizures do not include any content which flashes more than three times per second unless the flashes are small enough or dim enough to fall below the required thresholds. If the flashes contain very little of the colour red, they may also fall below the required threshold.

Key information

This standard is extremely important for people who have photosensitive seizure disorders, including photosensitive epilepsy. Any content which flashes more than three times per second and does not fall below the acceptable thresholds can cause seizures. Flashing content in eLearning resources could include an object such as a button which has been programmed to appear and disappear for visual effect, or a video clip or animated image which contains flashing content such as strobe lights or different types of lightning.

Many people are particularly sensitive to red flashing content, which is why it is specifically covered in the threshold requirements. The thresholds have specific size, brightness and red content requirements and are referenced in the Useful resources section.

Note: The advanced standard **2.3.2 Three Flashes** does not allow any content which flashes more than three times per second, even if the flashes are below the acceptable thresholds. This is considered to be best practice.

How to conform

Make sure that no content flashes more than three times per second unless it falls below the acceptable thresholds.

Exceptions

- Flashes which are small enough or dim enough to fall below the required thresholds are exempt.

- Flashes which contain very little of the colour red may also fall below the required threshold and be exempt.

Why?

Learners who benefit from this standard include:

- people with photosensitive seizure disorders, including photosensitive epilepsy, who can have seizures triggered by flashing content which does not fall below the acceptable thresholds.

How to test

Check that no content flashes more than three times per second unless it falls below the acceptable thresholds. A testing tool can be found in the Useful resources section.

Useful resources

- General flash and red flash thresholds[14]
  Recommendations from W3C on general flash and red flash thresholds.

- Photosensitive Epilepsy Analysis Tool[15]
  Information on photosensitive epilepsy and a testing tool from the Trace Research and Development Center.

- Photosensitive epilepsy[16]
  Information from Epilepsy Action on photosensitive epilepsy.
- 2.3.1 Three Flashes or Below Threshold – Level A[17]
  W3C quick reference guide and further information for this standard.

2.4.1 Bypass Blocks – Level A

Make sure learners who navigate using a keyboard or keyboard interface can skip blocks of content repeated over multiple pages and move directly to the main content of a page. In eLearning resources this most often applies to navigation items such as menus which are repeated on multiple pages.

Key information

While visual learners can choose to start reading a page wherever they want and often jump straight to the main content on a page, learners who use a keyboard or a keyboard interface to navigate have to access the content sequentially. This standard benefits these learners because it allows them to 'bypass' or skip to the main content of the page without having to tab through or, in the case of screen reader users, listen to blocks of content which are repeated across multiple pages. These could include links in a header or a sidebar menu, or items which appear in the course player, such as links to resources, glossaries and notes. They could also include blocks of text repeated across multiple pages such as course navigation instructions.

Some authoring tools provide bypass links such as 'Skip to main content' or 'Skip navigation' links which are always visible. Others provide bypass links which become visible only when the 'Tab' key is used to navigate through the content. If the authoring tool doesn't automatically provide bypass links, it is the responsibility of the content author to create a mechanism which allows learners to bypass blocks of repeated content.

How to conform

Make sure that keyboard users can skip content which is repeated across multiple pages.

Exception

- This standard does not apply to small, repeated sections of content such as individual words, phrases or single links.

Why?

Learners who benefit from this standard include:

- people who have motor impairments who use a keyboard or keyboard interface to navigate. A mechanism which allows them to skip repeated content requires fewer keystrokes to reach the main content of a page. This is extremely important as each keystroke can take a long time and can even cause discomfort or physical pain for some learners;
- people who are blind and use screen readers. They will not have to hear the screen reader repeatedly voice the same navigational content before they can hear the main content of the page;
- people affected by situational impairments, eg someone who has a wireless mouse which has run out of charge or battery power and has to navigate using the keyboard.

Example

FIGURE 9.7   Skip to lesson bypass link (Articulate Rise)

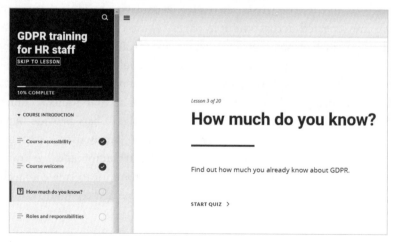

The 'Skip to lesson' bypass link in the menu of a resource created using the Articulate Rise authoring tool. This appears when learners use the 'Tab' key to navigate through the menu and prevents them having to tab through each item in the menu before they can access the content of a lesson.
SOURCE ©Articulate Global, Inc. Used with permission, all other rights reserved

How to test

Check that keyboard users can skip blocks of content which are repeated across multiple pages.

Useful resources

- 'Skip navigation' links[18]
  Article from WebAIM with detailed information regarding different methods which allow learners to skip links.
- Add a 'Skip Navigation' Link to Help Keyboard Users Reach Main Content Faster[19]
  Article from Deque University with sample HTML coding for creating skip navigation links.
- 2.4.1 Bypass Blocks – Level A[20]
  W3C quick reference guide and further information for this standard.

2.4.2 Page Titled – Level A

Give each page in the eLearning resource a descriptive title which explains the topic or purpose of the page.

Key information

This standard helps everyone to quickly understand what the topic or purpose of a page is before they access the content. It is particularly important for people who use assistive technology such as screen reader users who hear this information before they reach any other content on the page. With some authoring tools, page titles are coded using the <title> element. If this is the case, depending on how the resource is displayed, the title appears in the browser's title bar, or in the name of the tab if there are multiple pages open. This helps learners to navigate and to find information. This is also true if page titles are displayed in the menu of an eLearning resource.

A good way to check how effective your page titles are is to read them out of context. This is done for you automatically if your tool uses page titles to create a menu. Otherwise you can create your own list in a separate document to check that they can be understood when they stand alone without any supporting information. It should be possible for learners to understand exactly what they will cover on the page just from the title. Making sure that each title clearly explains the purpose of the page is also a great way of ensuring that any content included on that page keeps to topic when you are designing the resource. In addition to being descriptive, best practice is to ensure that page titles are concise and wherever possible, unique.

How to conform

Make sure that all pages have a descriptive title which explains the topic or purpose of the page.

Why?

Learners who benefit from this standard include:

- people with cognitive impairments which affect memory and reading ability. They will find it easier to understand the topic or purpose of a page if it has a concise and descriptive title;
- people who use assistive technology such as screen readers and refreshable braille displays which recognize and announce page titles before the content is reached;
- all learners, as being able to quickly and easily understand the topic or purpose of pages is good user experience for everyone.

Example

FIGURE 9.8   Page titles displayed in a menu (Articulate Rise)

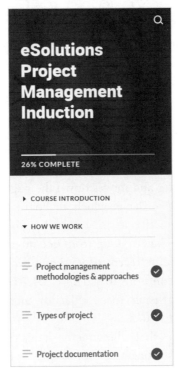

A course menu created with the Articulate Rise authoring tool showing unique, concise and descriptive titles for each page in an eLearning resource. Titles such as 'Project management methodologies & approaches', 'Types of project' and 'Project documentation' allow learners to quickly understand what information they will find on the page and can also help them to navigate to content that is relevant for them.

SOURCE ©Articulate Global, Inc. Used with permission, all other rights reserved

How to test

1   Check that each page in the eLearning resource has a unique, concise and descriptive title which explains the topic or purpose of the page's content.

2   Use a screen reader to make sure that assistive technology recognizes and announces page titles correctly.

Useful resources

- 2.4.2 Page Titled – Level A[21]
  W3C quick reference guide and further information for this standard.

2.4.3 Focus Order – Level A

Make sure that when learners navigate using a keyboard or keyboard interface, they move through interactive items in a logical linear order.

Key information

When visual learners read a page, they can choose to view the content in any order that suits them. Assistive technology, however, works by moving through content in a linear order. For English content, the order begins in the top right-hand corner and moves down the page until it finishes in the bottom right. This is the order in which keyboard navigation moves from interactive item to interactive item. Standard keyboard navigation allows learners to use the 'Tab' key to jump from one interactive item to the next. When an item is reached, it 'receives focus' and becomes active. As long as the eLearning resource conforms to standard **2.4.7 Focus Visible**, each interactive item will have a visible focus indicator such as a coloured border which appears when it has focus.

This standard requires that all interactive items receive focus in a logical order. Imagine how frustrating and confusing it would be if this wasn't the case – for example, if learners were trying to enter data into input fields on a form and when they used the 'Tab' key to move to the next field they were jumped instead to a field near the bottom of the form.

Authoring tools have various ways to make sure that interactive items are ordered correctly, and tool providers should give instructions on how this is possible. With some tools, simply placing interactive items in the correct visual order on the page ensures that they are in the correct order for keyboard navigation. Other authoring tools may require content authors to set the correct tab or focus order, or to layer objects in the correct order on the page.

Note: This standard is similar to standard **1.3.2 Meaningful Sequence**, but instead of referring to all content, it applies only to interactive items such as navigation items, input items and links.

How to conform

Make sure that when learners navigate using a keyboard, they move through interactive items in a logical linear order.

Exception

- This standard doesn't apply if there is no logical sequence needed to navigate interactive items, for example a random series of links presented in a word cloud. In this case the order in which the links are selected doesn't make any difference to the meaning so they can be navigated in any order.

Why?

Learners who benefit from this standard include:

- people who are blind or have low vision and use screen readers to navigate;
- people who have motor impairments and use a keyboard or keyboard interface to navigate;
- people with temporary impairments, eg someone who has an injured wrist or arm and needs to use a keyboard rather than a mouse to navigate.

Example

FIGURE 9.9   Logical focus order for interactive items (Articulate Storyline)

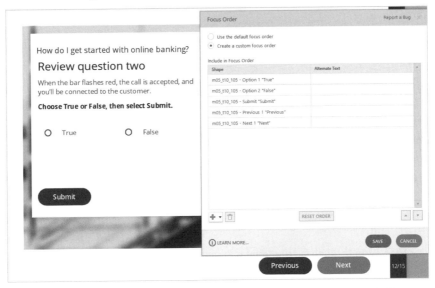

In the Articulate Storyline authoring tool the interactive items you add to a slide automatically appear in the Focus Order list. The items appear in the order in which you add them on the page. You often need to create a custom focus order so you can rearrange the items to be announced in a logical order by a screen reader. This True or False question example shows the interactive items in a logical order. The 'True' radio button appears first followed by the 'False' radio button. These are then followed by the 'Submit' button and then the 'Previous' and 'Next' buttons.

How to test

Navigate through the eLearning resource using only the keyboard. Check that the order for focusable interactive items is logical for both meaning and navigation.

Useful resources

- 2.4.3 Focus Order – Level A[22]
  W3C quick reference guide and further information for this standard.

2.4.4 Link Purpose (in Context) – Level A

Make sure that learners know where they will be taken when they select a link. You can do this either by using information in the link text itself or by adding information in the text surrounding the link. Underlying code should also be used so that assistive technology users know where links will take them.

Key information

This standard requires that learners are able to identify the 'purpose' of a link. Since the function of a link is to take learners to another destination, this means that learners need to know where a link will take them either from the link text itself or from the link text and information in the text surrounding the link eg in the same sentence, paragraph, list item or table cell, etc. For example:

Destination through link text alone
The difference between accessibility and usability.

Destination through surrounding text and link text
Before you start this assignment, it is important that you research the difference between accessibility and usability. Find out more.

Note: If the destination of the link is given in the surrounding text, best practice is to make sure this information is easy to find, eg it comes before the link rather than after it.

Assistive technology users must be able to identify links and where they will be taken when they select them. This is done through the underlying code of the tool. For example:

Text Link

<a href="/definition/computer">Computer Definition</a>

Image Link

<a href="https://techterms.com/definition/computer"><img src="/images/computer.jpg" alt="desktop PC"></a>

More information about coding for links can be found in the Useful links section.

Best practice for links

The advanced standard **2.4.9 Link Purpose (Link Only)** recommends that the link text alone should let learners predict where the link will take them, ie it does not allow this information to be provided in the surrounding text. This is considered to be best practice for accessible links. One of the reasons for this is due to the way that some assistive technology users navigate content. While visual learners can read the content of a page in any order they choose, assistive technology can only access content in a linear order. This means that screen reader users, for example, have to listen to every item on a page in the set order. Sometimes they will choose instead to 'scan listen' the contents of a page by jumping from heading to heading or from link to link. This works well for links if the link text itself tells learners where they will be taken. It doesn't work, however, if links use text such as 'Click here' or 'Find out more' and learners are expected to search in the surrounding text to find out the destination of the links. See Figures 9.10 and 9.11 to see examples of a screen reader Elements List which clarify this.

Another best practice recommendation for links is to avoid using full URLs (Uniform Resource Locaters), eg: https://www.bbc.co.uk/blogs/internet/entries/7a072979-8e30-49c6-a44e-a5bed647e12c.

Using full URLs for links is not good user experience for any learners because it often makes it more difficult for people to work where the link will take them. In the URL above, for example, the text doesn't contain the topic of the blog, only a series of numbers. This makes it impossible for learners to know from the link itself the content of the blog. Full URL links also cause problems for assistive technology users. For example, screen readers announce all the words and letters of a full URL. They may also announce all the punctuation depending on the punctuation settings that the screen reader user has chosen. Imagine how time-consuming and frustrating it would be to have to listen to a screen reader read out the full URL above.

If links open in a new window it is good practice to make learners aware of this, eg by adding text. For example, The difference between usability and accessibility (opens in a new window). The same information should be added to the underlying code so that it is also clear for assistive technology users. More information on how to achieve this can be found in the Useful resources section.

A final best-practice recommendation refers to the link text itself. It should always be clear, concise and informative. If possible, it should also either be the same as or very similar to the title of the destination page. This makes it easier for learners once they have arrived at the link's destination to be sure that they have selected the correct link and have been taken to the correct destination.

Note: Multiple links within an eLearning resource or on a page are covered by standard **3.2.4 Consistent Identification**. This requires that if there are multiple links to the same destination, these should be consistently labelled, ie have the same link text throughout.

How to conform

1 Make sure that learners can predict where links will take them, either through the link text itself or through the link text and information in the surrounding text.

2 Make sure that assistive technology users can recognize links and predict where the links will take them.

Exceptions

- Ambiguous links are exempt if they are deliberate. For example, it would be acceptable for the text of links to be ambiguous such as Portal 1 or Portal 2 if you wanted to create an element of surprise in a game.

- This standard does not apply if the purpose of the link is ambiguous for everyone. For example, if an eLearning resource for the travel industry had a link on a page which said Civil Aviation Authority (CAA), this could be ambiguous because the link could go to anything connected to the CAA. For example, it could take learners to a list of senior staff, or to an article about the history of the organization. These types of links are exempt because they are ambiguous for everyone.

Why?

Learners who benefit from this standard include:

- people who are blind or have low vision and use screen readers to voice the link text and to navigate;

- people who have motor impairments which affect dexterity and may have difficulty navigating to other pages. They will benefit by being sure that they only select links that are relevant for them;

- people who use speech recognition software. They will benefit from concise and informative links as they may need to voice the links in order activate them;

- all learners, as being able to easily identify where links will take them is good user experience for everyone.

Examples

FIGURE 9.10   Non-descriptive links shown in the Elements List of a screen reader (Articulate Rise)

Links in a resource created using the Articulate Storyline Rise authoring tool. These links conform to this standard because learners can identify where the links will take them due to the information in the surrounding text. The insert shows the Elements List from a screen reader. This functionality allows screen reader users to quickly navigate the content by jumping from link to link. If the information about the destination of links is given only in the surrounding text, however, this makes it impossible for screen reader users to make use of this functionality because a series of links with text that reads 'Find out more' is meaningless.

FIGURE 9.11   Descriptive links shown in the Elements List of a screen reader (Articulate Rise)

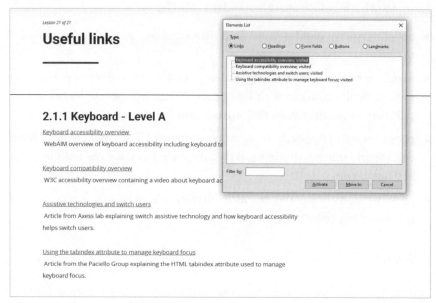

Links in a resource created using the Articulate Rise authoring tool. These links comply with the advanced standard 2.4.9 LINK PURPOSE (LINK ONLY) which recommends that the link text alone should let learners predict where they will be taken. The screen reader Elements List shown in the insert demonstrates how descriptive links such as 'Keyboard accessibility overview' allow screen reader users to use the Elements List to easily identify and navigate to the links which are relevant to them on a page.
SOURCE ©Articulate Global, Inc. Used with permission, all other rights reserved

How to test

1 Check that learners can predict where links will take them, either through the link text and information in the surrounding text or, for best practice, through the link text alone.

2 Use a screen reader to check that assistive technology users can recognize links and can predict where the links will take them.

Useful resources

- <a>: The Anchor element
  Guidance on the HTML <a> element from MDN web docs.

- Links and Hypertext – Link Text and Appearance[23]
  Guidance on text for accessible links from WebAIM.

- Usability & Web Accessibility – Links[24]
  Guidance from Yale University on creating accessible links.

- G201: Giving users advanced warning when opening a new window[25]
  Guidance from W3C on alerting learners when links open in a new window.

- 2.4.4 Link Purpose (in Context) – Level A[26]
  W3C quick reference guide and further information for this standard.

2.4.5 Multiple Ways – Level AA

Give learners more than one way to navigate content in eLearning resources. For example, provide a 'Home' icon, a menu and a search facility.

Key information

This standard gives learners control over how they navigate the content of eLearning resources. By giving them more than one way to navigate pages it ensures that learners can choose an option which best suits their needs. This can be achieved using various techniques, including:

- a 'Home' icon which allows learners to access links to other pages in the site;
- menus displayed in a sidebar or accessed via a 'Hamburger' icon;
- a search facility and tags;
- interactive page numbers;
- page navigation controls such as 'Forward' and 'Back' buttons;
- a breadcrumb trail.

Most authoring tools allow you to give learners the option to navigate content in more than one way. This could involve adding or enabling a search facility in the settings, adding or enabling a menu, adding links to pages or adding page navigation items such as 'Next' or forward arrow icons.

Note: Some eLearning resources are deliberately 'step locked'. This means that learners can only follow content in a particular order, eg they cannot move to the next module until they have completed the one before. It could be argued that this is allowed because one exception to this standard applies to any content which is part of a process that must be followed in a particular order. Good practice, however, would be to open up the content after learners have accessed it for the first time. They should then be able to navigate the content in multiple ways.

How to conform

Make sure learners have more than one way to navigate the content in eLearning resources.

Exception

- An exception to this standard applies to content which is part of a process and which needs to be followed in sequence. Website examples include e-commerce sites with a series of pages which are part of the shopping process, or banking sites with a series of pages to complete a loan application. In the case of eLearning resources it could apply to content which is step locked due to a required learner journey.

Why?

Learners who benefit from this standard include:

- people who have visual impairments who may find it easier to use a search facility to find content rather than navigating through a menu;
- people who have cognitive impairments which affect memory and who may find it easier to use a menu to find content rather than accessing it sequentially using page navigation;
- all learners, as being able to choose how they navigate content depending on their preferences or needs is good user experience for everyone.

Example

FIGURE 9.12   Multiple ways to navigate (Articulate Rise)

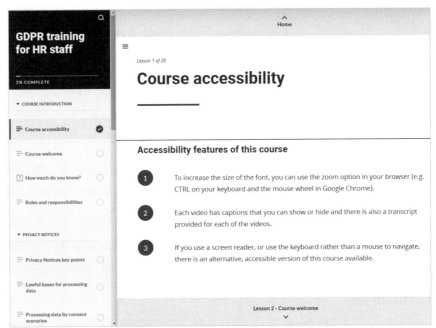

An eLearning resource created with the Articulate Rise authoring tool which provides learners with multiple ways to navigate the course. They can use the menu in the left-hand navigation or use the next lesson option at the bottom of the page to access lessons. There is also a search facility shown by a magnifying glass icon above the title of the course. This offers another way for learners to navigate content.

SOURCE ©Articulate Global, Inc. Used with permission, all other rights reserved

How to test

Check that learners have more than one way to navigate content in eLearning resources.

Useful resources

- Site Searches, Indexes and Site Maps[27]
  Article from WebAIM detailing different techniques for achieving this standard.
- 2.4.5 Multiple Ways – Level AA[28]
  W3C quick reference guide and further information for this standard.

2.4.6 Headings and Labels – Level AA

Make sure that any page headings describe the topic or purpose of the page and section headings explain the topic or purpose of the text that follows. Also make sure that the labels provided for interactive items make it clear what the purpose of the item is.

Key information

This standard doesn't require that headings or labels are used, only that if they are, they are descriptive. Descriptive page headings help learners to quickly understand the topic or purpose of a page and section headings to understand the purpose of the text that follows. Descriptive labels for inter-active items make it clear what the item is for. For example, a descriptive label for a data entry field which requires learners to enter their first name would be 'First name'. A descriptive label for a button which allows learners to magnify an image could be 'Zoom in'.

Note: This standard doesn't make any requirements about the coding of headings or labels for assistive technology. Coding requirements for headings are covered under standard **1.2.1 Info and relationships** and for labels are covered under standard **4.1.2 Name, Role and Value**.

The advanced standard **2.4.10 Section Headings** recommends that content authors use section headings, ie it doesn't refer to whether the section headings are descriptive or not but recommends that they are used.

How to conform

1 Make sure that any page headings clearly describe the topic or purpose of the page and any section headings explain the topic or purpose of the text that follows.

2 Make sure that labels for interactive items such as buttons describe the purpose of the item. Also make sure that labels for data entry fields describe the purpose of the field, ie make it clear what learners need to enter into the field.

Why?

Learners who benefit from this standard include:

- people who use screen readers and typically listen to content at a much higher speed than normal human speech. This 'skim listening' skill is made much easier if descriptive headings and section headings are used;

- people who have cognitive impairments which affect memory or reading ability who benefit from clear and descriptive signposting to help them understand and navigate content;

- all learners, as being able to clearly understand the topic and purpose of a page's content and understand the purpose of interactive items is good user experience for everyone.

How to test

1 Check that any page headings clearly describe the topic or purpose of the page and any section headings explain the topic or purpose of the text that follows.

2 Check that labels for interactive items such as buttons describe the purpose of the item. Also check that labels for data entry fields describe the purpose of the field, ie make it clear what learners need to enter into the field.

Useful resources

- Content design: planning, writing and managing content[29]
  Guidance from the UK Government Digital Service on how to write better online content.

- How people read online: New and old findings[30]
  Article from Nielsen Norman Group detailing survey results about how people read online content which highlights the importance of using descriptive headings and subheadings.

- 2.4.6 Headings and Labels – Level AA[31]
  W3C quick reference guide and further information for this standard.

2.4.7 Focus Visible – Level AA

Make sure that when learners navigate using a keyboard or keyboard interface there is a visible focus indicator for interactive items. This means there is a visible sign to show that these items have been selected. This could be with a change in the appearance of a button or a coloured border around a link, etc.

Key information

Many people are not able to use a mouse and the onscreen mouse pointer. Instead they use a standard keyboard, an adapted keyboard or an equivalent keyboard interface such as an onscreen keyboard to navigate and interact with content. Standard keyboard navigation allows learners to use the 'Tab' key to jump from one interactive item to the next. This normally applies to navigation items, input items and links, although it can also include tooltips or widgets such as calendar pickers.

When an item is reached, it 'receives focus' and becomes active. Whenever this happens there should be a clearly visible change to the item. This could involve a button or text changing colour, or a visible border appearing around the item which is in focus. It is important for visual keyboard users to be able to see when an item receives focus, so that it is clear where they are on the page and which item is selected and can therefore be activated. It is also important that the focus indicator is not time limited ie that it remains visible as long as the item has keyboard focus.

Note: The functionality of the visible focus indicator is usually controlled by the authoring tool, although some authoring tools do allow content authors to customize its colour and sometimes width. If this is the case make sure that the selected focus indicator colour has a colour contrast ratio of at least 3:1 against the background it appears on. This minimum contrast ratio is also recommended for the contrast between the colour of the interactive item and the focus indicator.

How to conform

Make sure there is a visible focus indicator which tells visual keyboard users when interactive items have been selected.

Why?

Learners who benefit from this standard include:

- visual learners with motor impairments which affect dexterity and who use a keyboard or keyboard interface to navigate. They can clearly see where they are on a page and when interactive items have been selected;

- people who have low vision and who navigate using screen reader keyboard navigation. They will be able to use the focus indicator to help them navigate quickly and efficiently;

- people with cognitive impairments such as those who experience attention or short-term memory issues who may find it beneficial to navigate using a keyboard so that they have a visual indicator which shows them where they are on a page;

- visual learners who prefer to navigate using a keyboard because they find it faster to interact with content, particularly when entering data into data entry fields. They will benefit from being able to see which fields are active when they are inputting data.

Examples

FIGURE 9.13   Visible focus indicator for radio buttons (CourseArc)

A multiple choice question created using the CourseArc authoring tool. Visual learners navigating using the keyboard can see which radio button is selected due to the visible focus border which appears around the radio button. In this case, the visible focus indicator shows that the first answer is currently selected. To choose this option learners could then use standard keyboard navigation and press the space bar.

SOURCE Reproduced with permission of CourseArc

FIGURE 9.14   Customizable focus indicator (Lectora Online)

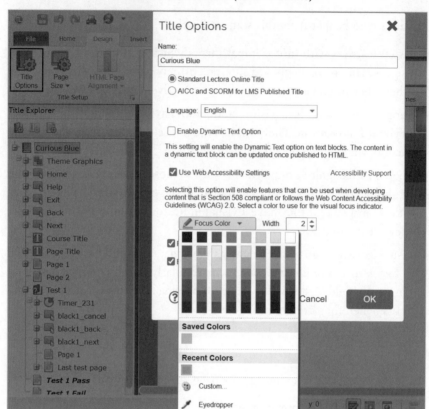

Some authoring tools allow you to customize the visible focus indicator. The Lectora Online authoring tool allows you to change the default colour and the width of the focus indicator in the Title Options to make it easier for visual learners to see.
SOURCE Reproduced with permission of eLearning Brothers

How to test

Navigate through the eLearning resource using only the keyboard. Check that each interactive item has a clear visual indicator when it receives keyboard focus.

Useful resources

- Why the focus indicator is important[32]
  Video from Nomensa explaining why the focus indicator is important for accessibility.

- Give Your Site Some Focus! Tips for Designing Useful and Usable Focus Indicators[33]
Article from Deque on designing accessible focus indicators.

- 2.4.7 Focus Visible – Level AA[34]
W3C quick reference guide and further information for this standard.

2.5.1 Pointer Gestures – Level A

Added in 2.1

For any interactions which need learners to carry out complex gestures, provide an alternative simple gesture which needs only a single point of contact. Complex gestures include 'multipoint' gestures which need two fingers, such as a two-finger pinch to zoom, and 'path-based' gestures where the path that the finger takes is important, such as a touch-and-drag interaction to pan.

Key information

This standard applies to pointer gestures which allow learners to interact with content. Its primary aim is to ensure that touchscreen gestures on mobile devices are accessible. It doesn't apply only to mobile devices, however. The same gestures could be used by someone using a trackpad on a laptop or desktop, or on a touchscreen laptop or monitor. Equally it doesn't only apply to finger gestures. The pointer gesture could be carried out by a mouse or joystick, or assistive technology devices such as a head or mouth pointer or an eye-gaze system.

The standard applies to both 'multipoint' and 'path-based' gestures:

- **Multipoint gesture.** This is a gesture that needs more than a single point of contact with a device such as where more than one finger or pointer touch is required. A two-finger pinch to zoom interaction is a multipoint gesture because it needs two fingers to carry out the pinch interaction. Other examples include split taps where learners need to keep one finger on the screen and tap with another, or two or three finger taps or swipes.

- **Path-based gesture**. This is a gesture where the path taken in the gesture is important as well as the end point. A gesture that requires swiping down and then right, rather than just simple swiping up or down, is a path-based gesture because the interaction works only if the path followed is correct.

This standard requires that any multipoint or path-based gestures have a single point interaction provided as an alternative. On a touchscreen, a single point interaction relies on only one point of contact with the screen to work. Single or double tap or click gestures, or a simple swiping gesture, are examples of single point interactions.

How to conform

Make sure that an alternative action which requires only a single point of contact is provided for all interactions which need learners to carry out complex multipoint or path-based gestures.

Exceptions

- This standard does not apply if multipoint or path-based gestures are essential. This would be the case, for example, if the learner needed to enter their signature with a pointer or finger, or for a game where a particular path-based gesture was needed.
- Complex gestures which are required to operate the user agent such as the web browser or assistive technology are also exempt.

Why?

Learners who benefit from this standard include:

- people who have motor impairments which affect dexterity and who are not able to carry out multipoint or path-based gestures;
- older people who often have dexterity issues and who may find it difficult to carry out complex gestures;
- people with temporary motor impairments, eg someone with a hand injury which means they cannot carry out complex gestures with their fingers.

How to test

Check that an alternative action which requires only a single point of contact is provided for all interactions which need learners to carry out complex multipoint or path-based gestures.

Useful resources

- 2.5.1 Pointer Gestures – Level A[35]
  W3C quick reference guide and further information for this standard.

2.5.2 Pointer Cancellation – Level A

Added in 2.1

Stop learners accidentally activating interactive items by triggering functionality on the up-event rather than the down-event unless they can undo or reverse the action. The up-event is when learners release their finger, the pointer or the mouse click. The down-event is when they press their finger, the pointer or the mouse click down.

Key information

Common or 'native' behaviour for any interactive item that can be activated by a single gesture such as the click of a mouse is that the action is triggered on the up-event rather than the down-event. This means that learners select an item by clicking on it, which is known as the down-event, but the interactivity of the item is not triggered until they release the mouse click, which is known as the up-event. This gives learners the chance to undo the action if they have clicked on something unintentionally. For example, if someone clicks on a link and then changes their mind, they can move the mouse pointer away from the link and release the mouse without being taken to the link's destination. They will only trigger the functionality and open the link if it is still selected and they release the mouse click.

This standard helps people who have motor impairments and may accidently activate interactions if they are triggered on the down-event rather than the up-event. In addition to mouse interactions, this standard requires the same behaviour for touchscreen and mobile device interactions. In these cases the down-event is when a finger or any pointing device such as a pointer or stylus touches the screen, while the up-event is when a finger or device is lifted away from the screen.

How to conform

Make sure that at least one of the following criteria is true for any interactive items which are triggered by only one click of the mouse or touch of the touchscreen:

- No functionality is triggered on the down-event.

- The functionality is completed on the up-event and learners can abort the action before it is completed, or can undo the action once it has been completed. A good example to demonstrate this is drag-and-drop interactions where selecting and moving an item takes place on the down-event, while dropping it on the intended target takes place on the up-event. If learners realize they have selected the wrong item, they can release the mouse, finger or pointer before they reach the intended target and the item reverts to its original position.

- The down-event triggers an event but that event is cancelled out by the up-event. An example would be with a press-and-hold action like a pop-up which appears when an item is pressed or clicked but disappears again when it is released.

Exceptions

- This standard applies only to interactions which are triggered by a single point gesture, ie a gesture which uses only one touch point and no movement.

- Any functionality in which the down-event is an essential interaction, such as selecting the letters on an onscreen keyboard or touching the keys on a simulated piano keyboard, is exempt.

- Actions which are needed to operate the user agent such as the web browser or assistive technology are also exempt.

Why?

Learners who benefit from this standard include:

- people who have motor impairments such as tremors which make it easy to accidently activate the functionality of interactive items;
- people with low vision who may find it more difficult to distinguish and locate interactive items, making it easier to select them by mistake;
- people who use assistive devices such as mouth or headsticks which may make it easier to select interactive items by mistake;
- people affected by situational impairments who may be more likely to select interactive items on mobile devices by mistake, eg someone on a jolting train journey.

How to test

Check that learners activate interactive items by triggering functionality on the up-event rather than the down-event. If this is not possible, make sure that if they are triggered on the up-event, any actions can be aborted or undone, or that the up-event cancels the functionality of the down-event.

Useful resources

- Exploring WCAG 2.1 — 2.5.2 Pointer Cancellation[36]
  Article from Knowability with examples and further explanations.
- 2.5.2 Pointer Cancellation – Level A[37]
  W3C quick reference guide and further information for this standard.

2.5.3 Label in Name – Level A

Added in 2.1

Make sure that interactive items which have a visible label such as the text on buttons have the same accessible name which can be recognized by assistive technology.

Key information

The purpose of this standard is to make it easier for users of assistive technology such as voice recognition software or screen readers to operate interactive items in eLearning resources. Many of these items have a visible name or label, for example a 'Next' button. The word 'Next' is the visible label which tells learners what will happen when they interact with the button. In addition to the visible label, the 'Next' button should have an accessible name. This is the alternative text for the label recognized by assistive technology. This standard requires that the label and the accessible name match.

This standard is particularly important for learners using speech recognition software who use spoken commands to operate functionality. Imagine how frustrating it would be to try to activate a button which is visibly labelled 'Start' by saying 'Select start' to speech recognition software, only to find that this doesn't work because the accessible name for the button is 'Begin'. For screen reader users who have low vision or who use the screen reader to navigate because they have a motor impairment, this standard is also helpful. It avoids confusion and disorientation by making sure that the visible label matches what is voiced by the screen reader.

Note: Sometimes the visible label is different from the accessible name because of the functionality of the item, for example a button which has the visible label 'B' to show that it is for bold functionality. In this case the accessible name should be 'Bold' and not 'B'. Another common example in eLearning resources is a visible label such as the 'greater than' symbol '>' on a button to signify play. This should have the accessible name 'Play', not 'Greater than'.

How to conform

Make sure that interactive items with visible labels have an accessible text alternative that matches the visible label.

Why?

Learners who benefit from this standard include:

- people with motor impairments who use voice recognition software and will be able to successfully activate interactive items by voicing the visible name;

- visual screen reader users who will not be disorientated by seeing a visible label on an interactive item on screen and hearing the screen reader announce a different name.

Example

FIGURE 9.15   Visible name and accessible name mismatch (Articulate Storyline)

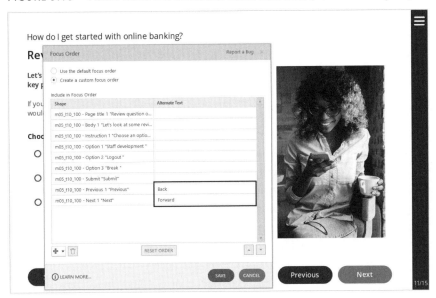

An eLearning resource created using Articulate Storyline which shows a mismatch between visible labels and the accessible names. The visible labels for the navigation buttons are 'Previous' and 'Next', but the accessible names in the Focus Order list are 'Back' and 'Forward'. This can often happen if the visible names of buttons are changed mid-way through an eLearning project but the corresponding accessible names are forgotten.
SOURCE ©Articulate Global, Inc. Used with permission, all other rights reserved

How to test

Use a screen reader to check that the accessible name for all interactive items matches the visible label.

Useful resources

- 2.5.3 Label in Name – Level A[38]
  W3C quick reference guide and further information for this standard.

2.5.4 Motion Actuation – Level A

Added in 2.1

Make sure that learners can disable functionality which is triggered by movement such as shaking or tilting a device to undo an action. Also make sure that the same functionality can be activated using standard controls such as a button or a link.

Key information

Mobile devices have accelerometer and gyroscope sensors which can detect the movement of a device very precisely. As a result, these sensors allow certain types of movement to act as an input. A common example is tilting a device to the right or left to move forwards or backwards through a series of steps. This is known as 'motion actuation'. Other examples of functionality triggered by motion include using a hand gesture to a camera to trigger moving forward in an event sequence, or the movement of eyes with an eye-tracking device which advances to the next page when the movement of the eyes signals that the end of a page has been reached.

This standard improves the experience of learners who may struggle to activate functionality that relies on the use of movements due to motor impairments such as tremors. It provides these learners with an accessible alternative way of carrying out the functionality triggered by motion actuation. It also benefits these learners because it allows them to disable motion actuation and so stops the possibility that it can be accidentally triggered.

How to conform

Make sure that learners can disable functionality which is triggered by movement and that the same functionality can be activated using standard single touch controls such as a button or a link.

Exceptions

- Any movement which is supported by assistive technology or by the accessibility features in user agents such as browsers is exempt.

- Any movement which is essential to functionality such as a pedometer which has the purpose of measuring the number of steps someone has taken is also exempt.

Why?

Learners who benefit from this standard include:

- people who have mobility impairments which affect dexterity, such as tremors, who may inadvertently trigger motion actuation;
- people who have mobility impairments which affect dexterity and may not be able to perform the particular movements needed to trigger functionality;
- people who have devices mounted on fixed holders on mobility aids such as wheelchairs and who may not be able to carry out the motion needed to trigger functionality;
- learners who benefit from having an alternative to motion actuation if they do not know the functionality exists or do not feel comfortable operating it.

How to test

Check that learners can disable functionality that is triggered by movement and that the same functionality can be activated using standard single touch controls such as a button or a link.

Useful resources

- 2.5.4 Motion Actuation – Level A[39]
  W3C quick reference guide and further information for this standard.

Endnotes

[1] H5P (Updated 2020) Recommendations and overviews of content types, 27 November, https://documentation.h5p.com/content/1290410474004879128 (archived at https://perma.cc/JA3D-2ZEH)
[2] WebAIM (Updated 2018) Keyboard Accessibility, 20 November, https://webaim.org/techniques/keyboard/ (archived at https://perma.cc/C8MB-QQMX)

3   W3C Web Accessibility Initiative (Updated 2019) Keyboard Compatibility, 23 January, https://www.w3.org/WAI/perspective-videos/keyboard/ (archived at https://perma.cc/99S5-6A5K)

4   Watson, L (2014) Using the tabindex attribute, The Paciello Group, 4 August, https://developer.paciellogroup.com/blog/2014/08/using-the-tabindex-attribute/ (archived at https://perma.cc/LB43-2RGY)

5   W3C (Updated 2019) How to Meet WCAG (quick reference), 4 October, https://www.w3.org/WAI/WCAG21/quickref/#keyboard (archived at https://perma.cc/TL7G-8AY9)

6   WebAIM (Updated 2018) Keyboard Accessibility, 20 November, https://webaim.org/techniques/keyboard/ (archived at https://perma.cc/C8MB-QQMX)

7   W3C Web Accessibility Initiative (Updated 2019) Keyboard Compatibility, 23 January, https://www.w3.org/WAI/perspective-videos/keyboard/ (archived at https://perma.cc/99S5-6A5K)

8   W3C (Updated 2019) How to Meet WCAG (quick reference), 4 October, https://www.w3.org/WAI/WCAG21/quickref/#no-keyboard-trap (archived at https://perma.cc/XT9J-HMD5)

9   Patch, K (2017) Single character key shortcuts affecting speech input – example 1 [Online video] https://www.youtube.com/watch?v=xzSyIA4OWYE&feature=youtu.be (archived at https://perma.cc/CE3A-3WUL)

10   Lucas, D (2018) WCAG 2.1 – What is character key shortcuts, 12 December, https://diginclusion.com/industry-updates/wcag-2-1-what-is-character-keyboard-shortcuts/ (archived at https://perma.cc/KN4P-S63X)

11   W3C (Updated 2019) How to Meet WCAG (quick reference), 4 October, https://www.w3.org/WAI/WCAG21/quickref/#character-key-shortcuts (archived at https://perma.cc/Q9S6-56FU)

12   W3C (Updated 2019) How to Meet WCAG (quick reference), 4 October, https://www.w3.org/WAI/WCAG21/quickref/#timing-adjustable (archived at https://perma.cc/B6B9-DJMR)

13   W3C (Updated 2019) How to Meet WCAG (quick reference), 4 October, https://www.w3.org/WAI/WCAG21/quickref/#pause-stop-hide (archived at https://perma.cc/3C8Y-V9SY)

14   W3C Recommendation (2008) General flash and red flash thresholds, 11 December, https://www.w3.org/TR/2008/REC-WCAG20-20081211/#general-thresholddef (archived at https://perma.cc/MJY6-E8F7)

15   University of Maryland College of Information Studies, Trace Center, Photosensitive Epilepsy Analysis Tool, https://trace.umd.edu/peat (archived at https://perma.cc/7MDR-M2HM)

16   Epilepsy Action (Updated 2018) Photosensitive epilepsy, June, https://www.epilepsy.org.uk/info/photosensitive-epilepsy (archived at https://perma.cc/Y59Q-5YT4)

17 W3C (Updated 2019) How to Meet WCAG (quick reference), 4 October, https://www.w3.org/WAI/WCAG21/quickref/#three-flashes-or-below-threshold (archived at https://perma.cc/5XZ2-63MS)

18 WebAIM (Updated 2013) 'Skip navigation' links, 25 October, https://webaim.org/techniques/skipnav/ (archived at https://perma.cc/5TC6-64A4)

19 Deque University, Add a 'Skip Navigation' Link to Help Keyboard Users Reach Main Content Faster, https://dequeuniversity.com/tips/add-skip-navigation-link (archived at https://perma.cc/BKN8-KWFK)

20 W3C (Updated 2019) How to Meet WCAG (quick reference), 4 October, https://www.w3.org/WAI/WCAG21/quickref/#bypass-blocks (archived at https://perma.cc/Q2XC-LRJM)

21 W3C (Updated 2019) How to Meet WCAG (quick reference), 4 October, https://www.w3.org/WAI/WCAG21/quickref/#page-titled (archived at https://perma.cc/3ZAS-5BHJ)

22 W3C (Updated 2019) How to Meet WCAG (quick reference), 4 October, https://www.w3.org/WAI/WCAG21/quickref/#focus-order (archived at https://perma.cc/5T3P-AJV6)

23 WebAIM (Updated 2019) Links and Hypertext – Link Text and Appearance, 24 October, https://webaim.org/techniques/hypertext/link_text (archived at https://perma.cc/WP57-STH2)

24 Yale University, Usability & Web Accessibility – Links, https://usability.yale.edu/web-accessibility/articles/links (archived at https://perma.cc/VH7S-RFYD)

25 W3C (2016) G201: Giving users advanced warning when opening a new window, https://www.w3.org/TR/WCAG20-TECHS/G201.html (archived at https://perma.cc/VL3V-MV3C)

26 W3C (Updated 2019) How to Meet WCAG (quick reference), 4 October, https://www.w3.org/WAI/WCAG21/quickref/#link-purpose-in-context (archived at https://perma.cc/G4D8-6MMX)

27 WebAIM (Updated 2013) Site Searches, Indexes and Site Maps, 25 October, https://webaim.org/techniques/sitetools/ (archived at https://perma.cc/U38A-UUJG)

28 W3C (Updated 2019) How to Meet WCAG (quick reference), 4 October, https://www.w3.org/WAI/WCAG21/quickref/#multiple-ways (archived at https://perma.cc/9XH4-D3JN)

29 GOV.UK, Content design: planning, writing and managing content, https://www.gov.uk/guidance/content-design/writing-for-gov-uk (archived at https://perma.cc/49MD-RZT2)

30 Moran, K (2020) How people read online: New and old findings, 5 April, https://www.nngroup.com/articles/how-people-read-online/?lm=how-users-read-on-the-web&pt=article (archived at https://perma.cc/9PJZ-D8G4)

31 W3C (Updated 2019) How to Meet WCAG (quick reference), 4 October, https://www.w3.org/WAI/WCAG21/quickref/#headings-and-labels (archived at https://perma.cc/9DCA-8G7P)

32 Bradbury, K (2013) Why the focus indicator is important, 19 September [Online video] https://www.youtube.com/watch?v=R-mfWJsJ7rE&feature=youtu.be (archived at https://perma.cc/3C6H-J4VJ)

33 Geier, C (2016) Give Your Site Some Focus! Tips for Designing Useful and Usable Focus Indicators, 29 June, https://www.deque.com/blog/give-site-focus-tips-designing-usable-focus-indicators/ (archived at https://perma.cc/QH42-UQLF)

34 W3C (Updated 2019) How to Meet WCAG (quick reference), 4 October, https://www.w3.org/WAI/WCAG21/quickref/#focus-visible (archived at https://perma.cc/AG28-TQNR)

35 W3C (Updated 2019) How to Meet WCAG (quick reference), 4 October, https://www.w3.org/WAI/WCAG21/quickref/#pointer-gestures (archived at https://perma.cc/3ZKV-JVYP)

36 Gibson, B and Eggert, E (2018) Exploring WCAG 2.1 – 2.5.2 Pointer Cancellation, 27 June, https://knowbility.org/blog/2018/WCAG21-252PointerCancellation/ (archived at https://perma.cc/3326-XVJW)

37 W3C (Updated 2019) How to Meet WCAG (quick reference), 4 October, https://www.w3.org/WAI/WCAG21/quickref/#pointer-cancellation (archived at https://perma.cc/798J-YUTC)

38 W3C (Updated 2019) How to Meet WCAG (quick reference), 4 October, https://www.w3.org/WAI/WCAG21/quickref/#label-in-name (archived at https://perma.cc/5ZH8-VA4P)

39 W3C (Updated 2019) How to Meet WCAG (quick reference), 4 October, https://www.w3.org/WAI/WCAG21/quickref/#motion-actuation (archived at https://perma.cc/3ZNC-QT9F)

10

Understandable

Note: The explanations given in this chapter are interpretations of WCAG standards and do not guarantee that content will be fully compliant with legal regulations. For further guidance and the full W3C wording for each of the standards, see: How to Meet WCAG (quick reference). Any W3C wording used is copyright. Copyright © 2019 W3C® (MIT, ERCIM, Keio, Beihang).

3.1.1 Language of Page – Level A

Identify the main text language used in the eLearning resource so that assistive technology can correctly pronounce and display the language.

Key information

This standard ensures that assistive technology is able to correctly interpret and communicate the text in eLearning resources. This is particularly important for screen readers as it allows them to access the correct pronunciation guide. If the wrong default language is specified such as French for an eLearning resource which has English text, the screen reader will voice all the text with a French accent. This requirement is also important for tools such as media players which have captioning functionality. The language needs to be specified in this case so that it is displayed using the correct characters, punctuation and reading direction of the text.

Authoring tools should provide a mechanism which allows the default language to be set. This is often done in the tool settings and automatically changes the underlying code. Further coding information can be found in the Useful resources section.

Note: If an eLearning resource has text in multiple languages, the language which appears the most should be selected as the main language. The additional standard **3.1.2 Language of Parts** covers the requirements for languages used in individual passages or phrases.

How to conform

Make sure that the main language used for text in the eLearning resource can be correctly identified by assistive technology.

Why?

Learners who benefit from this standard include:

- people who use screen readers or text-to-speech software and who will hear the text voiced with the correct pronunciation;
- people who use captions such as those with a hearing or cognitive impairment or second language learners, who will be able to see the captions in the correct language format.

Example

FIGURE 10.1   Language of page tool settings (Xerte Online Toolkits)

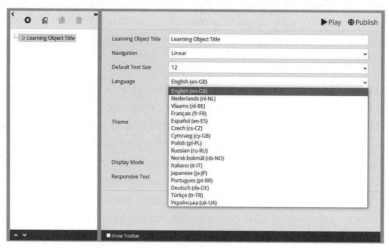

Tool settings in the Xerte Online Toolkit showing how to set the language of the resource to English and the other language options available.
SOURCE Reproduced with permission of The Xerte Project

How to test

Use a screen reader to voice the content of the eLearning resource and check that the language is read out using the correct accent and pronunciation.

Useful resources

- Designing for Screen Reader Compatibility[1]
  Guidance from WebAIM with an audio example of a screen reader set to the Czech language voicing English content.
- Lang[2]
  Guidance from MDN web docs on the coding required for this standard.
- 3.1.1 Language of Page – Level A[3]
  W3C quick reference guide and further information for this standard.

3.1.2 Language of Parts – Level AA

Identify the language of text used in individual passages or phrases if this is different from the main text language used in the eLearning resource.

Key information

Standard **3.1.1. Language of Page** requires that the language used for the main text in an eLearning resource is identified. This standard is very similar, but it requires that any additional languages used in the resource are also identified. This could apply to passages, phrases or even single words. An English eLearning resource which teaches Spanish, for example, would have both English and Spanish text. It would be important to be able to identify any passages or phrases in the eLearning resource which were in Spanish, as without this functionality a screen reader would voice the Spanish text with an English accent.

How to conform

Make sure that the language of text used in individual passages or phrases is identified if it is different from the main language of the eLearning resource.

Exceptions

The following types of text do not need to be identified as a language which is different from the main language:

- Proper nouns, ie the names of people, places or organizations.
- Technical terms in another language, eg homo sapiens, habeas corpus.
- Words in another language which are commonly used and understood in the main language, eg the French word 'rendezvous' which means meeting and is commonly used and understood in English.
- Words in an unknown language.

Why?

Learners who benefit from this standard include people who use screen readers or text-to-speech software and who will hear text used in languages other than the main language of the resource voiced with the correct pronunciation.

Example

FIGURE 10.2   Identify the language of an individual phrase (Adobe Captivate)

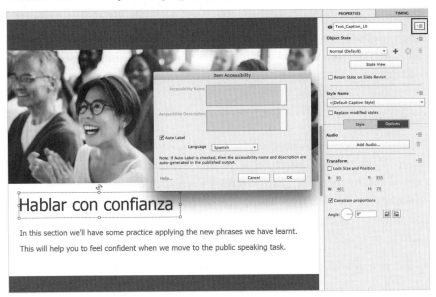

In the Adobe Captivate authoring tool you can set the language of individual phrases so that they can be correctly interpreted by assistive technology and browsers. The example shows an eLearning resource created to teach Spanish. The main language of the resource is set to English, but the language for any individual phrases in the resource which are in Spanish can be set to this language so that a screen reader correctly pronounces the phrase and doesn't announce it with an English accent.
SOURCE Reproduced with permission of Adobe Captivate

How to test

Use a screen reader to voice the content of the eLearning resource and check that each of the languages used is read out using the correct pronunciation.

Useful resources

- Designing for Screen Reader Compatibility[4]
  Guidance from WebAIM with an audio example of a screen reader set to the Czech language voicing English content.

- Lang[5]
  Guidance from MDN web docs on the coding required for this standard.

- 3.1.2 Language of Parts – Level AA[6]
  W3C quick reference guide and further information for this standard.

3.2.1 On Focus – Level A

When learners move the focus to interactive items, make sure this does not cause anything unexpected to happen, such as a new window opening without warning.

Key information

This standard ensures that no events which are unpredictable or unexpected occur when learners move focus to any interactive items. This could be done either by using the 'Tab' key on a keyboard for keyboard users, or by selecting the item with a mouse or another assistive technology device. Examples of unexpected events which could occur when learners move focus to interactive items include:

- a new window opens when learners move focus to a button;
- a link in a dropdown menu takes learners to the destination page when they move focus to the link rather than when they select it.
- a question answer is submitted as soon as a submit button receives focus, instead of when it is selected.

How to conform

Make sure that when learners move the focus to interactive items this does not cause anything unexpected to happen.

Why?

Learners who benefit from this standard include:

- people who have low vision and use screen magnifiers. Unexpected events which occur when they move the focus to interactive items are particularly disorientating when only a portion of the page is visible at a time;
- people who use screen readers who will not be confused by unexpected content suddenly being voiced by the screen reader when they move the focus to interactive items;

- people who have cognitive impairments which affect attention and concentration and who may find it distracting if page content changes unexpectedly;
- all learners, as unexpected events occurring when they move the focus to interactive items is poor user experience for everyone.

How to test

Check that nothing unexpected happens when learners move focus to interactive items.

Useful resources

- 3.2.1 On Focus – Level A[7]
  W3C quick reference guide and further information for this standard.

3.2.2 On Input – Level A

Make sure when learners interact with input items such as entering data into a data entry field or selecting a radio button, this doesn't cause anything unexpected to happen unless learners are warned what to expect before it happens.

Key information

This standard applies specifically to interactive items which allow learners to 'change the setting' of the item. This means that the interaction causes something to change with the item which persists even when learners are no longer interacting with it. It is commonly understood to refer to data entry fields, radio buttons and check boxes, etc. It does not apply to interactive items such as a 'Submit' button or a link. This is because selecting these items does not change the setting of the item, it just triggers an expected action such as submitting a form or moving to another destination.

The standard ensures that no events which would be considered unexpected occur when learners interact with input items, unless they are given warning that this will happen. For example, the standard behaviour of interacting with a radio button on a quiz question is that learners select the correct radio button and then select a 'Submit' button to submit their answer. If their answer was submitted as soon as they selected a radio button, this would be considered non-standard behaviour. It would be allowed only if learners were given prior warning that this was going to happen.

How to conform

Make sure that when learners interact with input fields this does not cause anything unexpected to happen unless they are given prior warning.

Why?

Learners who benefit from this standard include:

- people who have cognitive impairments which affect attention and concentration and who may find it distracting if unexpected events occur without warning when they interact with input items;
- all learners, as unexpected events that occur without warning when they interact with input items are distracting and this is poor user experience for everyone.

How to test

Check that nothing unexpected happens when learners interact with input items unless they are given prior warning.

Useful resources

- 3.2.1 On Input – Level A[8]
  W3C quick reference guide and further information for this standard.

3.2.3 Consistent Navigation – Level AA

Make sure that navigation items such as 'Home' icons or links to other pages which are repeated throughout the eLearning resource appear in the same order in the layout.

Key information

To ease cognitive load on learners it should be simple and clear for them to navigate through eLearning resources. This standard is an important way to make navigation straightforward for everyone because once learners are familiar with a particular layout for navigation items, this doesn't change throughout the eLearning resource. If navigation items are repeated over multiple pages, they always appear in the same order.

Note: This standard allows new items to be added to the navigation, as long as existing items stay in the same order throughout the eLearning resource.

How to conform

Make sure that navigation items such as 'Home' icons or links to other pages which are repeated throughout the eLearning resource appear in the same order in the layout.

Exception

- This standard doesn't apply if learners are able to change the layout of navigation items themselves, for example by using assistive technology or setting preferences.

Why?

Learners who benefit from this standard include:

- people who have low vision and use screen magnifiers. They will be able to navigate through the eLearning resource easily as the position of navigation items won't change unexpectedly. Many learners who use screen magnifiers also use visual cues such as the edge of the page to help them locate navigation items, so it is important that the position of these does not change;

- people with cognitive impairments which affect memory who will be able to navigate more easily if the layout of navigation items stays constant;

- people with situational impairments, eg someone working in a noisy and distracting working environment who is finding it difficult to concentrate;

- all learners, as consistent navigation ensures that less cognitive load is needed to navigate the resource and is good user experience for everyone.

How to test

Check that navigation items such as home icons or links to other pages which are repeated throughout the eLearning resource appear in the same order in the layout.

Useful resources

- 3.2.3 Consistent Navigation – Level AA[9]
  W3C quick reference guide and further information for this standard.

3.2.4 Consistent Identification – Level AA

Make sure that if interactive items with the same function have a visible label, eg the text or icon on a button, the visible label remains the same throughout the eLearning resource. Also make sure that the accessible name for interactive items with the same function remains consistent.

Key information

This standard is an important way to make interaction in eLearning resources straightforward for everyone. It does this by making sure that the visible labels or icons for interactive items are consistent throughout the eLearning resource. Imagine how frustrating it would be if a 'Search' facility field had a different visible label depending on where it appeared. For example, it could have a text label which said 'Search' in one section, another text label which said 'Find' in a second section and it could be shown by a magnifying glass icon in a third. Learners would spend unnecessary time trying to work out how to search for something each time they were in a new section.

Links are also included in this standard. If there are multiple links to the same destination in the eLearning resource, these should all be consistently labelled, ie have the same link text. For example, a link which takes learners to the landing page for BBC news should not have the text 'BBC news home page' in one link and 'Find out the latest from the BBC news' in another. It is also good practice to make sure that the same link text is not used for links which have different destinations. For example, a link which has the text 'Mental health awareness guidance' which takes learners to a company HR policy on one link should not take them to advice from an external organization on another link. This standard also helps users of assistive technology by requiring that in addition to the visible label, the accessible name is consistent throughout the eLearning resource.

Note: In some circumstances it is possible that there is a consistent visible label or icon but it might not make sense to have the same accessible name. For example, it may be clear to visual learners that a 'Print' icon in one section of the resource allows them to print a glossary and in another section the 'Print' icon allows them to print a checklist. In this case, the accessible names would still meet this standard if they were different, eg 'Print glossary' and 'Print checklist'.

How to conform

Make sure that interactive items which have the same functionality throughout the eLearning resource have a consistent visible label or icon and a consistent accessible name recognized by assistive technology.

Why?

Learners who benefit from this standard include:

- people with cognitive impairments which affect memory who will be able to navigate more easily if the visible text label or icon of interactive items remains the same throughout the eLearning resource;

- people who use assistive technology and who will be able to navigate and operate the functionality of the eLearning resource more easily because the accessible name of interactive items remains the same throughout.

How to test

1 Check that all interactive items have a consistent visual label or icon throughout the eLearning resource.
2 Use a screen reader to voice the accessible names of all interactive items to check that these are consistent throughout the eLearning resource.

Useful resources

- 3.2.4 Consistent Identification – Level AA[10]
  W3C quick reference guide and further information for this standard.

3.3.1 Error Identification – Level A

If learners make a mistake when they interact with input items such as radio buttons or data entry fields, make sure it is clear which input item the error applies to. Also make sure that the error is described to learners using text.

Key information

This standard is designed to make it easier for all learners to recognize errors when interacting with input fields. It requires not only that learners are informed if they make a mistake but also that it is clear which input item the error refers to and that the mistake is described using text. Communicating the error via text is important to ensure that the information is not missed by any learners. This could be the case if mistakes are communicated only through devices such as colour or icons. If an error is shown by using a red border around the input item, for example, this could cause problems for colour blind learners who may not be able to recognize the colour change. Similarly, if only an icon such as a cross is used to indicate an error, this could cause problems for learners with cognitive impairments who have difficulty interpreting visual cues such as icons. Learners with visual impairments may also not be able to see the change in colour or the icon used. Describing the error information in text avoids these issues. It also allows assistive technology such as screen readers to recognize and announce the information.

Note: This standard does not restrict the use of colour and icons to convey error information, it only requires that they are supplemented with text.

On standard websites, this guideline most commonly applies to input fields on a form which collect data. As a result, W3C's definition of an error applies specifically to 'information provided by the user that is not accepted'. This definition specifies two types of errors. The first is users not giving information that is required, for example not filling in the data in a mandatory field. The second is filling in fields with data in the wrong format, or with values that are outside the range of the field. Examples include filling in an email address without the @ symbol, or making a bid on a bidding site which is below the previous bid. If learners make errors when inputting data into fields, they must be able to identify which of the fields their errors relate to and this must also be communicated in text. This most commonly happens when the form is submitted. Good practice on forms which have many data entry fields is also to have summary error information detailing all the errors on the form which appears at the top of the page when the form is submitted.

Although some eLearning resources have input fields which collect data, in the majority of cases this standard is more likely to apply to input fields such as radio buttons or check boxes and text entry fields which are used to answer quiz or assessment questions. In this case, the most common error that learners make, which falls under the W3C definition of an error, is when they select 'Submit' before they have answered the question. Most authoring tools automatically provide error messages in this situation. If this is the case, the errors must be described in text to conform to this standard.

The narrow W3C definition of an error is a good demonstration of the limitations of the WCAG in relation to learning content. In a learning context I believe that learners answering a question incorrectly could also be considered an error. With the exception of certain situations such as for compliance assessments when content authors may deliberately not want to give feedback, I would suggest that good practice is always to make learners aware if they have answered a question incorrectly. If this is the case, best practice again would be to make sure that the requirements of this standard apply. This means that learners should be made aware which questions they have answered incorrectly and this should be conveyed in text. An example of good practice can be seen in Figure 10.3.

How to conform

Make sure that if learners make a mistake when they interact with input items such as radio buttons or data entry fields, it is clear what they have done wrong and the error is described to them using text.

Why?

Learners who benefit from this standard include:

- people who are colour blind and who may not realize that they have made a mistake if this is only highlighted with colour rather than text;
- people with cognitive impairments who may struggle to understand the meaning of visual clues such as colour and icons. They may be more easily able to identify when they have made a mistake if it is communicated in text;
- people who are blind and use screen readers who will miss error information if it is not conveyed in text which can be recognized by assistive technology;
- all learners, as being able to quickly identify and correct errors is good user experience for everyone.

Example

FIGURE 10.3   Quiz answer error feedback message (Articulate Rise)

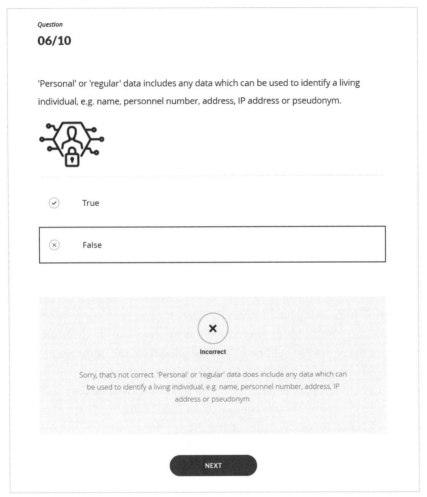

An error message in the Articulate Rise authoring tool which demonstrates good practice for communicating to learners that a quiz question has been answered incorrectly. The message has the word 'Incorrect' to supplement the cross icon to tell the learner that they have selected the wrong answer.

How to test

Check that if learners make a mistake when they interact with input items such as radio buttons or data entry fields, it is clear what they have done wrong and the error is described to them using text.

Useful resources

- 3.3.1 Error Identification – Level A[11]
  W3C quick reference guide and further information for this standard.

3.3.2 Labels or Instructions – Level A

When learners interact with input items such as radio buttons or data entry fields, make sure they are given instructions or labels which explain what they need to do. Also make sure they are given information about how any data they need to enter should be formatted and whether it is mandatory.

Key information

Giving learners clear instructions when they need to answer quiz questions or enter information into data entry fields is key to creating a good learner experience. If the eLearning resource requires learners to input information into data entry fields, these should have instructions in the form of labels. Each data entry field should be clearly labelled with the input requirement, such as 'First name' or 'Email address'. If there is any further information needed to help learners enter data into a field, it should be easy to find, eg available in an information box close to the field. If any fields are mandatory this should also be made clear, as should any formatting requirements. In addition, good practice when giving learners instructions about how to input data into fields is to provide examples.

While this standard doesn't specifically mention instructions for quiz questions, good practice for learning content is to be clear and specific about how to answer questions. For example, in a multiple choice question which allows learners to select only one answer, the instruction could be: 'Select the correct answer from the options given below.' If the question was a multiple response question which had more than one answer, the instruction could be: 'Select the correct answers from the options below (select all that apply).' If particular formatting is required, this should be explained in the instructions. For example, 'What does GDPR stand for? (Case sensitive).'

How to conform

Make sure that when learners interact with input items such as radio buttons or data entry fields, they are given instructions or labels which explain what they need to do. Also make sure they are given information about how any data should be formatted and whether it is mandatory.

Why?

Learners who benefit from this standard include:

- people who have cognitive impairments who will find it easier to interact with the eLearning resource if they are given clear instructions for answering quiz questions and filling in data entry fields;
- all learners, as having straightforward and easy-to-follow instructions when answering quiz questions and filling in data entry fields is good user experience for everyone.

Example

FIGURE 10.4   Formatting information in a quiz question (Articulate Rise)

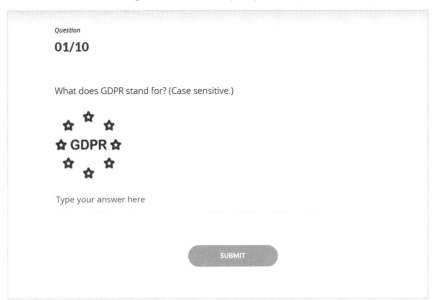

A quiz question created using the Articulate Rise authoring tool. The content author has provided extra formatting information to explain that the answer is case sensitive.
SOURCE ©Articulate Global, Inc. Used with permission, all other rights reserved

How to test

Check that when learners interact with input fields such as radio buttons and data entry fields, they are given instructions or labels which explain what they need to do and how any information they need to input should be formatted.

Useful resources

- 3.3.2 Labels or Instructions – Level A[12]
  W3C quick reference guide and further information for this standard.

3.3.3 Error Suggestion – Level A

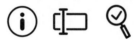

Give learners suggestions to help them correct any mistakes they make when they interact with input items such as radio buttons or data entry fields.

Key information

While standard **3.3.1 Error Identification** requires that learners are made aware of any mistakes they make when they interact with input fields, this standard requires that they are given suggestions about how to correct those mistakes. This helps all learners, including those with cognitive impairments who may find it easier to correct errors if they are given suggestions on how to do this.

On standard websites, this guideline most commonly applies to input fields on a form which collect data. As a result, W3C's definition of an error applies specifically to 'information provided by the user that is not accepted'. This definition specifies two types of errors. The first is users not giving information that is required, for example not filling in the data in a mandatory field. The second is filling in fields with data in the wrong format, or with values that are outside the range of the field. Examples include filling in the date in the wrong format, or making a bid on a bidding site which is below the previous bid. If learners make errors when inputting data into fields, when the form is submitted they must be given suggestions on how to correct these. If mandatory fields are missed, for example, the error suggestion could be highlighting those fields and explaining that they must be completed before the form can be submitted. If formatting errors are made, these could be highlighted and an example given of the data formatted correctly, such as the correct dd/mm/yy format. In the case of an entry falling outside the required range of the field, the error suggestion could include giving the accepted values which apply to the field.

Although some eLearning resources have input fields which collect data, in the majority of cases this standard is more likely to apply to input fields such as radio buttons or check boxes and text entry fields which are used to answer quiz or assessment questions. In this case, the most common error that learners make, which falls under the W3C definition of an error, is when they select 'Submit' before they have answered the question. Most authoring tools automatically provide error messages in this situation, but the message may not make it clear what learners need to do to correct the error. Content authors can sometimes change the wording in these error messages to include suggestions about how to correct the error (see Figure 10.5). It may also be possible to manually program the tool to display extra information, such as a layer or a pop-up message with suggestions about how learners can correct their mistakes.

The narrow W3C definition of an error is a good demonstration of the limitations of the WCAG in relation to learning content. In a learning context I believe that learners answering a question incorrectly could also be considered an error. If this is the case, then explaining why their answer is incorrect or giving the correct answer could be considered a form of error suggestion. With the exception of certain situations such as for compliance assessments when content authors may deliberately not want to give feedback, I would suggest that best practice is always to give an error suggestion as it helps to reinforce the learning point conveyed by the question. A good practice example of an error suggestion for a quiz question can be seen in Figure 10.3 in the explanation for standard **3.3.1 Error identification**.

How to conform

Make sure that learners are given suggestions to help them correct any mistakes they make when they interact with input items such as radio buttons or data entry fields.

Exception

- If the suggestion for the mistake could be a threat to security, such as giving hints for a password, or could invalidate the purpose of the interaction, this is exempt.

Why?

Learners who benefit from error suggestion include:

- people with cognitive impairments who will more easily be able to correct errors;
- all learners, as any suggestions to help correct errors is good user experience for everyone.

Example

FIGURE 10.5   Error suggestion message (Articulate Storyline)

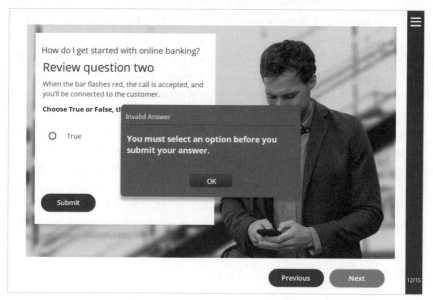

An error message which automatically appears in a resource developed using the Articulate Storyline authoring tool. The error message appears when learners do not select an option before selecting the 'Submit' button. The content author has changed the default error message to include the suggestion that learners need to select an option before they can submit an answer.

How to test

Check that learners are given suggestions to help them correct any mistakes they make when they interact with input items such as radio buttons or data entry fields.

Useful resources

- 3.3.3 Error Suggestion – Level AA[13]
  W3C quick reference guide and further information for this standard.

3.3.4 Error Prevention (Legal, Financial, Data) – Level AA

When learners input any information using input items such as data entry fields or check boxes, make sure they can reverse, check and correct or confirm their data before they submit it. This applies if the interaction has legal or financial implications. It also applies if the interaction changes or deletes information held in data storage systems and if the interaction submits test responses.

Key information

For commercial websites, this standard prevents people from making mistakes which could have serious consequences. Common examples include transferring money on a banking website, buying a non-refundable ticket on a ticketing website, or deleting personal data held on a public sector service website. In an eLearning context, while there are rarely legal or financial implications to learner interactions, the standard does refer specifically to submitting test results. If any interactions are applicable, then the requirement is that learners must be given the opportunity to do one of the following:

- **Reverse:** undo the interaction once they have submitted or deleted the information.
- **Check:** correct the information once it has been checked and they have been informed of any errors they have made when they input information.

- **Confirm**: review, confirm and correct the information before they submit it.

This standard is another example of where there are no W3C-specific recommendations which are applicable for eLearning content. As a result, it leaves how to conform to this standard open to interpretation. This can be seen in the difference of opinions among authoring tool providers on how it should be achieved. One provider suggests that this standard is not applicable despite the fact that its tool allows learners to submit test results because it states that the tool 'does not include any legal or financial transactions'.[14] Another suggests that having a quiz question with a 'Submit' button is enough to comply since 'this ensures all users have an opportunity to correct mistakes before submission'.[15] A third provider suggests that it is the responsibility of the content author to 'ask learners to confirm their responses before submitting them'.[16] They advise that when learners are required to enter text in a data entry field, for example, they are asked whether the information is correct and given the opportunity to change it before moving on.

This leaves content authors in a dilemma for a number of reasons. First, the standard offers no guidance on what constitutes submitting a test result. For example, should it apply to all quiz questions even if they are included for learner engagement only, or does it apply only to test results which are formally collected and recorded and held on a data system such as in an LMS? Second, it doesn't clarify exactly what qualifies as meeting the requirement of this criterion for learning content. For example, would it be possible to argue that allowing learners to retry a question or a test constitutes checking since it allows them to correct the information once their answer has been checked and they have been informed of any errors? Finally, it doesn't give any clarification about test results which are submitted as part of a compliance test with a set, possibly legally required, pass mark, which deliberately does not give learners the opportunity to reverse, check or confirm their answers.

As a result of these limitations, I believe that conforming to this standard can only be at the discretion of the content author. At some point in the future, industry support or standardized guidance from authoring tool providers may offer definitive clarification. In the meantime, however, I believe that good practice would be to give learners the opportunity to reverse, check or confirm their interaction wherever possible when they submit test results. One suggested solution is to give learners the opportunity to check or reset their answers for quiz questions as demonstrated in Figure 10.6. Another option could be to display a 'Yes/No' confirmation question on a layer. If learners select 'Yes' to confirm that the information is correct, they move to the next slide. If they select 'No', the layer is closed and learners are given the chance to change their responses before continuing. A final option could be to create a page where learners are given the opportunity to review all the answers of a quiz before they submit their final results.

How to conform

When learners input any information which has legal or financial implications, updates or changes personal data or submits test results, make sure they can reverse, check and correct or confirm their data before it is submitted.

Why?

Learners who benefit from this standard include:

- people with cognitive impairments which affect comprehension and memory who may inadvertently delete data or submit test answers by mistake;
- people with motor impairments which affect dexterity who may find it more difficult to interact with input items and who may inadvertently make mistakes such as submitting incorrect test answers;
- people affected by temporary impairments, eg someone who is tired and distracted and who may be at a higher risk of making mistakes.

Example

FIGURE 10.6   Check and reset option for quiz question (CourseArc)

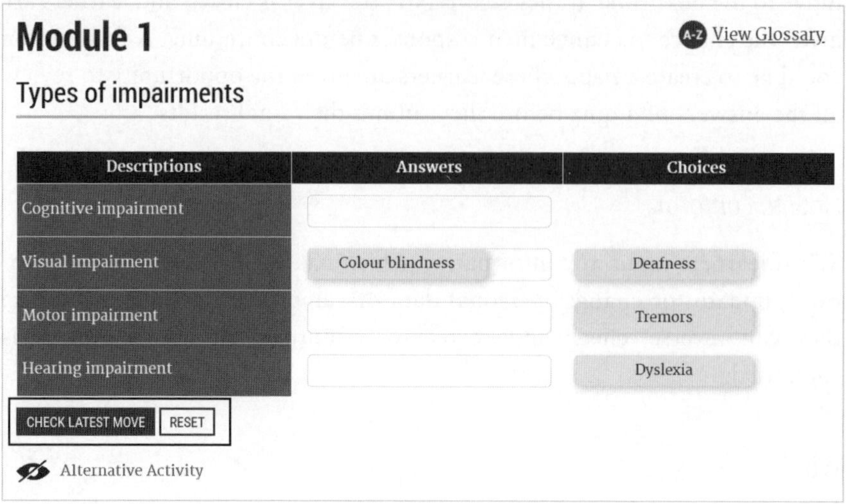

An example of a drag and drop question created using the CourseArc authoring tool which allows learners to check their answer or reset the question.
SOURCE Reproduced with permission of CourseArc

How to test

Check that when learners input any information which has legal or financial implications, updates or changes personal data or submits test results, they can reverse, check and correct or confirm their data before it is submitted.

Useful resources

- 3.3.4 Error Prevention (Legal, Financial, Data) AA[17]
  W3C quick reference guide and further information for this standard.

Endnotes

1   WebAIM (Updated 2017) Designing for screen reader compatibility, 21 April, https://webaim.org/techniques/screenreader/ (archived at https://perma.cc/U9XB-B5R4)

2   MDN contributors (Updated 2020) Lang, 5 November, https://developer.mozilla.org/en-US/docs/Web/HTML/Global_attributes/lang#Language_tag_syntax (archived at https://perma.cc/2N8T-AJQU)

3   W3C (Updated 2019) How to Meet WCAG (quick reference), 4 October, https://www.w3.org/WAI/WCAG21/quickref/#language-of-page (archived at https://perma.cc/DR66-WMLD)

4   WebAIM (Updated 2017) Designing for screen reader compatibility, 21 April, https://webaim.org/techniques/screenreader/ (archived at https://perma.cc/U9XB-B5R4)

5   MDN contributors (Updated 2020) Lang, 5 November, https://developer.mozilla.org/en-US/docs/Web/HTML/Global_attributes/lang#Language_tag_syntax (archived at https://perma.cc/2N8T-AJQU)

6   W3C (Updated 2019) How to Meet WCAG (quick reference), 4 October, https://www.w3.org/WAI/WCAG21/quickref/#language-of-parts (archived at https://perma.cc/A38L-ACCH)

7   W3C (Updated 2019) How to Meet WCAG (quick reference), 4 October, https://www.w3.org/WAI/WCAG21/quickref/#on-focus (archived at https://perma.cc/VHH3-9T5W)

8   W3C (Updated 2019) How to Meet WCAG (quick reference), 4 October, https://www.w3.org/WAI/WCAG21/quickref/#on-input (archived at https://perma.cc/9FHB-GK4J)

9   W3C (Updated 2019) How to Meet WCAG (quick reference), 4 October, https://www.w3.org/WAI/WCAG21/quickref/#consistent-navigation (archived at https://perma.cc/2VJE-CEDX)

10 W3C (Updated 2019) How to Meet WCAG (quick reference), 4 October, https://www.w3.org/WAI/WCAG21/quickref/#consistent-identification (archived at https://perma.cc/8RT2-M5FY)

11 W3C (Updated 2019) How to Meet WCAG (quick reference), 4 October, https://www.w3.org/WAI/WCAG21/quickref/#error-identification (archived at https://perma.cc/9JVF-89YG)

12 W3C (Updated 2019) How to Meet WCAG (quick reference), 4 October, https://www.w3.org/WAI/WCAG21/quickref/#labels-or-instructions (archived at https://perma.cc/QG5C-HGGN)

13 W3C (Updated 2019) How to Meet WCAG (quick reference), 4 October, https://www.w3.org/WAI/WCAG21/quickref/#error-suggestion (archived at https://perma.cc/SW6E-VTXC)

14 CourseArc, Voluntary product accessibility template, https://www.coursearc.com/vpat/ (archived at https://perma.cc/GCG8-KDJH)

15 Adapt Framework, https://www.adaptlearning.org/wp-content/uploads/2016/01/Adapt-Framework-v2-accessibility-matrix.pdf (archived at https://perma.cc/DN5S-HMNV)

16 Articulate Storyline 360 Accessibility Conformance Report https://articulate.com/support/article/Storyline-360-Accessibility-Conformance-Report-VPAT (archived at https://perma.cc/LRF4-YDHS)

[17] W3C (Updated 2019) How to Meet WCAG (quick reference), 4 October, https://www.w3.org/WAI/WCAG21/quickref/#error-prevention-legal-financial-data (archived at https://perma.cc/CW54-ZLM9)

11

Robust

Note: The explanations given in this chapter are interpretations of WCAG standards and do not guarantee that content will be fully compliant with legal regulations. For further guidance and the full W3C wording for each of the standards, see: How to Meet WCAG (quick reference). Any W3C wording used is copyright. Copyright © 2019 W3C® (MIT, ERCIM, Keio, Beihang).

4.1.1 Parsing – Level A

If the authoring tool uses a markup language such as HTML, make sure that the code doesn't cause any issues for assistive technology. This can happen if there are errors in the code such as when elements are missing complete start and end tags.

Key information

This standard refers to the underlying code which is analysed and interpreted by web browsers and assistive technology. As a result of the wide range of assistive technologies used by disabled people, it is difficult to predict when a code quality issue will have an impact. Making sure that there are no parsing errors such as duplicate IDs and poor nesting of elements, however, helps to ensure that there will be no issues such as content not being recognized and announced by screen readers.

Incomplete start and end tags are a common issue. For example:

Incomplete start tag

<h1Designing accessible learning content</h1>

This code is incorrect because the first tag is missing an angle bracket. This means that assistive technology may not identify the text as a heading level 1.

Complete start tag

<h1>Designing accessible learning content</h1>

This code has complete start and end tags, which allows assistive technology to identify the text as a heading level 1.

How to conform

Make sure that:

- HTML elements have complete start and end tags;
- HTML elements are nested according to their specifications, for example list items are within an ordered or unordered list;
- HTML elements do not have duplicate attributes;
- HTML IDs are unique within a page.

Why?

Learners who use assistive technology benefit from this standard as it prevents issues caused by coding errors.

How to test

Use the markup validation service which can be found in the Useful resources section to check the validity of the underlying code of the eLearning resource. If this is not possible, another option is to test this standard with the support of an accessibility expert, or to check with your authoring tool provider that the output of the tool conforms to this standard.

Note: Since the W3C markup validation service checks for a whole range of validation errors, not just those required by this standard, it can be difficult to identify the relevant errors. Accessibility auditors often use an experimental parsing bookmarklet to check only for WCAG parsing requirements. More information can be found in the Useful resources section.

Useful resources

- W3C Markup Validation Service[1]
  Validation service from W3C which checks the markup validity of web documents.
- Parsing error bookmarklet[2]
  Information about experimental bookmarklet used to test WCAG parsing requirements.
- 4.1.1 Parsing – Level A[3]
  W3C quick reference guide and further information for this standard.

4.1.2 Name, Role, Value – Level A

Make sure that all interactive items have an accessible name and role and that the state of items, eg whether they are expanded or collapsed, is communicated to assistive technology.

Key information

The purpose of this standard is to make sure that assistive technology users understand what interactive items are for, what they can do and what state they are in. For example, in a quiz question which had a 'True' or 'False' answer, in the case of the interactive 'True' radio button:

- the name of the interactive item is 'True';
- the role of the interactive item is a radio button;
- the value or state of the interactive item is either selected or not selected.

The requirements of this standard are met automatically if content authors use standard HTML controls such as links or buttons. If, however, content authors use custom controls such as sliders or tab controls, the code they use must also conform to this standard. Information on how this can be achieved can be found in the Useful resources section.

How to conform

Make sure that underlying code is used to provide an accessible name and role for interactive items and that the state of items is also communicated to assistive technology.

Why?

People who use assistive technology will benefit from this standard as they will be able to understand what interactive items are for, what they can do and what state they are in.

How to test

Check that the underlying code conforms with the requirements of this standard. If this is not possible, another option is to test this standard with the support of an accessibility expert, or to check with your authoring tool provider that the output of the tool conforms to this standard.

Useful resources

- WAI-ARIA Authoring Practices 1.1[4]
  Information from the Web Accessibility Initiative on how to use ARIA to make custom widgets, navigation and behaviours accessible using roles, states and properties.
- Use of ARIA with assistive technologies[5]
  Overview of ARIA from Dig Inclusion.
- 4.1.2 Name, Role, Value – Level A[6]
  W3C quick reference guide and further information for this standard.

4.1.3 Status Messages – Level AA

Added in 2.1

If the authoring tool uses a markup language such as HTML, make sure that assistive technology can recognize and announce status messages. This applies to status messages which appear on a page but do not receive keyboard focus.

Key information

Status messages can have several different functions. They can inform learners that they have successfully carried out an action, or that there are errors on a page. They can let learners know that they need to wait for an event such as a page updating. In addition they can report on the progress of events, eg with a progress bar. This standard ensures that status messages are coded correctly so that they are recognized and announced by assistive technology, even if they do not receive keyboard focus. This is often achieved using ARIA alerts or live regions.

While many status messages are coded so that they receive keyboard focus and are therefore automatically recognized and announced by assistive technology, some messages occur without receiving focus and therefore risk being missed – for example, the counter on a scoreboard quiz which shows learners how many points they have scored so far, and which is updated every time learners answer a question correctly. To conform with this standard, the change in score needs to be recognized by assistive technology and announced every time it changes, even if the counter does not receive keyboard focus.

How to conform

Assign roles or properties to status messages which ensure they are correctly recognized and announced by assistive technology.

Why?

Learners who benefit from this standard include:

- people who use assistive technology such as screen readers who will miss important information if status messages which do not receive focus are not recognized and announced;
- people who use screen magnifiers with screen readers who may miss important information if it appears outside the magnified view of the page and does not receive focus.

How to test

Use a screen reader to check that all status messages and updates are correctly recognized and announced even if they do not receive keyboard focus.

Useful resources

- GOV.UK WCAG 2.1 Primer 4.1.3 information[7]
  Examples and techniques on how to meet this standard from GOV.UK.

- Exploring WCAG 2.1 – 4.1.3 Status Messages[8]
  Article from Knowbility with a video demonstration of a time-out warning voiced by the NVDA screen reader.

- 4.1.3 Status Messages – Level AA[9]
  W3C quick reference guide and further information for this standard.

Endnotes

[1] W3C Markup Validation Service, https://validator.w3.org/ (archived at https://perma.cc/XG6G-PY7S)

[2] Faulkner, S (Updated 2019) WCAG 2.1 parsing error bookmarklet, 25 February, https://developer.paciellogroup.com/blog/2019/02/wcag-2-0-parsing-error-bookmarklet/ (archived at https://perma.cc/RYR4-T9J8)

[3] W3C (Updated 2019) How to Meet WCAG (quick reference), 4 October, https://www.w3.org/WAI/WCAG21/quickref/#parsing (archived at https://perma.cc/PZA9-8YDX)

[4] W3C Working Group Note (2019) WAI-ARIA authoring practices 1.1, 14 August, https://www.w3.org/TR/wai-aria-practices-1.1/ (archived at https://perma.cc/XYP9-JYJK)

[5] Blake, K (2019) Use of ARIA with assistive technologies, 9 September, https://diginclusion.com/industry-updates/use-of-aria-with-assistive-technologies/ (archived at https://perma.cc/A4AL-F6DR)

[6] W3C (Updated 2019) How to Meet WCAG (quick reference), 4 October, https://www.w3.org/WAI/WCAG21/quickref/#name-role-value (archived at https://perma.cc/TQA6-YS55)

[7] GOV.UK, WCAG 2.1 Primer 4.1.3 information, https://alphagov.github.io/wcag-primer/all.html#4-1-3-status-messages-aa (archived at https://perma.cc/EB4T-FB4R)

[8]   Gibson, B (2018) Exploring WCAG 2.1 – 4.1.3 Status Messages, 28 August, https://knowbility.org/blog/2018/WCAG21-413StatusMessages/ (archived at https://perma.cc/23D6-ERP9)

[9]   W3C (Updated 2019) How to Meet WCAG (quick reference), 4 October, https://www.w3.org/WAI/WCAG21/quickref/#status-messages (archived at https://perma.cc/KPV3-BUPV)

WCAG 2.1 level AAA and WCAG 2.2 draft accessibility standards

12

WCAG 2.1 level AAA accessibility standards

Introduction

This chapter provides an overview of the 28 level AAA WCAG standards. Level AAA is the advanced level for WCAG accessibility requirements. The standards at this level are considered best-practice guidelines but are not a legal requirement in most countries. W3C gives the following information about achieving this level: 'It is not recommended that Level AAA conformance be required as a general policy for entire sites because it is not possible to satisfy all Level AAA Success Criteria for some content.'[1]

Bearing in mind that conforming to this level requires 28 additional standards, it is understandable that content authors are often primarily concerned with meeting the requirements of levels A and AA. This leads to many of the AAA requirements being overlooked, which is unfortunate, particularly for eLearning content since many of them contribute to a better learning experience. To avoid this, any of the AAA standards which are particularly relevant to designing learning content are incorporated into the eLearning Accessibility Framework in Part Two and referred to in the full WCAG explanations in Part Three.

Note: The explanations given in this chapter are interpretations of WCAG standards and do not guarantee that content will be fully compliant with legal regulations. For further guidance and the full W3C wording for each of the standards, see: How to Meet WCAG (quick reference). Any W3C wording used is copyright. Copyright © 2019 W3C® (MIT, ERCIM, Keio, Beihang).

Principle 1 – Perceivable

Guideline 1.2 – Time-based Media

1.2.6 SIGN LANGUAGE (PRERECORDED)

Provide sign language interpretation for all prerecorded videos with sound. Sign language provides expression, intonation and emotion and therefore offers a much closer equivalent than just captions. Sign language is also the primary form of communication for many people with hearing impairments and written text in captions and transcripts is considered a second language.

1.2.7 EXTENDED AUDIO DESCRIPTION (PRERECORDED)

This standard refers to prerecorded videos with sound which do not have long enough pauses between the dialogue and the action to add audio description. If this is the case, edit the video to manually extend the existing pauses, or to add further pauses so that the background descriptive information can be added. This means that the video content pauses temporarily while the narrator continues describing the important visual details.

1.2.8 MEDIA ALTERNATIVE (PRERECORDED)

Provide a descriptive text transcript (media alternative) for all prerecorded videos with sound. The AA standard requires either audio description or a descriptive text transcript is provided, whereas this standard requires a transcript in all cases. This is strongly recommended by accessibility experts as it accommodates a wide range of accessibility needs. For example, providing descriptive transcripts is essential for deafblind learners who use refreshable braille displays and who may not be able to hear or see the content.

1.2.9 AUDIO-ONLY (LIVE)

Provide synchronized captions or an alternative such as a transcript for all live audio-only content such as podcasts, radio plays or speeches.

Guideline 1.3 – Adaptable

1.3.6 IDENTIFY PURPOSE

Added in 2.1

Make sure that assistive technology users can identify the purpose of interactive items, icons and page regions. This allows people to customize content, for example replacing interactive items with icons or hiding content that isn't important to them.

Guideline 1.4 – Distinguishable

1.4.6 CONTRAST (ENHANCED)

For any text and the background it appears on, choose colours that have a contrast ratio of at least 7:1. This applies to 'normal' size text which W3C defines as 17 point or smaller for regular text and 13 point or smaller for bold text. 'Large' text, ie 18 point or larger for regular text and 14 point or larger for bold text, has a contrast ratio requirement of at least 4.5:1. This standard applies both to text and images of text.

Exceptions:

- Text which is incidental. This includes text in deactivated interactive items such as disabled buttons, text in decorative images and text in images which is not important to convey meaning.
- Text which is part of a logo or a brand name.

1.4.7 LOW OR NO BACKGROUND AUDIO

For prerecorded audio-only content which primarily has speech in the foreground and background audio such as music, make sure that at least one of the following is true:

- The learner can switch off the background audio.
- The background audio is approximately four times quieter than the foreground audio, ie 20 decibels lower.

Exceptions:

- Audio CAPTCHAs or audio logos.
- Tracks where the foreground audio track is singing or rapping.

1.4.8 VISUAL PRESENTATION

Meet all the following requirements for blocks of text:

- Learners can change the foreground and background colours.
- The width of a block of text is no longer than 80 characters (40 characters if the language is Chinese, Japanese or Korean).

- The text is not justified to both left and right margins. For left to right languages such as English, text should be left aligned.

- The spacing between lines is at least a space-and-a-half (ie the space is 150% larger than the default space between lines, or 1.5 in formatting options). The spacing between paragraphs is at least 1.5 times larger than the line spacing.

- When learners enlarge the text up to 200% with standard browser functionality, they do not need to use a horizontal scroll bar, ie scroll from left to right, to view the text.

1.4.9 IMAGES OF TEXT (NO EXCEPTION)

Use onscreen text rather than images of text to convey information unless images of text are used only for decoration or are essential.

Exceptions:

Images of text can be used only in the following essential situations:

- The image of text conveys a visual identity such as a logo or a brand name.

- The image of text conveys a visual aspect of the text such as a particular font family.

Principle 2 – Operable

Guideline 2.1 – Keyboard Accessible

2.1.3 KEYBOARD (NO EXCEPTION)

Make sure that everything in the eLearning resource is usable with a keyboard or a keyboard interface. This includes interactive items and audio and video player controls. Also make sure that 'keystrokes', ie pressing the keys, do not have any time constraints. Unlike standard **2.1.1 Keyboard** this standard has no exceptions such as a handwriting tool or a freehand painting or drawing program.

Guideline 2.2 – Enough Time

2.2.3 NO TIMING

Do not set time limits for any activity or let any content move or scroll automatically.

Exceptions:

The only exceptions are for real-time events, eg:

- online auctions such as eBay;
- webcasts, ie live online broadcasts of the audio or video feed from meetings or events.

2.2.4 INTERRUPTIONS

Make sure learners can postpone or switch off any interruptions such as updates and alerts.

Exception: Interruptions which are considered an emergency are exempt, eg messages which warn of a loss of connection, a danger to health and safety or data loss.

2.2.5 RE-AUTHENTICATING

Make sure that if learners need to authenticate to access a session, any data they enter during that session is not lost when they are timed out and have to re-authenticate to access the content again.

2.2.6 TIMEOUTS

Added in 2.1

This standard applies to pages which allow learners to input data and have a time out mechanism that means any data entered could be lost if the page remains inactive. Learners must be informed of the period of time the page can remain inactive before the time out mechanism is activated.

Exception: This standard applies unless the data entered into the page is preserved for more then 20 hours during any periods of inactivity.

Guideline 2.3 – Seizures and Physical Reactions

2.3.2 THREE FLASHES

Do not include any content which flashes more than three times per second.

2.3.3 ANIMATION FROM INTERACTIONS

Added in 2.1

In order to prevent issues for learners with motion sensitivity do not include any animation which creates the illusion of motion and is triggered by learner interaction unless it can be disabled. Examples include spinning or vortex effects and parallax scrolling.

Exception: Any animation which is essential such as the preview function of an application which allows content authors to create animated sequences.

Guideline 2.4 – Navigable

2.4.8 LOCATION

Make sure learners can identify where the page that they are on is located in the eLearning resource. This could be done with the following example devices:

- A breadcrumb trail.
- A sitemap.
- An indicator which gives the page number and the total number of pages in the section, eg 3/14.
- An indicator which tells learners which step they are on in a process, eg Step 2 of 5.

2.4.9 LINK PURPOSE (LINK ONLY)

Make sure learners know where they will be taken when they select a link just from the link text itself, not from the link text and information in the surrounding text.

Exception: Ambiguous links if they are deliberate, eg to create the element of surprise in a game.

2.4.10 SECTION HEADINGS

Use section headings to organize and give structure to content and to help learners process information and navigate.

Guideline 2.5 – Input Modalities

2.5.5 TARGET SIZE

Added in 2.1

Make sure that interactive items are large enough to select easily. The size of the target for pointer input should be at least 44 × 44 CSS pixels (9 mm square on most mobile devices).

Exceptions:

This standard applies unless:

- there is an equivalent target on the same page which meets the size requirement of 44 × 44 CSS pixels;
- the target is inline, ie in a sentence or a block of text;
- the size of the target cannot be changed by the author;
- the size of the target is essential to the information that it is being used to convey, eg a target in the shape of a small bone on an anatomical interaction.

2.5.6 CONCURRENT INPUT MECHANISMS

Added in 2.1

Make sure learners can switch between input mechanisms to accommodate their preferences or accessibility needs. Input mechanisms include keyboards, keyboard interfaces, trackpads, mice, touch screens and voice recognition software.

Exceptions:

This standard applies unless:

- input mechanisms are limited in order to protect the security of the content;
- a particular input mechanism is essential, eg an app for teaching people how to touch type which is limited to keyboard interaction.

Principle 3 – Understandable

Guideline 3.1 – Readable

3.1.3 UNUSUAL WORDS
Explain words or phrases which might be difficult for some people to understand. These could include jargon, eg 'drill down' to mean 'look at a problem in detail', or idioms, eg 'over the moon' to mean 'very happy'.

3.1.4 ABBREVIATIONS

Explain the meaning of all abbreviations by putting the expanded definition in brackets after the abbreviation, eg CAD (Computer Aided Design), or by providing a definition or a glossary.

3.1.5 READING LEVEL

Provide an easily readable alternative or supplementary content if language is too difficult to understand for someone with a lower secondary education reading level, ie with about nine years of education.

Exceptions:

- Proper names, ie a specific name for a particular person, place or thing, eg Bernardine, Paris, or Neptune.

- Titles, including the titles of people, documents, books, movies, etc.

3.1.6 PRONUNCIATION

If the meaning of a word can only be understood because of the way it is pronounced, give learners extra help to make it clear what is meant. This can be done either with information in the surrounding text or by giving the pronunciation of the word. For example, the word desert can mean either 'to abandon' or 'dry area of land' depending on the pronunciation. If the surrounding text has information describing average rainfalls in arid regions, it would be clear that in this context desert means 'dry area of land'. If the surrounding text doesn't contain enough information for learners to understand the meaning, a solution could be to supply a link to the audio file of someone reading the word aloud.

Guideline 3.2 – Predictable

3.2.5 CHANGE ON REQUEST

Make sure that nothing unexpected happens on a page which could confuse or disorientate learners. This could include new pages opening, automatic page updates or forms submitting when learners complete a field instead of selecting a 'Submit' button. Anything which changes on a page should always be the direct result of learner input. Alternatively they should have the option to switch off or disable automatic changes.

Guideline 3.3 – Input Assistance

3.3.5 HELP

Provide 'context-sensitive' help for learners when they are filling in data entry fields. This means help is provided at the exact point they need to enter data into each field. Normally this is achieved through labels, eg a field labelled 'First Name' clearly explains what learners are required to fill in. If more information is needed, however, content authors should provide extra support. An example could be information icons next to each field which take learners to extra guidance and example answers.

3.3.6 ERROR PREVENTION (ALL)

When learners input *any* information using input items such as data entry fields or check boxes, make sure they are given the opportunity to do one of the following:

- **Reverse:** undo the interaction once they have submitted or deleted the information.

- **Check:** correct the information once it has been checked and they have been informed of any errors they have made when they input information.

- **Confirm:** review, confirm and correct the information before they submit it.

Endnotes

1   W3C Working Group Note (2016) Understanding conformance, https://www.w3.org/TR/UNDERSTANDING-WCAG20/conformance.html (archived at https://perma.cc/TE3X-PRT5)

13

WCAG 2.2 draft accessibility standards

Introduction

This chapter provides the nine WCAG 2.2 standards which were released in August 2020. As with all new W3C standards they are first released in draft form and are then finalized after feedback from accessibility experts has been taken into consideration.[1] They are included for reference and because they give an indication of future requirements and best practice. The standards in this chapter are not plain English interpretations of the guidelines but simply the W3C wording. Both the wording and the levels assigned are subject to change. At the time of publishing there was no definitive date available for when these standards would be finalized and officially published. It is important to be aware, however, that there is normally a significant lag between the release of new standards and changes in legislation which make them a legal requirement.

Note: For further guidance on requirements for meeting these standards see: Web Content Accessibility Guidelines (WCAG) 2.2 W3C Working Draft 11 August 2020.[2] All wording used is copyright. Copyright © 2019 W3C® (MIT, ERCIM, Keio, Beihang).

Principle 2 – Operable

Guideline 2.4 – Navigable

2.4.11 FOCUS APPEARANCE (MINIMUM) – LEVEL AA

For the keyboard focus indicator of each user interface component, all of the following are true:

- **Minimum area:** The focus indication area is greater than or equal to a 1 CSS pixel border of the focused control, or has a thickness of at least 8 CSS pixels along the shortest side of the element.

- **Change of contrast:** The colour change for the focus indication area has a contrast ratio of at least 3:1 with the colours of the unfocused state.

- **Adjacent contrast:** The focus indication area has a contrast ratio of at least 3:1 against all adjacent colours for the minimum area or greater, or has a thickness of at least 2 CSS pixels.

- **Unobscured:** The item with focus is not entirely hidden by author-created content.

2.4.12 FOCUS APPEARANCE (ENHANCED) – LEVEL AAA

For the keyboard focus indicator of each user interface component, all of the following are true:

- **Minimum area:** The focus indication area is greater than or equal to a 2 CSS pixel solid border around the control.

- **Change of contrast:** Colour changes used to indicate focus have a contrast ratio of at least 4.5:1 with the colours changed from the unfocused control.

- **Unobscured:** No part of the focus indicator is hidden by author-created content.

2.4.13 FIXED REFERENCE POINTS – LEVEL A

When a web page or set of web pages is an electronic publication with page break locators, a mechanism is available to navigate to each locator and each locator maintains its place in the flow of content, even when the formatting or platform change.

Guideline 2.5 – Input Modalities

2.5.7 DRAGGING – LEVEL AA

All functionality that uses a dragging movement for operation can be operated by a single pointer without dragging, unless dragging is essential.

2.5.8 POINTER TARGET SPACING – LEVEL AA

For each target, there is an area with a width and height of at least 44 CSS pixels that includes it, and no other targets, except when:

- **Enlarge:** A mechanism is available to change the CSS pixel size of each target, or its spacing, so there is an area with a width and height of at least 44 CSS pixels that includes it, and no other targets;

- **Inline:** The target is in a sentence or block of text;

- **User agent:** The size of the target is controlled by the user agent and is not modified by the author;

- **Essential:** A particular presentation of the target is essential to the information being conveyed.

Principle 3 – Understandable

Guideline 3.2 – Predictable

3.2.6 FINDABLE HELP – LEVEL A

For single-page web applications or any set of web pages, if one of the following is available, then access to at least one option is included in the same relative order on each page:

- human contact details;
- human contact mechanism;
- self-help option;
- a fully automated contact mechanism.

3.2.7 HIDDEN CONTROLS – LEVEL AA

Controls needed to progress or complete a process are visible at the time they are needed without requiring pointer hover or keyboard focus, or a mechanism is available to make them persistently visible.

Guideline 3.3 – Input Assistance

3.3.7 ACCESSIBLE AUTHENTICATION – LEVEL A

If an authentication process relies on a cognitive function test, at least one other method must also be available that does not rely on a cognitive function test.

3.3.8 REDUNDANT ENTRY – LEVEL A

For steps in a process, information previously entered by or provided to the user that is required on subsequent steps is either:

- auto-populated; or
- available for the user to select.

Exception: When re-entering the information is essential.

Note: WCAG 2.2 also changes the level of WCAG 2.1 standard **2.4.7 Focus Visible** from level AA to level A.

Endnotes

1   Smith, J (2020) WCAG 2.2 overview and feedback, 31 August, https://webaim.org/blog/wcag-2-2-overview-and-feedback/ (archived at https://perma.cc/E4J6-FV5Q)

2   Adams, C, Campbell, A, Montgomery, R, Cooper, M and Kirkpatrick, A (2020) Web Content Accessibility Guidelines (WCAG) 2.2 W3C Working Draft, 11 August, https://www.w3.org/TR/2020/WD-WCAG22-20200811/ (archived at https://perma.cc/AJ34-DWMD)

Conclusion

A few years ago I carried out some research on assistive technology at the Henry Tyndale School in Surrey in the UK. The school is a 'Specialist College for Cognition and Learning' and caters for pupils with complex learning difficulties and disabilities. In a break between observing lessons, I was invited to watch Ananya Chittolla, one of the school's pupils, play her favourite 'custard pie' digital game. Ananya loved this game so much that she was happy to give up her free time to play it. I soon discovered that one of the main reasons for this was that Ananya's teachers had customized the game so that it featured photographs of some of the school's staff and her classmates. The purpose of the game was to 'splat' these pictures by moving custard pies on the screen with eye-tracking software. Ananya's teacher explained that this helped to strengthen her eye muscles and allowed her to practise the complex movements needed to master eye-tracking technology. She pointed out how the software automatically detected any weaknesses and responded accordingly. In Ananya's case, her response times were slower for targets on the left side of the screen. This made the program automatically deliver more targets on that side, in order to develop her coordination and strengthen those particular eye muscles.

I had seen a few demonstrations of eye-tracking software online before my visit and had always been amazed at the speed and the precision of the eye movements involved. But this was the first time that I realized the amount of work, effort and determination needed to master this form of assistive technology, both from the people who used it and from the people who taught them. This proved to be another lightbulb moment in my accessibility journey. It was a powerful demonstration of my responsibility as an eLearning professional to design accessible learning content. It has served as an abiding reminder that if I create inaccessible eLearning resources, I directly undervalue and undermine this same work, effort and

FIGURE C.1   Key takeaways eLearning resource slide

Designing Accessible Learning Content

Key takeaways

1. Learning content which is accessible provides a better learning experience for all of our learners.

2. Making eLearning content accessible allows us to "dramatically improve people's lives, just by doing our job a little better." Steve Krug

3. eLearning accessibility is a journey, not a destination. We should aim for progress rather than perfection.

4. Designing accessible learning content can transform our industry and help us to ensure that accessibility becomes the norm rather than the exception.

5. "I know that if people learn how to help, they will." Haben Girma

Exit course

The final page of an eLearning resource which summarises the key takeaways of this book. These are: 1. Learning content which is accessible provides a better learning experience for all of our learners. 2. Making eLearning content accessible allows us to 'dramatically improve people's lives, just by doing our job a little better'(Steve Krug). 3. eLearning accessibility is a journey, not a destination. We should aim for progress rather than perfection. 4. Designing accessible learning content can transform our industry and help us to ensure that accessibility becomes the norm rather than the exception. 5. 'I know that if people learn how to help, they will' (Haben Girma).

determination. I also create unnecessary barriers which deny learners the opportunity to fulfil their potential.

Haben Girma, a disability rights advocate, and the first deafblind graduate of Harvard Law School, made a memorable comment in her TED Talk on removing access barriers for students with disabilities. As part of her call to action to make digital content accessible, she said, 'I know that if people learn how to help, they will.'[1] My objective in writing this book was to make it easier for eLearning professionals to learn how to help. I wanted to 'democratize'[2] eLearning accessibility so that as many content authors as possible could finally make sense of it and apply it to their learning content. But while a key objective of this book is to make it easier for people to meet accessibility standards in order to comply with legislation, it is important to remember that this is not the only way that we can make a difference. Our help can be as simple as implementing a few key standards and recommendations, becoming better informed advocates for eLearning accessibility, or even just using more inclusive imagery in our learning content.

Despite its imperfections, I hope that *Designing Accessible Learning Content* achieves its objectives and allows you to offer the eLearning accessibility help that you can. By doing so, I also hope that it contributes to a culture shift in the eLearning profession whereby accessibility becomes the default rather than the exception for learning content.

Endnotes

[1]   Haben, G (2014) Why I work to remove access barriers for students with disabilities (Online video), https://youtu.be/Mvoj-ku8zk0 (archived at https://perma.cc/D9HX-9AYK)

[2]   Smyth, P (2020) Techshare Podcast TSP39: Accessibility insights with Paul Smyth of Barclays (Podcast), 8 September, https://abilitynet.org.uk/accessibility-services/techshare-procast-abilitynets-podcast (archived at https://perma.cc/QG32-8WCC)

ACKNOWLEDGEMENTS

Special thanks to my husband, Tim, for his unfailing belief in me and unwavering support – you make it easy. To my parents Franz and Pauline for their kindness and generosity, to my sister Karin for her encouragement and praise, to my brother Marc for transatlantic Mullins advice, and to my daughters Izzy and Freya for their patience and love.

Thanks to the following for their contributions and help with the book. I'm deeply grateful for the improvements they've made and the support they've given me.

Kirsty Major, Esi Hardy, Luke Westwood, Jake Harrison and Jill Bussien. Bethany Meyer and the team at CourseArc, Paul Schneider at dominKnow Inc, Lisa Logan at Elucidat, Rory Lawson and Matt Leathes at Kineo. Aron Janecki at Dig Inclusion, Sam Cook at Intellum, Alistair McNaught from the Xerte Project, Maria Varankina at iSpring, Simon Taghioff at Articulate, Chris Willis and Sheryl Coggins at eLearning Brothers, Will Butler and Sanne Byrgesen at Be My Eyes, Jonathan Hassell at Hassell Inclusion, Heather Giles and all the staff and pupils at Henry Tyndale School.

Thanks to everyone who has supported me in my first steps into the worlds of eLearning accessibility, business ownership and writing.

Alistair McNaught, Abi James, Rory Lawson, Laura Clark, Ben Watson, Ghizzi Dunlop, Matthew Deeprose, Zoran Birimisa, Sabine de Kamps, Katrin Kircheis, Michael Buckfield, Neil Milliken, George Rhodes, Jayne Davids, Louise Talbot, Lindsey Coode, Jenna Reardon, Michael Osborne, Joan Keevill, Leonard Houx, Jonathon Lightfoot, Alice Harris, David Wrigley, Toby Gilchrist, Vickie Birnie, Ailsa Duncan, Kirsty Lewis, Suzanne Bourne, Kim Mason, Sam Barber, Jan Carlyle, Simon Howes, Sue Thomas, Felicity Dwyer, Karen Williams, Anne-Marie Heeney, Lucy Carter and The Old Alresford Book Club.

Finally, heartfelt thanks to my wonderful support network who have encouraged me and kept me going. Without them I would have given up countless times.

Debbie Hands, Melanie Locke, Clare Spence, Tina Thompson, Liz Brant, Sally Page, James Allen, Mimi Lee, Sheila Miller, Ali and Steve Law, Maria Gonoude, Trish Sherry, Sinead and Matt Knell, Rachel Webb, Sam Garner, Elizabeth James, Alison Haverly, Anna Hallett, Elaine Secluna and last, but definitely not least, Andrew Spence and Matt Locke.

ACKNOWLEDGEMENTS

INDEX

The main index is filed in alphabetical, word-by-word order. Acronyms are filed as presented. Page locators in italics denote information within a figure or table; those in roman numerals denote information within the preface. WCAG and eLa standards are filed by subject headings within the main index; a separate index is also presented for each by standard number.

abbreviations 69, 115, 316
ableism 37
accessibility, defined 13, 15, 45
Accessibility Guidelines 3.0 18, 19
accessibility statements 26–27, 34, 75
accessibility testing 30–32, 47
    see also operable standards testing;
        perceivable standards testing;
        robust standards testing;
        understandable standards testing
achromatopsia 40
ADA (Americans with Disabilities Act)
    38, 76
ADA Title I 76
ADA Title III 76
Adapt 29, 85
adaptability 97–98, 310–11
adaptive keyboards 65–66
ADHD 42, 43, 237, 238, 279, 280
adjacent contrast 319
adjustable time limits 62, 103, 118, 136,
    141, 142–43, 233–36, 312–13
Adobe Captivate *232, 277*
ageing population 44
    see also older learners
alerting devices 64, 303, 313
alternative activity links 26, 46, 81, 226
alternative text 94–95, 117, 125–26,
    130–31, 140, 153–59
    see also non-text content
ambiguous links 250
Android 59
animation paths 224, 227
animations 61, 95, 137, 141, 161, 224,
    227, 233–34, 237, 313–14
    see also progress bars
anticipatory duty 74
Apple 59, 66
apps 1–3, 58, 171
ARIA 179, 302, 303
ARIA11 179

arrow keys 67, 102, 223, 228–29
Articulate Rise *242, 245, 251–53, 255,*
    287, 289
Articulate Storyline 24, *292*
    operable standards *225, 227, 247,*
        251–52, 267
    perceivable standards *158, 166, 181,*
        197
assessments 23, 52–53, 67, *94,* 135–37,
    285, 291
    disability 50–51
assistive listening devices 64
astigmatism 39
attention deficit hyperactivity disorder
    (ADHD) 42, 43, 237, 238, 279,
    280
audio content *94,* 137–41, 155
    background 64, 311
    live 164, 171, 172, 310
    prerecorded 95, 96, 159–63, 311
    standards testing 162, 194
audio control 99, 140, 192–94
audio description 95–97, 137–39, 160–62,
    167–71, 173–75, 310
audio narration 141, 167–68, 192
audio-only content 64, 95, 137–38, 141,
    159–63, 164, 172, 310, 311
auditory cues 98, 184, 185
auditory processing disorders 40
authentication 313, 321
Authoring Tool Accessibility Guidelines
    (ATAG) 23–24, 28, 34
authoring tool settings *94,* 118, 199, 214,
    273–74
authoring tools 15, 20–30, 164, 176, 179,
    180–81
    see also Adapt; Adobe Captivate;
        Articulate Rise; Articulate
        Storyline; CourseArc; Evolve;
        iSpring; Lectora Online; Xerte
        Online Toolkit

autocomplete 187–88, 189
automatic captions 49, 164, 166, 171–72, 173
automatic tables 176
automatic testing tools 31
automatically moving and updating content (autoplay) 69, 103, 142–43, 193–94, 233–34, 237–39
Axe 31

background audio 64, 141, 311
background contrast 116, 120, 195, 196, 198
banking sites 254, 293
    see also Barclays
bar charts 126, 127, 190, 206–07
Barclays 78
Be My Eyes 1–3
best practice 28–30
    see also Level AAA WCAG standards
blank page authoring tools 21
blindness 39, 46–47, 167
    see also colour blindness; deafblindness
blinking content 103, 142, 237–38, 239
blur functionality 78–79
Bmibaby 74
bold text 99, 116, 122, 266
braille xviii
braille displays 62, 168, 182, 211, 244
braille keyboards 65
brand enhancement 78
British Sign Language (BSL) 47, 48
browsers 31, 58, 62, 188, 264
buttons 154, 196, 197, 207–08, 232, 239, 265–67, 282–84
    see also radio buttons; submit buttons
bypass blocks 104, 241–43
    see also skipping repeated blocks of content
bypass links 241–43

capital letters 122
CAPTCHA 155, 311
captions 47–49, 64, 96, 99, 101, 138–39, 163–67, 171–73, 274
Carol (Simmonds, Carol) 56, 58
Casey, Caroline 78
Center for Applied Special Technology 79
cerebral palsy 50–51
change on request 316
character key shortcuts 61, 66, 102, 145, 230–33
charities 75
check boxes 67, 110, 132, 183–84, 285, 317

checking information 293, 296
cheek sensor switches 66
Chittolla, Ananya 322
chording keyboards 65
chronic conditions 51–53, 224
Cisco 78
closed captions 163, 166
Coblis colour blind simulator 192
coding 21–22, 32, 61, 94, 147–49, 189, 299–301
    see also HTML
coding errors 149
cognitive impairments 41–42, 45, 51–53, 68–69, 169, 183–84, 188, 193, 205, 286
    see also ADHD; dyslexia; memory
Colorcop colour picking tool 198
colour 48, 49, 98–99, 104, 116, 123–24, 134, 135, 189–92
    standards testing 198, 209
colour blindness 39–40, 63, 183, 185, 189–92
colour contrast checkers 31, 195, 196, 198, 209
colour contrast ratios 16, 99, 100–01, 116, 120, 126–27, 128, 194–98, 206–09, 311
    visible focus indicators 258
    see also adjacent contrast
colour pickers 196, 198, 209
colour values 195, 207
commonly used words 108, 122, 149, 276
communication support workers 48
complete start tags 300
complex gestures 67, 106, 146–47, 261–63
complex images 126, 154, 157, 205
concurrent input mechanisms 315
conductive hearing loss 40
confirmation 294, 295, 317
conforming alternate versions 25–26
consistent identification 109, 129, 250, 282–84
consistent navigation 67, 108–09, 131–32, 281–82
content authors 14, 81
content blocks 22, 67
    ordering 181, 182
    skipping 132, 145
content on hover 101, 124, 128, 196, 212–15
content reflow 100, 145–46, 199, 204–05
content structure 147–48, 179
controls
    audio 99, 140, 192–94
    hidden 321
    volume 99, 192, 193

Convention on the Rights of Persons with
     Disabilities (UN) 38, 72–73
core values 84, 85
Cortana 66
course menus 245
CourseArc 24, 81–82
     alternative interactivity 26
     alternative text 157
     check and reset options 296
     content block order 182
     drag-and-drop 226
     table headers 178
     text spacing 211
     transcript links 170
     visible focus indicators 259
COVID 19 73
credentials assessment 24, 84–85
CSS 13, 128, 314, 315, 319, 320
culture 45, 191
custom navigation 80, 114
customization 79, 80, 100, 114, 201, 210,
     260, 310–11, 322

data entry fields 23, 108, 256, 257, 279–80,
     317
     see also buttons; check boxes; error
          correction suggestions; error
          identification; error prevention;
          labelling
deactivated (inactive) buttons 99, 207
deafblindness 62, 323
deafness 47–49, 158, 164, 184, 185
decorative images 126, 155, 158, 161, 196,
     200–01
default language setting 273–74
Department of Commerce (US) 73
descriptive headings 105–06, 115, 119
descriptive labels 95, 126, 129, 155, 256
descriptive links 252
descriptive transcripts 61, 64, 68, 96,
     137–38, 139, 159–61, 167–71,
     173, 224
design theme 116
Designing for Screen Reader Compatibility
     (WebAIM) 60, 275
deuteranopia 39
diabetic retinopathy 39, 40
diagnosis 43–44
digital accessibility, defined 15
digital divide 73
disability 38, 42–44, 53
     attitudes towards xvii–xix
disability activism 45–46
disability assessments 50–51
Disability Discrimination Act (1995) 74

disability personas 46
disabled population 3, 38, 42–43
Disabled Students Allowance 48
disclosure 43
discrimination 37, 43, 51, 73, 74, 76
dismissible pop-up content 101, 124, 128,
     212, 213, 214
distance learning providers 46–47
distinguishable content 98–101, 311–12
dominKnow | ONE 29, 30, 82–83, 157
down-events 67–68, 106–07, 129, 147,
     263–64
Down syndrome 42
drag-and-drop 26, 224, 226, 227, 264, 296,
     320
dropdown lists 46, 224, 227, 231, 233, 278
dyslexia 28, 43, 112, 117, 198, 201, 202,
     211
Dyslexia friendly style guide 198
dyspraxia 51–53

e-commerce sites 254
eBooks 48
Edit HTML source code 22
eLa (eLearning accessibility) framework 10,
     112–50
eLearning 14
eLearning professionals 14
Elucidat 84
emails 78, 201, 285
embedded videos 164, 165–66
EN 301 549 75
enhanced text 116, 120
enlarged text 99–100, 119, 120, 186,
     198–200, 312
enter key 223
epilepsy 42, 69, 239, 240–41
Equality Act (2010) 38, 74–75
Equality and Human Rights Commission
     75
Equality Commission 75
ergonomic keyboards 65
error, defined 285, 290–91
error correction suggestions 109–10, 125,
     133, 136, 290–93
error feedback 137, 287
error identification 109, 125, 133, 136,
     284–88, 290, 291
error prevention 110, 133, 137, 293–96,
     317
essential images 202
ethics 72–73, 82, 85
European Union 75–76
Evolve 28, 29, 162, 203
expert support 7, 32

Exploring WCAG 2.1- 4.1.3 Status Messages 304
extended audio description 139, 174, 310
eye-tracking technology 66, 268, 322

Facebook Live 171
Farisai (Moyo, Farisai) xvii–xix
farsightedness 39, 199
FE Accessibility Maturity Model 33
feedback 137, 190, *191*, *287*
findable help 320
fixed holders 186, 187, 269
fixed reference points 319
flashing content 69, 104, 142, 237, 239–41, 313
focus 108, 128, 278–79
focus appearance 319
focus indication areas 319
focus order 67, 105, 117, 130, 144, *158*, *181*, 246–48, 267
    see also meaningful sequences
focus visible (visible focus indicators) 67, 106, 130, 144, 223, 246, 258–61, 319, 321
font 69, 175, 177, 201
    eLa standard 117, 122
    WCAG standard 16
footers 175
Fragile X 42
full URLs 249–50
functional images 126, 155

games 105, 147, 233, 250, 262, 322
gestures
    complex 67, 106, 146–47, 261–63
    hand 268
    multipoint 106, 146, 261, 262
    pointer 106, 147, 261–63
    single point 264
Girma, Haben 323
glaucoma 39
Glitch 209
global icon *94*
glossaries 115, 210, 241, 283, 316
Google Assistant 66
Google Lighthouse 31
Google Slides 173
Government Digital Service 46, 75, 179, 257
graphs 82, 99, 126, 127, 154, *157*, 190, 195, 206–07, 209
greyscale 31, *191*

halo effect 196
hand gestures 268

Hardy, Esi 50–51
Harrison, Jake 47–49
HE Accessibility Maturity Model 33
head wands (headsticks) 65–66, 265
headers 175, 176, *178*, 241
heading levels 61, 176–77
headings 61, 81, 105–06, 115, 119, 121, 175–77, 179, 256–57, 314
hearing impairments 40–41, 44, 45, 47–49, 63–64, 161, 165, 184
    see also deafblindness; deafness
help 317, 320
Henry Tyndale School 322
hex values 195, 207
hidden controls 321
hidden disabilities 43
higher education (HE) 33, 47–49, 73
    see also university education
home icons 105, 253
horizontal scroll bars 204–05, 312
hotspot interactions 224, *225*
hover function 101, 124, 128, 196, 212–15
HSL values 195, 207
HTML 22, 61, 176–79, 195, 207, 214, 243, 301
    see also parsing; status messages
human transcribers 171–72
hyperopia (farsightedness) 39, 199

IBM 78
icons 93–94, 105, 127, 190, 206, 282–85
    information 167, 317
identification, consistent 109, 129, 250, 282–84
image links 249
images 94, 95, 125–27, 154–59
    complex 205
    decorative 161, 196, 200–01
    essential 202
images of text 99, 100, 120, 121, 127, 196, 200–04, 312
inactive (deactivated) buttons 99, 207
inbuilt buttons 196, *197*
inbuilt screen readers 59
incidental content 99
inclusive design 79–80
Inclusive Design Subject Matter Expert Series 171
incomplete start tags 300
indicators 314
    see also visible focus indicators (focus visible)
individual phrases 31, 122, 149, *277*
infographics 201

information 94, 97–98, 123–25, 135, 167,
    175–79, 190, 317
innovation 78–79
input assistance 109–10, 317, 321
input fields 98, 133, 148, 175, 176,
    187–89, 225, 285
    see also concurrent input mechanisms
input items 94, 108, 124, 132–33, 135,
    279–80
    see also buttons; check boxes
input modalities see drag-and-drop;
        labelling; motion actuation;
        pointer cancellation; pointer
        gestures; pointer target spacing
input purpose 98, 187–89
instructions 94, 109, 123–25, 132, 135–36,
    183–85, 238, 288–90
interactive item target size 128, 314–15
interactive items 94, 127–34, 155, 158,
    247, 279–80
    see also input items; links; navigation
        items
internet 49, 53, 60, 76, 156, 203
interruptions 313
introductory pages 233
ISO 20071–1 33
iSpring 191, 226–27, 236
italics 122

JAWS 46, 60

key shortcuts 61, 66, 102, 145, 230–33
keyboard accessible 102, 130, 140, 144,
    224, 226, 228, 252, 312
keyboard commands 46, 59, 60, 61, 62,
    224
keyboard trap 67, 102, 130, 140, 144,
    228–30
keyboards 65–66, 94, 107, 143–45, 222–33
    standards testing 243, 248, 260
    see also visible focus indicators (focus
        visible)
keys 190
keystrokes 102, 242
Kindle 50
Kineo 84–85

label in name 57, 107, 129, 265–67
labelling 95, 105–06, 109, 115, 256–57,
    282–84, 288–90, 317
    descriptive 126, 129, 155
    see also label in name
labyrinthitis 42
landscape orientation 98, 186

language 48, 52, 61, 67, 69, 124, 135–36,
    211
    see also language; plain English;
        pronunciation; punctuation
language of individual phrases 31, 122,
    149, 277
language of page 107–08, 118, 121, 149,
    273–75
language of parts 19, 108, 122, 149, 274,
    275–77
language of resource 118, 121, 149
large size text 99, 195
learning content 14
learning management systems 23
Learning Technology Awards 71–72
Lectora Accessibility User Group 30
Lectora Online 22, 158, 165, 260
legislation 17, 20, 38, 73–77
    see also Public Sector Bodies
        Accessibility Regulations 2018
        (PSBAR)
letters spacing 210
    see also capital letters
Level A WCAG standards
    operable 102–05, 106–07, 222–53,
        261–69, 319
    perceivable 95–96, 97–99, 153–71,
        175–85, 189–94
    robust 110–11, 299–302
    understandable 108, 109, 273–75,
        278–80, 284–93, 320–21
Level AA WCAG standards
    operable 105–06, 253–61, 319, 320
    perceivable 96–97, 98, 99–101, 171–75,
        186–89, 194–215
    robust 111, 302–04
    understandable 108–10, 275–77,
        281–84, 293–96, 321
Level AAA WCAG standards 64, 112–13,
    309–17, 319
lightness sliders 195, 198, 207
lightness values 195
line spacing 122, 210, 312
link destination (purpose) 105, 134, 148,
    248–53, 283, 314
link destination through link alone 134,
    248, 249, 252, 314
link destination through surrounding text
        and link 134, 248, 249, 251
link text 80, 206, 249, 250
links 94, 157, 167, 176
    alternative activity 26, 46, 81, 226
    ambiguous 250
    descriptive 252

multiple 250, 283
non-descriptive *251*
see also link destination (purpose); link
       destination through link alone; link
       destination through surrounding
       text and link; link text
lists 176
live audio content 138, 164, 171, 172, 310
live captions 49, 96, 171–73
live video conferencing 47–49, 78–79, 172
live video content 1, 171, 172
location 115, 183, 314
logical focus order 67, 105, 117, 130, 144,
       158, *181*, 246–48, 267
see also meaningful sequences
logical reading order 117, 145, 148, 180,
       181–82, 184
logos 99, 100, 155
low background audio 141, 311

Mace, Ronald L 79
macular degeneration 39
main content 176, 177
Major, Kirsty 46–47
Make it accessible (Aston University) 166,
       171
meaningful sequences 31, 97, 117, 145,
       148, 180–85, 246
see also logical focus order
media alternative 310
see also audio description; descriptive
       transcripts
medical diagrams 207
memory 42, 244, 259, 295
Ménière's disease 42, 165
mental health problems 42, 51–53, 283
menus 176
Mercy xvii–xviii
Microsoft 66, 78, 80, 171
Microsoft Teams 48, 78–79
minimum focus indication area 319
mission statements 82, 84
mobile devices 59, 62, 67–68, 75, 94,
       146–47
see also apps; motion actuation
'more information' buttons 184
motion activated functionality 147
motion actuation 23, 107, 147, 268–69
motor impairments 41, 44–45, 50–51,
       65–68, 205, 224, 265
mouth sticks 65–66
moving content 61, *94*
       automatically 69, 103, 142–43, 193–94,
       233–34, 237–39

Moyo, Farisai xvii–xix
multiple choice options 26, 135, 223, 224,
       226–27, *259*, 288
multiple links 250, 283
multiple navigation points 105, 115, 131,
       253–55, 281
multipoint gestures 106, 146, 261, 262
myopia 39

names 111, 129, 131, 149, 256, 265–67,
       282–84, 301–02
see also label in name; proper nouns
       (names)
narration 141, 167–68, 192
Narrator 59, 60, 62
navigation
       consistent 67, 108–09, 131–32, 281–82
       custom 80, 114
       multiple points 105, 115, 131, 253–55,
       281
see also bypass blocks; fixed reference
       points; focus appearance; focus
       visible (visible focus indicators);
       headings; labelling; link
       destination (purpose); location;
       logical focus order; multiple
       navigation points; navigation
       items; navigation menus; page
       titles
navigation items 63, 67, 68, *94*, 104, 114,
       131–32, 253
navigation menus 176
nearsightedness 39
neurodiversity 1, 42, 43–44, 52
NoCoffee vision simulator 192
noise-sensitive environments 165
non-descriptive links *251*
non-governmental organizations 75
non-text content 95, 100–01, 153–59
see also bar charts; images; interactive
       items; text alternatives
non-text contrast 100–01, 116, 127, 128,
       195, 206–09
normal size text 99, 195
'nothing-about-us-without-us
       principle' 45–46
NVDA 60, 231, 304

older learners 44, 197, 199, 208, 262
see also ageing population
on focus see focus
on input see input items
online learning 46–51, 73, 82
onscreen keyboards 65, 66, 107

open captions 163
open orientation 118, 146
open source tools 21, 29–30, 60, 224
    see also Adapt; NVDA
operable principle 18, 102–07, 222–72,
    312–15, 319–20
operable standards testing
    content control 239
    content flashes 240
    headings 257
    keyboards 228, 230, 232–33, 243, 248,
        260
    labels 267
    links 252
    motion actuation 269
    navigation 255
    page titles 245
    pointer cancellation 265
    time limits 236
ordering dropdown lists 46, 224, 227, 231,
    233, 278
organization strategy 32–34, 78, 83
orientation 98, 118, 146, 186–87

page location 115
page regions 176
page titles 104, 115, 119, 243–45
paragraph spacing 122, 210, 212, 312
parsing 110, 149, 299–301
parsing error bookmarklet 301
path-based gestures 106, 262
patterns 190
pedometers 269
peer support 48
perceivable principle 18, 94–101, 153–221,
    310–12
perceivable standards testing
    audio content 162, 194
    audio description 174
    coding 189
    colour 191, 198, 209
    content on hover 215
    content reflow 205
    images 159
    information 179
    meaningful sequences 182
    orientation 187
    sensory characteristics 185
    text 200, 203, 212
    video content 162, 166, 170, 172
persistent pop-up content 213
personal data 23, 98, 133, 148, 187–89,
    293, 295
personas 46

photosensitive epilepsy 42, 69, 239,
    240–41
Photosensitive Epilepsy Analysis Tool 240
phrases, individual 31, 122, 149, 277
pie charts 154, 157
Pie Graph Transcript link 157
pixelation 128, 199, 205, 314–15, 319, 320
plain English 123
'play' label 266
pointer cancellation 106–07, 129, 147,
    263–65
pointer gestures 106, 147, 261–63
pointer target spacing 320
pop-up content 101, 124, 128, 212–15, 264
POUR principles 9, 17–18, 19, 93
    see also operable principle; perceivable
        principle; robust principle;
        understandable principle
pre-course registration 47
prerecorded audio content 95, 96, 137–38,
    141, 159–63, 311
prerecorded video content 95–97, 137–40,
    159–71, 173–75, 310
presentations 96, 101, 139, 171–73
press-and-hold 264
programmatically determined
        information 19, 176, 187
progress bars 103, 142, 190
pronunciation 61, 273, 316
proper nouns (names) 122, 276, 316
protanopia 39
public sector 37, 72, 75–76, 78, 83, 293
Public Sector Bodies Accessibility
        Regulations 2018 (PSBAR) 27,
        75–76, 172
puff switches 66
punctuation 49, 156, 250
purple pound 77–78
purpose 3, 310–11
    link 105, 134, 148, 248–53, 314

quizzes 110, 196, 224, 289, 294–96, 303
    feedback 190, 191, 287
    instructions 136, 183, 288
    navigation items 67, 223, 280, 301
    time limits 52, 103, 142–43, 233, 236

radio buttons 67, 108, 176, 183–84, 247,
    259, 280
rapid authoring tools see authoring tools
re-authenticating 313
reading level 19, 123, 316
reading order 117, 145, 148, 180, 181–82,
    184

real-time events 103, 143, 171, 173, 234, 235, 313
reasonable adjustments 50, 74–75
red flashing content 239–40
redundant entry 321
reflow 100, 145–46, 199, 204–05
refreshable braille displays 62, 168, *182, 211*, 244
Rehabilitation Act (1973) 76–77
remapping 231, *232*
resource design *94*, 114–17
revenue growth 77–78
reverse actions 293, 317
review workflows 29
reviewing answers 295, 317
RGB values 195
robust principle 18, 110–11, 299–305
robust standards testing 300, 302, 304
roles 111, 131, 149, 256, 301–02
Royal National Institute of Blind People 74

scoreboard quizzes 302
screen magnifiers 62–63, 154, 183, 185, 201, 278, 281–82, 303
screen reader testing 31, 60–61, 159
screen readers 56–57, 59–62, 153–54, 180, 183, 184, 192–94, 273–78
    and images 201, 238
    key shortcuts 231
    labelling 266, 267
    link access 249
    punctuation 156
    speed of 58, 169, 257
    see also JAWS
scroll bars 199, 204–05, 312
scrolling content 233–34, 237
    see also moving content
search icons 206
second-language learners 161, 235, 238, 274
Section 508 Program Maturity Levels 24, 33, 77, 82
section headings 105, 119, 256, 257, 314
seizures 42, 69, 104, 142, 237, 239–40, 313–14
Semantic Structure (WebAIM) 179
sensor switches 66
sensorineural hearing loss 41
sensory characteristics 98, 124, 135, 183–85
sensory cues 124, 135
sensory experiences 95, 155–56
settings change, interactive items 279–80
shape recognition 183–84

shift key 223, 229
shortcuts, key 61, 66, 102, 145, 230–33
sign language 47, 64, 140, 164, 235, 310
Sign Supported English 47
Silver project (taskforce) 18
Simmonds, Carol 56, 58
simulations (simulators) 39, *40*, 98, 136, 143, 146, 186, 191–92, 227, 234
single character key shortcuts 61, 66, 102, 145, 230–33
single point interactions (clicks) 262, 264
sip switches 66
Siri 50, 66
situational impairments 45, 156, 161, 169, 172, 191, 197, 200, 208, 265
skim listening 257
skipping repeated blocks of content 67, 132, 145
    see also bypass blocks
sliders 195, 198, 207, 301
social model of disability xix, 15–16, 38
Sony 78
sounds (sound effects) 64, 163, 171, 184
space bar 59, 223
spacing 63, 69, 101, 121, 122, 148, 202, 209–12, 312, 320
speech-input 231
speech (voice) recognition 66, 154, 156, 164, 251, 266–67
split taps 261
standalone content 103
Standard ISO 30071-1 33
start tags 300
status messages 111, 124–25, 149, 302–04
step locked resources 105, 253–54
strategy 32–34, 78, 83
stress 45, 51, 52, 211
submit buttons 132, 223, 278, 279–80, 285, 290–91, 294–96
subtitles 163, 166, 171
    see also captions
summary error information 285
swipe gestures 261–62
switches 66
synchronized captions 64, 163, 164, 166

tab key 223, 228–29, 241, *242*, 246, 258, 301
tables 175, 176, *178*, 205
Talkback 59
talking head videos 96, 168
team strategy 32–34
Teams (Microsoft) 48, 78–79
technical terms 52, 108, 122, 276

temporary impairments 44–45, 161, 165,
        197, 200, 225, 229, 247, 262,
        295
text *94*, 99–100, 119–23, 195–96, 311–12
    alignment of 69, 312
    enhancement 116
    enlargement 186, 198–200, 312
    error identification 285
    images of 127, 200–04, 312
    standards testing 200, 203, 212
    see also audio description; text links;
        text resizing; text spacing;
        transcripts
text alternatives 94–95, 117, 125–26,
        130–31, 140, 153–59
    see also non-text content
text block alignment 123
text block width 123
text links 80, 206, 249, 250
text on background image check 198
text resizing 31, 99–100, 119, 120,
        198–200
text spacing 63, 69, 101, 121, 148, 202,
        209–12
text-to-speech software 49, 58, 61, 274
theme selectors 29, *30*
third-party software 58, 60, 61, 62, 68–69
timeouts 313
timing *94*
timing adjustable 62, 103, 118, 136, 141,
        142–43, 233–36, 312–13
titles 316
    page 104, 115, 119, 243–45
tool settings *94*, 118–19, 199, 214, 273–74
training 31, 33, 52, 57, 159
transcribers 171–72
transcripts 61, 64, 68, 96, 137–38, 139,
        159–61, 167–71, 173, 224
trigger functionality 67–68, 101, 129, 147,
        213, 263–65, 268–69
tritanopia 40
Twitter 230
two-finger pinch gesture 261

underlining 68, 122, 134, 190
understandable principle 18, 107–10,
        273–98, 315–17, 320–21
understandable standards testing
    errors 287, 293, 296
    focus 279
    identification 284
    input 280
    labelling 290
    language 275, 277

names 302
navigation 282
parsing 300
status messages 304
undiagnosed disabilities 43–44
undisclosed disabilities 43
unexpected events 128, 133, 193, 278–80,
        316
United Nations (UN)
    Convention on the Rights of Persons
        with Disabilities 38, 72–73
    Universal Declaration of Human Rights
        (1948) xix
universal design for learning 79
university education 50–51, 71
    see also higher education (HE)
unobscured content 319
unusual words 115, 315
up-events 67–68, 106, 129, 147, 263–64,
        265
updating content 69, 103, 142–43, 193–94,
        233–34, 237–39
URLs 249–50
usability 80–81
user interface components 127, 206
    see also input items; interactive items;
        links; navigation items

Valuable 500 78
values 131, 149, 195, 256, 301–02
vestibular disorders 42, 237
video conferencing 47–49, 78–79, 172
video content 58–59, *94*, 137–41, 155,
        159–71
    embedded 164, *165–66*
    live 1, 171, 172
    prerecorded 95–97, 173–75, 310
    standards testing 162, 166, 172
    see also Evolve; talking head videos
virtual learning environments 23
visible focus indicators (focus visible) 67,
        106, 130, 144, 223, 246, 258–61,
        319, 321
visible labels 57, 107, 109, 129, 265–67,
        282–84
visible names *267*
visual impairments 1–3, 39–40, 44, 45,
        46–47, 59–63, 183, 184, 197,
        200
    see also blindness; deafblindness
visual location 183
visual presentation 100, 122, 123, 311–12
voice (speech) recognition 66, 154, 156,
        164, 251, 266–67

Voiceover 59, 60
volume control 99, 192, 193
voluntary product accessibility template
        (VPAT)™ 24, 28, 32

WAI-ARIA 13, 302
WAVE 31
WCAG framework 9–11, 13–14, 15,
        16–20, 21–23, 68, 73, 74–75,
        93–111
    see also operable principle; perceivable
        principle; robust principle;
        understanding principle
WCAG Level A standards
    operable 102–05, 106–07, 222–53,
        261–69, 319
    perceivable 95–96, 97–99, 153–71,
        175–85, 189–94
    robust 110–11, 299–302
    understandable 108, 109, 273–75,
        278–80, 284–93, 320–21
WCAG Level AA standards
    operable 105–06, 253–61, 319, 320
    perceivable 96–97, 98, 99–101, 171–75,
        186–89, 194–215
    robust 111, 302–04
    understandable 108–10, 275–77,
        281–84, 293–96, 321
WCAG Level AAA standards 64, 112–13,
        309–17, 319

web accessibility 15
Web Accessibility Initiative 16
Web Accessibility Tutorials (W3C) 179
Web Content Accessibility Guidelines see
        WCAG framework
WebAIM 60, 198, 209, 275
Westwood, Luke 51–53
Wiberg, Hans Jørgen 2
Windows 59–60
Windows Narrator 59, 60, 62
word clouds 247
word completion technology 65
    see also autocomplete
word spacing 210
words, commonly used 108, 122, 149, 276
W3C (World Wide Web Consortium) 9, 11,
        15, 16, 17, 25, 80, 93–94
    Accessibility Guidelines 3.0 18, 19
    Authoring Tool Accessibility Guidelines
        (ATAG) 23–24, 28, 34
    markup validation service 300–01
WYSIWYG tools 21, 22

Xerte Online Toolkit 28, 178, 274

Yes/No confirmation 295
YouTube 164, 166, 171

zoom function 31, 62, 63, 99, 199, 200,
        204

eLa standards

eLa 1.1 114–17	eLa 1.2.2 118	eLa 2.1.13 122
eLa 1.1.1 115	eLa 1.2.3 118	eLa 2.1.14 122
eLa 1.1.2 115	eLa 1.2.4 118	eLa 2.1.15 122
eLa 1.1.3 115	eLa 1.2.5 119	eLa 2.1.16 122
eLa 1.1.4 115	eLa 2.1 119–23	eLa 2.1.17 123
eLa 1.1.5 115	eLa 2.1.1 119	eLa 2.1.18 123
eLa 1.1.6 116	eLa 2.1.2 119	eLa 2.1.19 123
eLa 1.1.7 116	eLa 2.1.3 119	eLa 2.2 123–25
eLa 1.1.8 116	eLa 2.1.4 120	eLa 2.2.1 123
eLa 1.1.9 116	eLa 2.1.5 120	eLa 2.2.2 124
eLa 1.1.10 117	eLa 2.1.6 120	eLa 2.2.3 124
eLa 1.1.11 117	eLa 2.1.7 121	eLa 2.2.4 124
eLa 1.1.12 117	eLa 2.1.8 121	eLa 2.2.5 124
eLa 1.1.13 117	eLa 2.1.9 121	eLa 2.2.6 124–25
eLa 1.1.14 117	eLa 2.1.10 121	eLa 2.2.7 125
eLa 1.2 118–19	eLa 2.1.11 122	eLa 2.2.8 125
eLa 1.2.1 118	eLa 2.1.12 122	eLa 2.3 125–27

eLa 2.3.1 125–26
eLa 2.3.2 126
eLa 2.3.3 126
eLa 2.3.4 126
eLa 2.3.5 126–27
eLa 2.3.6 127
eLa 2.3.7 127
eLa 3.1 128–31
eLa 3.1.1 128
eLa 3.1.2 128
eLa 3.1.3 128
eLa 3.1.4 128
eLa 3.1.5 129
eLa 3.1.6 129
eLa 3.1.7 129
eLa 3.1.8 129
eLa 3.1.9 130
eLa 3.1.10 130
eLa 3.1.11 130
eLa 3.1.12 130
eLa 3.1.13 130–31
eLa 3.1.14 131
ela 3.2 131–32
eLa 3.2.1 131
eLa 3.2.2 131–32
eLa 3.2.3 132
eLa 3.3 132–33
eLa 3.3.1 132
eLa 3.3.2 133
eLa 3.3.3 133
eLa 3.3.4 133
eLa 3.3.5 133
eLa 3.3.6 133

eLa 3.4 134
eLa 3.4.1 134
eLa 3.4.2 134
eLa 3.4.3 134
eLa 3.5 135–37
eLa 3.5.1 135
eLa 3.5.2 135
eLa 3.5.3 135
eLa 3.5.4 135
eLa 3.5.5 136
eLa 3.5.6 136
eLa 3.5.7 136
eLa 3.5.8 136
eLa 3.5.9 136
eLa 3.5.10 137
eLa 3.5.11 137
eLa 4.1 137–41
eLa 4.1.1 137–38
eLa 4.1.2 138
eLa 4.1.3 138
eLa 4.1.4 138
eLa 4.1.5 139
eLa 4.1.6 139
eLa 4.1.7 139
eLa 4.1.8 140
eLa 4.1.9 140
eLa 4.1.10 140
eLa 4.1.11 140
eLa 4.1.12 140
eLa 4.1.13 141
eLa 4.1.14 141
eLa 4.2 141–42
ela 4.2.1 141

eLa 4.2.2 142
eLa 4.2.3 142
eLa 4.2.4 142
eLa 4.3 142–43
eLa 4.3.1 142–43
eLa 4.3.2 143
eLa 4.3.3 143
eLa 5.1 143–45
eLa 5.1.1 144
eLa 5.1.2 144
eLa 5.1.3 144
eLa 5.1.4 144
eLa 5.1.5 145
eLa 5.1.6 145
eLa 5.2 145–46
eLa 5.2.1 145
eLa 5.2.2 145–46
eLa 6.1 146–47
eLa 6.1.1 146
eLa 6.1.2 146–47
eLa 6.1.3 147
eLa 6.1.4 147
eLa 6.2. 147–49
eLa 6.2.1 147–48
eLa 6.2.2 148
eLa 6.2.3 148
eLa 6.2.4 148
eLa 6.2.5 148
eLa 6.2.6 149
eLa 6.2.7 149
eLa 6.2.8 149
eLa 6.2.9 149
eLa 6.2.10 149

WCAG standards

WCAG 1.0 9, 17, 94–95, 153–59
WCAG 1.1 9, 94–95, 153–59
WCAG 1.1.1 9, 153–59
WCAG 1.2 23, 95–97, 159–93, 256, 310
WCAG 1.2.1 95, 159–63, 256
WCAG 1.2.2 96, 163–67, 172
WCAG 1.2.3 96, 167–71
WCAG 1.2.4 23, 96, 171–73
WCAG 1.2.5 97, 168, 173–75
WCAG 1.2.6 164, 310
WCAG 1.2.7 174, 310
WCAG 1.2.8 168, 173, 310
WCAG 1.2.9 164, 172, 310
WCAG 1.3 97–98, 175–85, 310–11

WCAG 1.3.1 97, 175–79
WCAG 1.3.2 97, 180–85
WCAG 1.3.3 98, 183–85
WCAG 1.3.4 98, 186–87
WCAG 1.3.5 98, 187–89
WCAG 1.3.6 310–11
WCAG 1.4 98–101, 189–215, 310–12
WCAG 1.4.1 98–99, 189–92
WCAG 1.4.2 99, 192–94
WCAG 1.4.3 99, 194–98
WCAG 1.4.4 99–100, 198–200
WCAG 1.4.5 100, 200–04
WCAG 1.4.6 195, 311
WCAG 1.4.7 311

WCAG 1.4.8 311–12
WCAG 1.4.9 312
WCAG 1.4.10 100, 199, 204–05
WCAG 1.4.11 100–01, 195, 206–09
WCAG 1.4.12 101, 209–12
WCAG 1.4.13 101, 212–15
WCAG 2.0 17, 24, 77
WCAG 2.1 10–11, 17, 24, 77, 80–81, 98,
          100–03, 106–07, 151–317
WCAG 2.1.1 102, 222–28
WCAG 2.1.2 102, 228–30
WCAG 2.1.3 223, 312
WCAG 2.1.4 102, 230–33
WCAG 2.2 11, 17, 20, 103, 233–39,
          312–13, 318–21
WCAG 2.2.1 103, 233–36
WCAG 2.2.2 103, 237–39
WCAG 2.2.3 234, 312–13
WCAG 2.2.4 313
WCAG 2.2.5 313
WCAG 2.2.6 313
WCAG 2.3 104, 239–41, 313–14
WCAG 2.3.1 104, 239–41
WCAG 2.3.2 240, 313
WCAG 2.3.3 313–14
WCAG 2.4 104–06, 223, 241–61, 314,
          319
WCAG 2.4.1 104, 241–43
WCAG 2.4.2 104, 243–45
WCAG 2.4.3 105, 246–48
WCAG 2.4.4 105, 248–53
WCAG 2.4.5 105, 253–55
WCAG 2.4.6 105–06, 256–57
WCAG 2.4.7 106, 223, 246, 258–61
WCAG 2.4.8 314
WCAG 2.4.9 249, 314
WCAG 2.4.10 256, 314
WCAG 2.4.11 319
WCAG 2.4.12 319
WCAG 2.4.13 319

WCAG 2.5 23, 57, 106–07, 261–69,
          314–15, 320
WCAG 2.5.1 106, 261–63
WCAG 2.5.2 106–07, 263–65
WCAG 2.5.3 57, 107, 265–67
WCAG 2.5.4 23, 107, 268–69
WCAG 2.5.5 314–15
WCAG 2.5.6 315
WCAG 2.5.7 320
WCAG 2.5.8 320
WCAG 3.0 18, 19
WCAG 3.1 107–08, 123, 273–77, 315–16
WCAG 3.1.1 107, 273–75
WCAG 3.1.2 108, 274, 275–77
WCAG 3.1.3 315
WCAG 3.1.4 316
WCAG 3.1.5 123, 316
WCAG 3.1.6 316
WCAG 3.2 108–09, 250, 278–84, 316,
          320–21
WCAG 3.2.1 108, 278–79
WCAG 3.2.2 108, 279–80
WCAG 3.2.3 108–09, 281–84
WCAG 3.2.4 109, 250, 282–84
WCAG 3.2.5 316
WCAG 3.2.6 320
WCAG 3.2.7 321
WCAG 3.3 109–10, 284–96, 317, 321
WCAG 3.3.1 109, 284–88
WCAG 3.3.2 109, 288–90
WCAG 3.3.3 109–10, 290–93
WCAG 3.3.4 110, 293–96
WCAG 3.3.5 317
WCAG 3.3.6 317
WCAG 3.3.7 321
WCAG 3.3.8 321
WCAG 4.1 110–11
WCAG 4.1.1 110, 149, 299–301
WCAG 4.1.2 111, 256, 301–02
WCAG 4.1.3 111, 125, 149, 302–04